What people are saying about …

AQUACHURCH

"*AquaChurch* remains the best introduction to the art of postmodern leadership on the market. Through a skillful weaving of metaphor, narrative, practice, and current church examples, the book draws us into the engagement of Scripture and our culture. Recognizing that the medium is the message, the book reflects something of what it teaches. It is a must-read for those wrestling with how to live out the gospel in the twenty-first century."

Dr. Donald Goertz, director, MDiv in ministry, assistant professor of church history at Tyndale University College & Seminary, Toronto

"*AquaChurch* is worth taking the time to read. Len Sweet is someone I greatly respect and appreciate. You will agree when you have navigated through this book. Thanks, Len."

Dr. Walt Kallestad, senior pastor of Community Church of Joy

"Len Sweet is a master of the apt metaphor. He discerns today's invisible forces that make leadership more like a voyage than a march. His navigational aids help keep us on course."

Marshall Shelley, editor of *Leadership*

"Len Sweet is an ancient-future leader who navigates by Go[illegible]h Star. This book is a must-read for Jesus leaders who risk navi[illegible]d, postmodern seas."

Mike Slaughter, pastor [illegible] urch

"Len Sweet offers us a 'learning' manual on self-navigating the 'watery' world of Postmodernism. Instead of describing a one-size-fits-all type of instruction manual on leadership, he shares with us the 'leadership arts' that can help guide us through the turbulent currents of today."

Bill Easum, senior managing partner of Easum, Bandy and Associates

AQUACHURCH 2.0

AQUACHURCH 2.0

Piloting Your Church in Today's Fluid Culture

LEONARD SWEET

AQUACHURCH 2.0
Published by David C. Cook
4050 Lee Vance View
Colorado Springs, CO 80918 U.S.A.

David C. Cook Distribution Canada
55 Woodslee Avenue, Paris, Ontario, Canada N3L 3E5

David C. Cook U.K., Kingsway Communications
Eastbourne, East Sussex BN23 6NT, England

David C. Cook and the graphic circle C logo
are registered trademarks of Cook Communications Ministries.

LCCN 2008931906
ISBN 978-1-4347-6757-8

First edition published by Group Publishing in 1999 © Leonard Sweet, ISBN 0-7644-2151-4

The Team: John Blase, Amy Kiechlin, Jack Campbell, and Karen Athen
Cover Design: Rule29
Interior Design: The DesignWorks Group

Printed in the United States of America
Second Edition 2008

1 2 3 4 5 6 7 8 9 10

070308

To Thane,
a disciple of The Way

Your face, my Thane, is as a book where men
May read strange matters.

—LADY MACBETH

CONTENTS

INTRODUCTION

They that go down to the sea in ships,
that do business in great waters;
These see the works of the Lord, and his wonders in the deep.
—PSALM 107:23–24 KJV

AquaChurch.

I know what some of you are thinking: "Haven't I seen this before?" Yes, you have. I wrote *AquaChurch* back in 1999 and over time, it went out of print. However, constant cries of "how can I get a copy of this book?" were heard from individuals, pastors, and college and seminary faculty. The publisher David C. Cook approached me recently about getting *AquaChurch* back out in print and I enthusiastically said, "YES!" We both agreed, though, that in this fluid Aqua-culture, things have changed a little since 1999. Actually, quite a lot. So, the decision was made to bring the book back out as *AquaChurch 2.0*—same basic content, but some upgrades and updates.

AquaChurch, as a title, needed to remain the same because it's still fitting for what the church needs to become if it's going to thrive in today's culture. Notice I say "thrive," not "survive." In my 1999 book, *SoulTsunami*, I described the coming wave of culture change that could swamp and overwhelm the church. There I suggested strategies for surviving that tsunami of change and encouraged church leaders to think seriously about keeping the church afloat in the midst of that wave.

AquaChurch took that concept a nautical mile further, providing missional arts that allowed church leaders to successfully navigate the waters of a culture totally foreign to those of us who were born modern rationalists. It helped churches sail unknown seas as they sought to reach people drowning without hope in Jesus Christ.

AquaChurch 2.0 goes a little further still.

Our goal in the church must go beyond surviving to thriving in this new culture. We must provide Jesus' message in forms and language people in today's culture can understand and embrace. We must develop ministries that continually adjust and change with our continually changing culture. And we must be about leading people to the source of Living Water.

What we face can be seen as a threat, but also as an opportunity of perhaps unprecedented proportions. USAmericans today are more open to the supernatural—to spiritual things—than they've been for several generations. Even with the hostility toward the church and organized religion via Christopher Hitchens and the new atheism, people are still interested in spiritual things. The reality is the church is the last place they'd look for something "spiritual." More possibilities are available to us today for accomplishing our task than ever before. And God is still God! Our job is to serve our Creator and Sustainer God by presenting Jesus in containers out of which others will be clamoring to drink.

In *AquaChurch 2.0* you still won't find formulations, but invitations. Other resources promise to give you a map that charts out the route, a formula in which you fill in the blanks, a recipe for you to add water and stir. In a culture that still prefers the fake, the artificial, the simulation to the real thing, a lot of people will prefer going with the map.

We refuse to go in that direction. We won't give you anything but the real thing. Instead of maps, here you will receive travel guides that will help you in orienteering. Instead of maps, here you will find missional arts that will help you to navigate your ministry. Instead of some magic bullet "fill-in-the-blank" formula, instead of some quick-fix, "one-size-fits-all" pantyhose solution, here you will find navigational principles connected with nautical images. Plus here you will be encouraged as you encounter the Guide who goes with you wherever you go.

When he had finished speaking, he said to Simon, "Now go out where it is deeper, and let down your nets to catch some fish" (Luke 5:4). So get ready to set sail once again, going out "where it is deeper," in this great adventure called life and ministry.

THE CASE FOR AQUACHURCH

PART ONE: THE TRAPS OF MAPS

We're all explorers....
We're all in pursuit of fundamental truths.
That's what exploration is all about.[1]

—Explorer and *Titanic* discoverer Robert Ballard

A Postmodern Parable

You and your party have just landed at the Miami airport in the wee hours of the morning. You race to the car rental counter. Amidst your huffing and puffing you see in the distance a light still on behind the counter. When you collapse on the counter's ledge, a smiling attendant greets you by name and says, "We've been waiting for you." Hertz has stayed open for you after they learned your flight had been delayed.

After some pleasant, grateful banter, the attendant hands you the keys and inquires, "Where are you headed?"

"I'm going to the marina," you pant.

"Do you need a map?"

"Are you kidding? You think I'm driving through Miami at one in the morning without a map? I hear the motto for this city is 'Sorry We Missed You.' You bet I need a map."

You take the map, stuff it under your arm, collect the rest of your luggage, and head for the car with your party.

You're now driving out of the airport and trying to decide which way to go. But the signs are confusing. You take snapshot glances at the map while driving, but within a few miles you're hopelessly lost. You pull nervously to the side of the road and turn on the map light. You keep studying the map and looking at the road signs. Something's not right.

Then someone says, "Give it here." They begin examining the map more closely. They say, "Look at this date. It says 'copyright 1955.' Fear and disgust come into your eyes.

How would you like to get around a 2020 Miami using an 1895 map? Or a 1955 map? Or even a map to begin with? Would you rather have an up-to-the-minute computer on your dash (e.g., GPS), or a map?

In the ancient world, maps and globes were as valuable as rare spices and precious metals. No one wants to be like that misguided, misbegotten nineteenth-century army in Paris that set off for the Prussian border without the right maps.[2]

> Philosopher A. C. Grayling, in his preface to the Oxford University Press attempt at an introduction to philosophy, writes: "If you intend a journey, you do well to consult a map."[3]

No wonder "remapping" is such a buzzword in almost every discipline and field. We are entering a new future. There is no way back. We can only feel and find our way forward. Everyone everywhere is looking for the right maps.

Novelist Salman Rushdie speaks for the majority. "There is a need for political fiction, for books that draw new and better maps of reality,"[4] something which he himself tried to do in his cartography of East and West called *The Satanic Verses* (1989).

A World of Mapping

- Instead of taking linear notes, make "iMindMaps" with trees, pictures, colors, symbols, and patterns.[5] First developed by Britain's Tony Buzan, this method of storing information aims to imitate how the brain actually works—which is not through outlines, columns, or neat lines.[6]
- University of Chicago social anthropologist Ernest Gellner is convinced that the central task of social thought is this: "We need some kind of orientation, some kind of overall map of possible social forms, of the kind of features which go together, of plausible transitions, of incompatibilities."[7]
- The biggest section of the book *Shadow of Spirit: Postmodernism and Religion* (1993) is dedicated to "Maps and Positions." A whole new theological geography is emerging, a spiritual map of a "polycentric world" and a "polycentric Christianity."[8]

In the business world, the concept is "Go global—but get a map." That's why the biggest movement in corporate circles throughout last two decades of the twentieth century and the first decade of the twenty-first has been "re-engineering" or "reinventing." Re-engineering is the corporate name for remapping, and re-engineering has been the name of the game among the Fortune 500.[9] Maps come in the guise of recipes for organizational change, Total Quality Management (TQM), Future Visioning, Repositioning,[10] and Business Process Re-engineering, for example.

The same search for savior maps can be seen in the church as well. The argument states that churches must develop life "remapping" for people, and not just for burned-out boomers and their deflated life projects. This approach is highly seductive. Doesn't a road map tell you everything you need to know … except how to fold it back up again?

One's destination is never a place, but rather a new way of looking at things.[11]

—Author and artist Henry Miller

Or does it?

Maps Lie

Our problem is this: Jesus never gave us a map that says "turn left here" or "right turn only" or "no outlet." Jesus gave us signs and signposts, but not maps. Why?

Because Jesus never lied.

When the psalmist asks the question, "When the foundations are being destroyed, what can the righteous do?" (Ps. 11:3), the answer is not to find a new map. Why? Why don't we offer you a map for your outward-inward journey?

Because we don't want to lie either.

Every attempt to "draw a new map of reality" is really an exercise in lying. The title of geology professor Mark Monmonier's book on maps, *How to Lie with Maps* (1991), is playful and punning. But it's also true. Every map is, by definition, a lie: "A single map is but one of an indefinitely large number of maps that might be produced for the same situation or from the same data."[12] There has never been a map without omissions, concessions, and interpretations. The main purpose of a map is to help you find your way. The map is not the way, however.

Cartography is not topography. Don't believe me? Look at any city map. Do you remember seeing how simple the interchanges from one route to another appeared on paper, but when you drove through them they actually involved nervous breakdowns?

A party of economists was climbing in the Alps. After several hours they became hopelessly lost. One of them studied the map for some time, turning it up and down, sighting on the distant landmarks, consulting his compass, and finally using the sun.

Finally, he said: "Okay. I've got it. See that big mountain over there?"
"Yes," answered the others eagerly.
"Well, according to the map, we're standing on top of it."
You cannot get "the lay of the land" from maps.

> It is not down on any map; true places never are.[13]
>
> —Herman Melville

Maps lie big time. Take a look at the way maps trap us.

The Traps of Maps #1: No Map Is Accurate

The first reference to a map in the Bible is found in Ezekiel 4:1, where God told Ezekiel to outline on a clay tablet a plan to lay siege to Jerusalem. But the first written reference to a map was made by the Greek historian Herodotus, and it was a sneer: "For my part, I cannot but laugh when I see numbers of persons drawing maps of the world without having any reason to guide them."[14]

A map is a flat depiction of a huge sphere. Any two-dimensional mapping of a three-dimensional sphere distorts shapes, distances, or areas. One's choice is either to preserve true relationships between areas (equal area projections) or true angles and shapes (conformal projections). Most maps try to create a balance between the two and do neither very well.

The only truly accurate map would be the one in the fable by Jorge Luis Borges—a map so large and accurate that it would be the exact same size and shape as the place being represented.[15]

> Just as any truly accurate representation of a particular geography can only exist on a scale of 1:1 (imagine the vast, rustling map of Burgundy, say, settling over it like a freshly-starched sheet!) so it is with all our abandoned histories, those ignoble lines of succession that end in neither triumph nor

> disaster, but merely plunge on into deeper and deeper obscurity; only in the infinite ghost-libraries of the imagination—their only possible analogue—can their ends be pursued, the dull and terrible facts finally authenticated.[16]
>
> —François Aussemain

However, a one-to-one correspondence is not a map. It is the real thing, as this dialogue from Lewis Carroll makes clear:

> "We actually made a map of the country on the scale of a mile to the mile!"
>
> "Have you used it much?" I enquired.
>
> "It has never been spread out, yet," said Mein Herr. "The farmers objected: They said it would cover the whole country and shut out the sunlight! So now we use the country itself, as its own map, and I assure you it does nearly as well."[17]

One of my favorite Picasso stories tells how he was accosted by a stranger in a railway station one day. "Why don't you paint things as they really are?" the stranger asked. Picasso feigned not to understand what the gentleman meant. Whereupon the stranger pulled out of his wallet a photograph of his wife. "I mean," he said, "like that. That's how she is."

Picasso coughed softly and said, "She is rather small, isn't she? And somewhat flat?"[18]

The Traps of Maps #2: No Map Is Current

Forty-nine square miles of New Jersey are missing from the latest map. A decade ago the Garden State claimed 7,468 square miles of land. Now the state is down to 7,419 square miles. It has gone from being the 46th to the 47th largest state.

"You think we had parking problems before," said one legislator.[19]

A *New Yorker* cartoon shows a man returning home and asking his wife, slumped before the television, whether any new autonomous republics had declared themselves while he was out.

In the modern world—in which those of us who are boomers grew up—one could assume a "steady state" universe. No longer. Our environment is ever-changing, fast-paced, unpredictable. I fully expect to wake up to a different world than the one I went to bed in.

One of the greatest explorers of the past one hundred years is Robert Ballard. In terms of undersea discovery, he and Jacques Cousteau have no equals. He also found the *Titanic*, the *Bismarck*, and led more than 110 underwater expeditions. His advice for exploring, which begins with the declaration, "We're all explorers," ends with "Work today involves traveling in uncharted territory, navigating the unfamiliar terrain of a new economy for which no maps exist."[20]

In the first six months of 1992, so many rapid changes occurred that the National Geographic Society had to revise its world map six times. Newman Levy once depicted mapmakers Rand and McNally in a conversation about making world atlases in a world that changed so rapidly:

> "Time was when this business of ours was grand,"
> Said Mr. McNally to Mr. Rand,
> "When our toughest job was to sit and think
> Shall France be purple and Britain pink?"
> "Remember those days," McNally said,
> "When we'd plan a map a month ahead,
> And we'd know, if it came out at noon, let's say,
> It was up to date the entire day?"
> "Those days," said Rand, "are gone totally."
> "You said it, brother," said Mr. McNally.[21]

Change is happening so fast, we can't really imagine the world of our parents, and we can't really imagine what will be our children's world. There is a new Web page every two seconds, a new product every thirty seconds. World knowledge now doubles every eighteen months, with more new information having been produced in the last thirty years than in the previous five thousand. Decades are now measured in centuries and millenniums when one moves from chronological to cultural time.

Moore's Law states that microprocessing speed doubles every eighteen months, and computer costs drop by half in that same time. Ray Kurzweil has shown that Moore's Law will make possible a $1,000 purchase of the computing speed and capacity of the human brain by 2020. In fact, change has become so exponential that Moore's Law will be defunct as the type of technology known today is replaced by new forms of circuitry around 2020.[22] No wonder one study concluded with the observation that "the half-life of paradigms appears shorter and shorter as human affairs become increasingly complex."[23]

I bought the latest computer;
it came completely loaded.
It was guaranteed for ninety days,
but in thirty was outmoded.[24]
—Bill Ihlenfeldt

What is fresh and innovative today is stale and obsolete tomorrow. If you're doing church the same way you were a year ago, or even last week, you're falling behind and failing.

The Traps of Maps #3: No Map Is Impartial

There is an old expression: "as skewed as a medieval map."

Every map promotes politics.[25] Throughout history, to map a domain was to own that domain. Some historical atlases idealize the real world in order to

control it. Others are designed to embody a culture's common view of itself. But every map is a political statement. A map is a cultural construct, a model of what a generation "sees." Maps are never neutral. In fact, a map is the continuation of politics by other means. Each map portrays areas and presents information according to a particular vantage point. A map depends on the position from which it is drawn and the period in which it is conceived.

You can usually tell where a map is made by noting which country is positioned in the middle. For example, from the beginning of the Crusades to the sixteenth century, world maps produced by Christians always had Jerusalem, the "navel of the world," at the very center. While Marco Polo and his successors did their best to give cartographers accurate profiles of new lands, medieval scholars continued to draw circular maps that became worthless to navigators at sea because they positioned the East (where Christ will come again with the rising sun) at the top of the world, and Jerusalem at its center.

Remember the world map your grade-school teacher pulled down from the wall? Most likely it was a Mercator projection map. Gerard Mercator allowed pilots for the first time to chart a straight line on a navigational bearing. But he did so only by projecting massive distortions of parallel meridians, which inspired other cartographers to project their own distortions. Another projection map, by Van der Grinten, was a favorite of Cold War anti-communists, who used it to their benefit. It showed a larger-than-life Soviet Union at the top of the globe like a Sherwin-Williams can of paint, gradually spilling out and covering the earth.

The Soviets projected their own "Cold War map," which showed the USSR vast and central, and the USA divided and weak, split into two sections, with one half at each side of the map. Since 1989, USAmericans have switched to the Robinson projection, which reduces the Soviet Union from being 223 percent larger than life to only 18 percent larger.[26]

Australia, tired of Mercator's Eurocentric view of the world and weary of always being at the bottom, came up with the "McArthur's Universal Corrective Map of the World," which places the Southern Hemisphere at the top and Australia at the middle where Europe usually is. As weird as it looks, the McArthur Map is just as accurate as any of the others.

The Traps of Maps #4: No Map Will Get You There

Maps are notoriously difficult when it comes to application. A vast theological difference separates trying to find your way in life and being led through life. The former is based on human effort; the latter is based on the gift of arrival.

"Remapping" doesn't respect the self-organizing capacity of complex living systems. Mathematician Kurt Gödel proved in his famous *Incompleteness Theorem* (1931) that no system of mathematics, no scientific theory, no mental map can ever offer an absolutely complete description of anything.[27] Nothing is ever as it seems. Nothing is ever as is seen. To fathom the world at its core we must pass beyond maps and theories to risk reality through the fury of lived experience.

Margaret Wheatley, in her critically acclaimed *Leadership and the New Science*, argues that maps are the old paradigm.[28] Complexity theory makes a mockery of maps. That's why "remapping" always fails. "Re-engineering," "restructuring" or whatever name "remapping" comes wrapped in are the last gasps of the old rigid command-and-control models of movement.

In her inaugural address as president of the University of Puget Sound, Susan Resneck Pierce stated,

> I have come to recognize just how little, at the moment of my own entry into college, our educational system had anticipated the world in which we now live. The questions faculty asked my generation, the advice our parents gave us, and our own hopes and

> dreams did not anticipate the social changes that would come.... They did not prepare us for the new kinds of ethical and public policy questions that we would need to face as a society and as individuals, questions that often have been the direct results of medical advances and new technologies.[29]

Look at the Bible. Go from beginning to end, from Genesis to the maps. You can't reduce God's way of working with any biblical figure to a cute formula or a colorful map. Each person's map of the world is as peculiar to that individual as a voiceprint or a thumbprint or a heart song.

It's amazing to me that people still look at a church like Willow Creek Community Church in South Barrington, Illinois, and say, "We should be like that." Willow Creek is a unique church. There is only one Willow Creek. To seek simple formulas for complex missions is to incubate mediocrity if not misconduct of mission. One person's plan is another person's poison. Even Willow Creek has now decided that it needs to do Willow differently than it has for thirty years.

Becoming a Mariner

You can't create a map of terra incognita. You can't consult maps in a world where the terra is no longer firma. In a new world with no familiar landmarks, you can only explore the new world for yourself. Google culture is unmappable on flat surfaces. It cannot be reduced to two dimensions. Mapping is now nonlinear. It's more like "a spider spinning a web," says Brian Shannon of the Corps of Engineers. "You're moving back and forth, building something one line at a time until you have a complex network that captures a place."[30]

To lead by traditional maps is to set a whole train of losses in motion.

> The civilization characteristic of Christendom has not yet disappeared, yet another civilization

> had begun to take its place.[31]
>
> —Harvard's George Santayana in 1913

When you change the question, you change everything. When you change the question, you change the playing field, you change the mission field. *AquaChurch 2.0* changes the question from "Where is my map?" to "Where is God calling me to navigate my life and my ministry?" The top challenge of leadership is this: How do you get people to ask new questions, to think in different ways?

To navigate your church in the rapids of a fluid culture, forget the maps other people have drawn. Even for you personally to update redrawn maps becomes worthless when the very principles of mapping have changed. What leaders need to pilot the church on God's terms are navigational skills that can help chart the appropriate course.

Sailors in the Bible were known as "salites" (*mallahim*) or "ropers" (*hobhlim*). People who ventured on a boat to set sail were called in Hebrew *yorde*, which takes at least five English words to translate, most often "they that go down to the sea in ships" (Ps. 107:23 KJV; Isa. 42:10 KJV). The captain of the ship was called in Greek *kubernetes*. A captain was one who (1) knew from experience the ways of the sea; (2) could perform all the diverse duties on board the ship; (3) could set and keep a true course; (4) assumed responsibility for the welfare of the ship's passengers and cargo.

The captain was a "navigator" with skills that could take a ship from where it was docked to where it was destined to go. Today's leaders need navigational skills that can take them from where they find themselves or where God has placed them to where God is calling them to go. To be a mariner is to learn the cartographical skills that will enable you to create your own map.

In the words of another, the chair of the Peter F. Drucker Foundation, Frances Hesselbein, the leader of the future needs to be a "how to be" leader, not a "how to do it" leader.[32] This book will help you become that kind of leader.

The "Me" generations are on self-navigating journeys; we need to help voyagers on the routes of God-navigating journeys. Generation "Me" is being called to be "self-navigators"; we're calling you to be divine-navigators. It's time to get the church seaworthy and seagoing again. It's time for the church to rediscover the vocation of voyaging.

> 'Tis the Old Ship of Zion
> Get on board, Get on board.
> Ain't no danger in the water
> Get on board, Get on board.
> —African American spiritual

Let's now set off toward the new horizon. Get on your sailing gear as we prepare to embark on a voyage into the future.

THE CASE FOR AQUACHURCH

PART TWO: SCANNING THE HORIZON

To find your way in Postmodern Country
you need a different eye, ear, compass and map.[1]
—Gary Phillips

There is a vast difference between "learning" and "instruction." In "instruction," you are trained by rote in what to think and do and be. In "learning," you are trained contextually in how to think and do and be. This book is a learning manual, not an instruction manual.

Put Your Name on the Map

You need a map of your very own. Each leader must do his own mapping. Each person needs a map of her very own. Every one of us has unique spatial information that we need to integrate into our map-making. Every leader needs a map with his or her name on it.

No two churches are alike. No two pastors are alike. No two ministries are alike. No two people even understand their church the same way. You need a map of your ministry that is as unique as your thumbprint. To follow someone else's map is to reduce your You-ness, to diminish the You-ness of you.

In this new world, we will increasingly do things that have never been

done before. José Saramago received the Nobel Prize for Literature in 1998. In an essay after the award, he argued that it is as impossible for twenty-first-century musicians to compose a symphony as it would be for twenty-first-century carvers to build a Corinthian capital. These were unique genres for unique times, and the time in which we find ourselves is calling all artists, including novelists, to embark on an odyssey that resonates with our times.[2]

In such an ever-new world, navigation becomes the greatest leadership challenge. Every leader needs to create his or her own map. But no leader dare create a map in isolation. Leaders learn from other explorers about their maps. A river's course doesn't change quickly, but the character and complexion of the river changes daily, even hourly. When white-water rafting, a rise or fall of even one inch can change a river drastically.

Leaders talk to other mappers and glean their wisdom before they go out on the river with their own maps. Don't use others' maps, but learn as much as possible from other leaders about the rapids and dangers of the river. Mapping requires mentoring from others who have known and shown the way. In the words of Gilles Deleuze, "We learn nothing from those who say: 'Do as I do.' Our only teachers are those who tell us to 'do with me.'"[3]

The Church's Inboard Navigational System

The development of missional arts for spiritual navigation must be the top leadership agenda. How ironic that the U.S. Naval Academy in 1998 cut out its celestial navigation courses for the first time in its history. Cruise control is not going to get anyone to the future.

AquaChurch 2.0 is intended to be a Garmin Navigational System for your church that parallels the inboard navigational systems for cars and trucks that has made road maps obsolete. The eighteenth century founders of my tradition (Wesleyan) used to talk about the need for Christians to develop "disciplines" and even produced a "Book of Discipline" to help disciples become disciplined about their daily walk with God. What we used to call disciplines are now being called "spiritual practices." For reasons that will become manifest through the course of this book, our preferred vernacular is not "daily disciplines" or "spiritual practices," but "missional arts."

This book introduces 11 1/3 missional arts for spiritual navigation. Each one is a navigational thrival skill—"thrival" because it enables leaders to thrive, not just survive, in these chaotic waters. These missional arts define what must be done if life is to be lived and ministry and mission conducted in today's fluid culture.

Why not ten? Or twelve? Because a Google world is not balanced or uniform. It's odd, aberrant, ragged, and various.

Why one-third? Why a fraction? As mathematicians and philosophers tell us, life itself is fractal. Fractals derived their name from being structures that have fractional dimensions, not mere integers.

These missional arts will help you live the adventure that is your life—the life-adventure that you are partly making up and that is partly beyond your making. They will help you face the future, outface the present, and about-face the past—as well as help you get to the future first.

> … long ago by God's word the heavens existed and the earth
> was formed out of water and by water.
> —2 Peter 3:5

"Two if by Sea"

These missional arts are coming to you in the form of nautical images. Roberto Burle Marx's famous maxim—"I hate formulas but I love principles"—has been turned on its head in this book. We shun formulas, but we love images. Images reflect and images inflect. Images lead.

You say: This book is about the practice of ministry—why introduce here images and theories? There's nothing so practical as a good theory, as the saying goes—or a good image. A theory is a conceptual container, and even if that container needs to be altered or supplanted, it's better to work with a flawed conceptual container than to work with raw and runaway liquid.

Products change, images capitalize.[4]

—Oliviero Toscani, creative director of Italian clothing brand Benetton

The modern era (from the fifteenth century through much of the twentieth century) was built on landed images. "Modern" is but another name for a period in the West dominated by ordering life according to rational, scientific means, the relegation of religion to private choice, and the emergence of capitalism.

Modernity's mental map was one of landlocked "landscapes." Its spiritual sweep was "grounded" albeit rootless if not uprooted. Its definition of God was even docked: "Ground of Being." As one would expect of a culture whose favorite surfaces were solid, stable ones, it spent a lot of time drawing boundaries, fixing borders, building structures on "rock-solid" foundations, and fighting boundary disputes. It distrusted fluids so much that a bone-chilling slur was to say "watered down," "wishy-washy," "squishy," or "groundless."

We tried to make things hard-and-fast, "waterproof" and "watertight." To say something was "like Watergate" was to "open the floodgates" of criminality and immorality. One took "stands" and dared not "float" through life. In modern culture the sea posed danger and created the need for an anchor—something stable and secure. If you don't believe me, just read your hymnal.

If the Gutenberg world was a rage for order, regulation, stability, singularity, and fixity, the Google world is a rage for chaos, uncertainty, otherness, openness, multiplicity, and change. Google-world surfaces are not landscapes but wavescapes, with the waters always changing and the surface never the same. The sea knows no boundaries.

The shift from a Gutenberg world to a Google world is a change from images of landscape to images of seascape. If the Paul Revere signal was "one if by land, two if by sea," postmodern Paul Reveres are signaling "two."

Google culture is an aquaculture. The hottest color of this first decade is blue, the water color. Shades are known as Blue Moon, Blue Planet, Cancun

Blue, and Cobalt Blue. Color therapists (there really are such experts) tell us that the appeal of sea imagery and water colors is apparent not just in Bluetooth, but in people's homes, with bottled water, built-in spas, and steam saunas. The importance of water and sea imagery to postmodern culture cannot be overstated. It is one of the most substantive bridges postmoderns have to the first century.

In his wonderful book on teams and the church, George Cladis makes a case for there being "certain aspects of Postmodern culture that actually encourage the church to make needed reforms; reforms that are foundational to biblical Christianity."[5] In other words, incarnating ministry in Google culture may actually help the church capture certain features of the faith lost or muted in modernity. Aquaculture is one of them.

Getting Wet

Old Testament references to seafaring are not common, although there are enough for the Jewish historian Raphael Patai to write an entire book on *The Children of Noah: Jewish Seafaring in Ancient Times* (1998). Here Patai documents the ways in which ships played a prominent role in the intellectual and image-related worlds of the ancient Jewish people. In fact, the loaves of bread offered in the Jerusalem temple were in the form of a dancing ship. Even the ladle used to draw wine from the jug in the temple had the shape of a ship floating in the sea.[6]

Biblical language is a language of water—fitting for a water planet. Jesus' first disciples were hauled from the sea, and not surprisingly the earliest symbols of the church were likewise drawn from the sea: fish and boat. The church's earliest theologians used these metaphors extensively in their thinking. The letter X began as a picture of a fish. Clement of Alexandria loved to use as a metaphor of the church a "ship running in the wild."

> Let our seals be either a dove, or a fish, or a ship scudding before the wind, or a musician's lyre … or a ship's anchor … and

if there be one fishing, he will remember the Apostle, and the children drawn out of the water.[7]

—Clement of Alexandria (c.150–c.215)

The church's ministry must get aquatic. In fact, ministry today is so aquatic that our two patron saints should be Noah and Peter. Noah, the only shipbuilder mentioned in the Bible, built the oldest vessel mentioned in Hebrew literature. He built a new structure called an "ark" for the new world emerging in his day. Peter, a fisherman who loved and lived for the sea, learned how to walk on water.

It's time for the church to get wet, and get wet in ways it has never before even dreamed of. We must plunge in, "aquaesce" in this aquaculture, and learn to think in terms of water. Unless we fashion a ministry out of "living water" and understand water as a metaphor for ministry, we will not arrive at a place where anyone can find us. Ministry can't get-to-the-point without it first being willing to get-to-the-moment. Our moment is Aqua.

Earth is the only blue planet. Earth is the only life planet. What makes Earth blue? Aqua. This is an aquatic planet. Water covers 75 percent of the planet's surface, and half the world's population lives within sixty miles of the sea. By volume, oceans contain 97 percent of all the earth's living space. The word *water* comes from Arabic for "luster and splendor." It is used often by gemologists in talking about jewelry, especially the luster and transparency of the finest jewels. Water is nature's crown jewel. The human brain with its hundred million nerve cells is 78 percent water.

Creation required God's feet to get wet. Without the gathering of the waters and separating a heavenly dome out of them, there was no creation. "The voice of the Lord is over the waters" (Ps. 29:3). No water, no life. Anhydrobiosas, or "Life Without Water," is impossible for earthlings. Water is the very elixir of life.

Becoming Rainmakers

In the Hebrew Scriptures and in many other cultures, water is a symbol of chaos. Yet all traditions that relate Jesus to water present water in a positive way. Jesus' first miracle was the changing of water set aside for a ritual to produce wine for a party.

Chaos is one of the key words for the twenty-first century. How fitting that this word be associated with water. Spiritual awakening is "the knowledge of the glory of the Lord" cascading over a people "as the waters cover the sea" (Hab. 2:14). Spiritual awakening is the opening of the "floodgates of heaven" (Mal. 3:10) so that showers of blessing may fall. In other words, spiritual leaders are rainmakers. What "revivalists" were to the modern world, rainmakers are to the postmodern world. And every one of us is called to be a rainmaker.

The greatest rainmaker of all time, Jesus the Christ, had his own pet metaphor for ministry: "living water." Water is always going somewhere. The grace of God is like water that's being poured out—a celestial fluid poured out from above.

> By the gift of water You nourish and sustain us
> and all living things.
>
> —Baptismal rite of the Lutheran Church

Hard Rain

A liquid, no matter how yielding and transient it appears, can erode stone. Soft water wins out over hard rock every time. When people call you a "softie" or a "soft touch," remember the power of water's "soft touch" to carve a Grand Canyon.

Over time, there is nothing stronger than water. Water wears down even rock to make a new world. No matter how hardened and stony the human heart, softness defeats hardness … over time every time; gentleness beats rigidness … over time every time; fluidity overcomes flintiness … over time every time. The waters of abounding grace are even more powerful than death.[8]

> The Scripture is a tree, or rather a whole paradise of trees of life, which bring forth fruits every month, and the fruit thereof is for meat, and the leaves for medicine. It is not a pot of manna or a cruse of oil, which were for memory only, or for a meal's meat or two, but as it were a shower of heavenly bread sufficient for a whole host, be it never so great, and as it were a whole cellarfull of oil vessels; whereby all our necessities may be provided for, and our debts discharged. In a word it is a pantry of wholesome food against mouldy traditions; a pharmacist's shop (Saint Basil calleth it) of preservatives against poisoned heresies; a code of profitable laws against rebellious spirits; a treasury of most costly jewels against beggarly rudiments. Finally, a fountain of most pure water springing up into everlasting life.[9]
>
> —Prefix, "Address to the Reader," King James/Authorized Version (1611)

In cyberspace as in life, fluidity wins out over fixity every time. Instead of "structuring" and "ordering" and "solidifying" reality, it "bends" and "blends" and "melts." Life is more a fluid realm than solid. Keep in mind that "fluid" does not mean "anything goes," as some have argued, but a different kind of going.

Living Water

At noon a woman stops at the well of Sychar to draw water. The disciples are in a nearby village getting bread, and Jesus is alone as the woman approaches. He engages her in conversation and asks her for a drink. When the disciples return and see him in conversation with the woman (John 4:27), they are outraged.

First, the woman was an untouchable for a Jew, a Samaritan who represented the social dregs at the bottom of the cup. Second, social convention prohibited a first-century man from speaking with a woman in public unless that woman was his wife. Third, this woman was doubly "defiled" because she was living in adultery. Jesus put himself in a receiving posture to someone who was unclean from the standpoint of both ritual and reputation.

Finally, there were tremendous cultural and religious implications to offering or receiving a cup of water. To offer water, or to receive it, was like signing a contract that you would be that person's friend for a year. When you ate together, a "meal covenant" implied that you would be friends for life. When Jesus asked for a drink, he was offering to be this woman's friend. When the Samaritan woman asked why Jesus would make such a request, she was really asking, "How is it that you, a Jew, want to be the friend of me, an outsider and outcast?" Jesus offered her a friendship that would last, not just a year, but a lifetime. Jesus offered her his no-strings-attached presence through a metaphor: "living water."

No wonder the woman left her water jar. The living water that Jesus gives leaves all other water jars behind. The Samaritan woman came to see that what she first thought would be simply a labor-saving device that would free her from the wearying walk to the well would actually free her from life's ultimate bondages. Jesus did not promise us living water that would last a lifetime. Once we have tasted the "living water," we want more water, not less. The promise of the gospels is that this water is from a well that never runs dry. We thirst more for the living water because it is the only liquid that can truly quench thirst.

Running Dry

The church is in the midst of a water crisis. As the world grows thirstier, the church is in a period of extended drought. Water shortages are everywhere. In some cases the supply of water is deficient. In others the usable, potable water is insufficient.

You die without water, physically and spiritually. It takes less than a 1 percent deficiency in our body's water to make us thirsty. A 5 percent deficit causes a slight fever. An 8 percent shortage causes the glands to stop producing saliva and the skin to turn blue. A person cannot walk with a 10 percent deficiency, and a 12 percent deficiency brings death. Every day 9,500 children die from lack of water or from diseases caused by polluted water.

Part of the church's deficiency of supply is bad plumbing. In the modern world denominational pipes channeled the living water to the thirsty. But the delivery system created by denominational machinery has come undone. Either the pipes have gotten rusty, corroded, and clogged, or else the piping is so leaden and inflexible it is unsuited to this new world. Worst of all is when the bit of "living water" that trickles from the pipes is not the fresh rain of the Spirit but the rainfall collected by our ancestors and stored in cisterns. Water that sits for any length of time becomes stale, stagnant, and sometimes even toxic.

Like our physical bodies, our spiritual bodies are almost all water. People around us are dying of spiritual thirst. What can we do to get them to take a drink of fresh "living water"?

Titanium Rule Christianity

The psalmist created a marvelous mixed metaphor: "Taste and see that the Lord is good." The very next line reads "blessed is the man who takes refuge in him" (Ps. 34:8). Our mission is to lead people to water. We can't make them drink. But we can hand them or show them the containers that hold the living water. We can make sure the living water is clean and pure. If we muddy the water, we make it difficult to lead people to it, let alone persuade them to drink. When we've offered them the living water, our assignment ends, and the Spirit's mission begins.

But notice something about water: Water is a liquid that fills the shape of any receptacle. As long as we trust the water and don't tamper with the recipe—don't dilute it, thicken it, or separate its ingredients—the content can remain the same while containers change.

> My wife is a tea drinker. Her favorite container is a little cup with a handle so tiny I can't even get my finger through it. My favorite container is a Jadite coffee mug (I started collecting Fire King Jadite long before Martha Stewart inflated the market and made it uncollectible). Our eight-year-old Thane's favorite container is a little glass we put juice in. Our three-year-old Soren's favorite container is a Winnie the Pooh sippy cup. Eighteen-month-old Egil's favorite container is a bottle.

Every generation needs a shape that fits its own hands, its own soul. Each generation, every person, needs a different handle from which to receive the living waters of Jesus. Our task is to pour the living water into anything anyone will pick up. By "anything" I mean that literally: anything. If I want to reach my twenty-second-century children (they probably will live to see 2100) with the gospel of Jesus, I must be prepared to pour the living water into containers out of which I myself would never be caught dead drinking. This is what Paul meant when he talked about our "becoming all things to all men" that we might win some (1 Cor. 9:22).

> He had brought a large map representing the sea,
> Without the least vestige of land:
> And the crew were much pleased when they found it to be
> A map they could all understand.
>
> "What's the good of Mercator's North Poles and Equators,
> Tropics, Zones, and Meridian Lines?"
> So the Bellman would cry: and the crew would reply
> "They are merely conventional signs!"

"Other maps are such shapes, with their islands and capes!
But we've got our brave Captain to thank"
(So the crew would protest) "that he's bought us the best—
A perfect and absolute blank!"[10]
—Lewis Carroll

I am a virtual fundamentalist about content. I am a virtual libertarian about containers. Only in Jesus the Christ did container and content become one. Jesus' comments about new wine in old wineskins reminds us that we cannot make an idolatry of any form or container. We must not elevate an ecclesial form to the level of authority or primacy that belongs only to the content. Unfortunately, much of the church is as fundamentalist about containers as I am about content, and as libertarian about content as I am about containers. Too many churches will only pour the living water into something they like or would pick up. A lot of churches are languishing because they won't trust the gospel to fit and fill containers with handles they don't like.

The church is filled with too many Golden Rule Christians whose motto is "Do unto others as you would have them do unto you" and not enough Platinum Rule Christians: "Do unto others as they would have you do unto them."[11] What is most lacking, however, is "Titanium Rule" Christians, practicing the most powerful command of all: "Do unto to others as Christ has done unto you."[12]

The mystery of the gospel is this: It is always the same (content), and it is always changing (containers). In fact, for the gospel to remain the same, it has to change. The old, old story needs to be told in new, new ways. In fact, one of the ways you know the old, old truths are true is their ability to assume amazing and unfamiliar shapes while remaining themselves and without compromising their integrity.

The issue of whether changing the style changes substance is an important one, especially in a culture where containers and content seem to meld into one another. Does the shape of the container affect the content? Isn't it true that what we do in worship affects what we believe? Doesn't the shape and form of the liturgy impact the faith we confess? Yes and no. Yes, people's experience of God and of the gospel changes. But no, God and the gospel don't change. Our experience does, and it should change through time. But God remains the same. The gospel is timeless. Part of leadership is making sure that the containers don't alter the content, as they are wont to do.

To be conservative about content but liberal about container does not mean that one is not interested in the content itself. I am a theologian. I want to understand the properties of living water, this magic elixir that changes lives. Made up of two volatile gasses, hydrogen and oxygen, why does a glass of water not explode when I move it? When I push two ice cubes together, why don't I get one twice-as-dense cube? As a physicist explores the mysteries that bind molecules of oxygen and hydrogen to form the stable substance H_2O, I want to explore the true nature of the living water Jesus offers.

So it is with Google generations. When not watching *The Office, American Idol,* or *LOST,* today's culture is watching Discovery HD. We want to discover our universe—the physical and spiritual universe of inner and outer space. The spiritual universe is not just inner space.

There Is a Fountain

One of my favorite symbols is that of the fountain. Throughout the history of the Christian church, the fountain has been one of the supreme symbols of perfection. God is called the "Spring of Living Water" (Jer. 2:13), and Jesus is likewise called a "Fountain of Living Water" (John 4:14). Theologian Hildegard of Bingen defined the Holy Spirit as "an overflowing fountain that spreads to all sides."[13]

The power of the fountain as an image of voyaging in grace and journeying in the Spirit was never captured better than by St. Gregory of Nyssa:

> If anyone happened to be near the fountain which Scripture says rose from the earth at the beginning of creation … he would approach it marveling at the endless stream of water gushing

> forth and bubbling out. Never could he say that he had seen all the water.... In the same way, the person looking at the divine, invisible beauty will always discover it anew since he will see it as something newer and more wondrous in comparison to what he had already comprehended.[14]

A fountain is always changing, and always the same. A fountain is always still, and always in motion. A fountain is sensitive and savage. A fountain is welcoming and distancing. A fountain has a single source with no beginning, and a dead end with no ending.[15] A fountain breathes out and in, moves up and down, at the same time.

Like the church doing ministry in Google culture.

In God's name we are sailing
His grace we need:
May his power shield us,
And his holy sepulchre protect us.[16]
—Favorite hymn of German pilgrims in the later Middle Ages

MISSIONAL ART #1

ORIENTING BY THE NORTH STAR: JESUS THE CHRIST

What!
No star, and you are going out to sea?
Marching, and you have no music?
Traveling, and you have no book?
What!
No love, and you are going out to live?
—Ancient French proverb

The first essential of navigation, and the place to start in map making, is establishing any position at any place that can be located at any time. We need a reference point that enables us to plot any position on the earth's surface in relation to the stars.

In the art of sailsmanship, that reference point is magnetic north, the "pole star" or North Star. Fixed in the firmament like no other star, the North Star gives sailors a sense of direction and becomes their sure and constant guide.

But notice two things about this reference point known as Polaris.

First, what is fixed is not the point of reference itself, but one's orientation toward that North Star. Wherever you are in the universe, that North Star may appear differently, but it's the same guiding star. The pole star never changes. What changes is one's personal coordinates and orientation toward the North Star.

Second, the earth's axis of rotation points differently toward Polaris at different points in history. First described by Newton, the "wobble" in the earth's orbit fractionally alters the alignment of the poles. Sometimes the earth's axis of rotation points within one degree of the star Polaris. Other times it is farther apart. What this all means is simple: Sometimes the North Star appears brighter in the heavens than at other times.

> The value of a Jesuit education was summarized by one grateful student: "You showed us where north is."

What is our North Star, our fixing orientation?

Jesus of Nazareth is our North Star. The personal coordinates of Jesus, our "Morning Star," our "Day Star" (2 Peter 1:19), are what keep us on course. Jesus' last words to us were these: "I am … the Morning Star" (Rev. 22:16). You can find them on the last page of every Bible.

> We are all in the gutter, but some of us are looking at the stars.[1]

Christianity is a relationship religion. The core relationship is a relationship with Christ. Everything depends on the administration and management of that relationship. However, some of us are more careful about maintaining and managing relationships with our pets than our relationships with Jesus, God-made flesh.

With a cosmos changing at the speed of light, there are no fixed horizons. With a fix on the Jesus horizon, we have steering points to guide us in ever-new destinations.

> For the raindrop, joy is entering the river.[2]
>
> —Greatest Urdu poet Ghalib Mirza Asadullah Khan

Lose sight of Christ, and a sailor on the sea of life quickly becomes lost. When Peter took his eyes off Christ, he sank (Matt. 14:30–31). When we live by grace, we walk on water. Else we sink … in despair, in disease, in depression, in dread of the future.

Jesus and Today

French sociologist Jacques Ellul identifies three crowning achievements of the modern West: first, the emergence of a sense of self, resulting in the separation of the individual from the tribe, nature, or the cosmos; second, the development of the critical, scientific method; and third—most important—human freedom and individuality.[3] Each one of these three, which provided dependable charts and fixed bearings for modern journeys, is up for grabs in today's world. To navigate under such fluid conditions makes the certainty of a fixed point in the heavens more important than ever before.

> The greatest question of the New Testament is often said to be: "What do you think of Christ?" Or, in Jesus' own words: "Who do you say I am?" (Mark 8:29).

The closeness of identification between Jesus and the Christian community is more than metaphorical. Whenever John Wesley wrote in his journal, "I offered them Christ," he was saying, "I preached." Would that more churches had etched on their pulpits the words that admonish everyone who steps into the crow's nest of one West Virginia church: "Sir, we would see Jesus."

A biblical spirituality is relationship driven. It begins and ends with Jesus: does it sound like Jesus? see like Jesus? taste like Jesus? touch like Jesus? smell like Jesus? One of my favorite writers, the Canadian Robertson Davies, used to say that he read life and literature by the light of "a candle that is plainly marked 'Manufactured by C.G. Jung & Co., Zurich.'"[4] But as Christians, we read life by the light of a star that shone brightly one dark

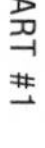

night in Bethlehem more than two thousand years ago and has lit up the skies ever since.

God lit up the skies more than two thousand years ago to show us how God can light up our skies today. Christians are people who live at the speed of light—the light of Jesus: "Christ in you, the hope of glory" (Col. 1:27). Christ is being "formed in you" (Gal. 4:19). For the indwelling Christ to be formed in us does not mean that we abandon our own space. Rather, it means that the indwelling Christ makes us more like ourselves at the same time we become more like Christ.

> Artist/visual allegorist Stanley Spencer one day asked Sir John Rothenstein, Director of the Tate: "Do you know what good art is? It's just saying 'ta' to God." Good sailsmanship is saying "ta" to Jesus. It is navigating one's life by the North Star.

One of the key influences on my thinking has been that of the missiologist Bishop Lesslie Newbigin. He reminded us that the key focus of the church's mission is not the church but the world. In one of the memorial addresses at his funeral in 1998, it was noted that Newbigin knew everybody. He knew on a first-name basis all sorts of kings, queens, prime ministers and presidents, celebrities and zillionaires.

But the only name he ever dropped was the name of Jesus.[5]

Jesus and Values

As pioneers on an earlier trek westward came to appreciate and articulate, today's explorers need to choose carefully the star to which they hitch their wagons. In the economic world, the guiding star is becoming EPIC values rather than profits. An approach to business that is values-driven and service-oriented rather than profit-driven and owner-oriented is perhaps the most significant stars-in-its-eyes transformation in twentieth- and twenty-first-century management.

I visited my friend today.
He's eighty-five
and travels light,
a wise and wonderful man.
We spoke of many things,
small talk and big talk,
and then he said,
"Yes, for most of our
comings and goings
maps are O.K.,
but for the Big Trip
we still follow the Star!"[6]
—Poet/seminary professor Gerhard Frost

In the global world of business, the most distinguishing quality of a leader has become the ability to lead through values. Value setting has replaced goal setting as the primary task of leadership. Swiss organizational consultant Peter Koenig argues that the issue is not whether values-driven business is profitable. In fact, values and profits don't necessarily go together. The issue is whether values are being followed for their own sake: "The only motive deserving of the name 'values driven' is one where the values are being expressed simply for their own sake—as a matter of radical principle."[7] Koenig reminds us that the charters of incorporation were given to businesses because they existed "for the common good" and were trusted to act in the interests of "the common good."

What is due north for values-driven entrepreneurs? When James F. Keenan shoots for the stars, he finds four cardinal virtues: justice, fidelity, self-care, and prudence.[8] Another management theorist has compiled another top ten value skills list: "honesty," "integrity," "commitment," "loyalty," "fairness," "concern for others," "respect," "obedience to the law," "pursuit of excellence," and "personal accountability."[9]

In many ways the values-oriented revolution of the 1990s has been but

another attempt to restate the classic Christian virtues embodied by Jesus and embedded in his life—faith, hope, love, prudence, justice, temperance, fortitude, fidelity, self-care—in more contemporary form. Some books don't even bother separating out the principles of Christ from the person of Jesus. For example, see *Jesus CEO* by Laurie Beth Jones and *Jesus on Leadership* by C. Gene Wilkes.

Values for values' sake? What about Jesus for Jesus' sake? All of us are "on the way." Christians are people who follow the "Living Way" of Jesus the Christ. Our star is the Star of Bethlehem. We journey the ways The Way went and cherish the ways The Way cherished.

Guiding by the Star

People often ask megachurch pastor Mike Slaughter what he's going to do next, where he sees himself in five or ten years. Mike responds that if he is in charge of his own life, he knows the answer to that question. But if God is in charge of his life, he has no idea how to answer that question.

Leaders help people ask questions like: Who is in control of your life? Who's piloting your ship? Are you at the helm, or is God? Are you going your own way, or going God's way?

> Jesus, Savior, pilot me
> Over life's tempestuous sea;
> Unknown waves before me roll,
> Hiding rock and treacherous shoal;
> Chart and compass come from Thee:
> Jesus, Savior, pilot me.[10]
> —Edward Hopper, 1871

Christian leaders are not customer-centric but Christo-centric. Their focus is not "what the customer wants," but "what Christ wants." They look to Christ themselves, to help others find Christ in their own lives, to help the word made flesh be made fresh again. Missional art #1 is the ability to help people understand that the fullness of truth is not propositions or principles. The fullness of truth is Christ.

> Christ is in the Church
> in the same way as the sun
> is before our eyes.
> We see the same sun as our fathers saw,
> and yet we understand it
> in a much more magnificent way.[11]
> —Teilhard de Chardin

Disciples of Jesus begin faith's journey with Christ as a fixed reference point. But two points are needed if there is to be true fixity of faith: space and time. The North Star tells us where we are in the space of the soul. But time as well as space is necessary to accurately calculate longitude. Hence the chronometer of history and culture.

The chronometer—the ship's clock—was one of the most important instruments onboard ship. Often actual diamonds were used to jewel its mechanisms, so special was it. Only one or two sailors would have the key to open its lock and adjust it. Today one of those early chronometers can command six figures.

What made the chronometer so special? The only way navigators could tell longitude was by looking at the time. Today's leader must ask the question "What time is it?" while being guided by the North Star. The difference between finding your way in life and losing your way is often a matter of a few degrees of longitude. When the longitudinal questions of time are asked alongside the directional questions of space, two things become clear about Jesus the Christ, two things that parallel the two things we noted earlier about the North Star.

> The way is often rough for a pilgrim and hard going, but
> pilgrims must keep going resolutely and courageously. They

> are lost if they stop looking for the right way to reach their destination. But there is one who is on the lookout to guide us; it is the Son of God, who is the way, the truth and the life.[12]
>
> —Basil Hume

Sighting Jesus in Every Culture

First, Jesus the Christ remains the same yesterday, today, and forever. But our experiences of Christ depend on our personal and cultural coordinates. Jesus is not an alien force, a nonnative source, or an import that comes into a culture. Jesus is an indigenous illumination of what is already there.

> Some years ago, the distinguished southern churchman and theologian Albert Mollegen was lecturing to a group of laypeople in Virginia on the topic of "Revelation." It was loaded with technical distinctions and sophisticated analysis. At the end, the professor entertained questions from the audience, and a bewildered and slightly defeated woman arose and said, "Dr. Mollegen, how does God speak to you?" The great man thought about that for a moment, and then abandoned his professorial demeanor. "In English, ma'am. With a Tidewater accent."

Jesus transcends every known culture. God comes to the Chinese in a Chinese accent. Jesus appears to the African in a Swahili cadence. Jesus appears to the American Indian in a Shoshone beat. Jesus appears to a West Virginian in an Appalachian accent. All cultures share in the pre-Incarnation mystery. Even the culture of first-century Palestine couldn't contain but one look at Jesus—there is not a single story of Jesus, but four basic stories, with multiple stories within those stories.

When Jesus rose from the dead and ascended, he became the exalted Christ, a universalized presence and power. He did not take his Jewishness

with him into heaven. In the garden with Mary, Jesus says "touch me not" or "do not hold on to me" (John 20:17). In other words, Mary, I'm not what I used to be. Things are different now. Or in Paul's way of putting it to the church at Corinth: "Though we have known Christ after the flesh, yet now henceforth know we him no more" (2 Cor. 5:16 KJV).

> "You accept the historical existence of Jesus?"
>
> "Unquestionably! No one can read the Gospels without feeling the actual presence of Jesus. His personality pulsates in every word. No myth is filled with such life."[13]
>
> —Interview with Albert Einstein in *The Saturday Evening Post* (1929)

Letting Jesus Shine

Second, as we spin on our Google Earth axis, Jesus is shining brighter and brighter. Christianity may appear to be dying in the West, but interest in Jesus has never been higher in the West and Christianity is rising in the East and the South.

People today are antireligious but deeply spiritual. Twenty-first-century culture is filled with day trippers asking for direction, some with feet on the ground, others stuck in the mud, still others with heads in the clouds—but all scouring the horizon for hope, wonder, genuineness, and a way out of their mazes of aimless living.

Say "I'm a Christian" to these pilgrims, and they flee for their lives. Say "I'm a disciple of Jesus," and they gather round to hear more. People have stars in their eyes about Jesus and the stomach for a fight about Christianity. The "global boom" in books about Jesus, with an average of four new books coming out every single day, attests to the brightness of this one star in the postmodern firmament. Worldwide, more than sixty-six thousand

books have been written about Jesus, claims missiologist David Barrett. The quest for the historical Jesus has never been more frenzied. Even in a roundabout way the irreverent and highly modern "Jesus Seminar" and "The Da Vinci Code" frenzies are backhanded compliments to this obsession with Jesus.

> I will not doubt, though all my ships at sea
> Come drifting home with broken masts and sails;
> I shall believe the Hand which never fails.
> And, though I weep because those sails are battered,
> Still will I cry, while my best hopes lie shattered,
> "I trust in Thee!"[14]
>
> —Ella Wheeler Wilcox

When too many people picture "Christians," the image that comes to mind is not a good one. It used to be that negative images of Christians featured people who couldn't dance, drink, smoke, gamble (as a kid I never could find those prohibitions in the Bible). Negative images of Christians today are of people who are mean, judgmental, hysterical, homophobic, condemn people to hell, and want to leave everyone not like them behind.

A friend of mine, who is an outspoken supporter of a certain political candidate, tells of receiving scores of hate e-mails, many from acquaintances who profess to be devout Christians. They either write abusive letters themselves or forward invective messages they have received from other individuals or religious groups. One message discounted the candidate's Christian faith because the candidate's social and political stands didn't fit within the mold of the writer's beliefs. Another correspondent went so far as to suggest that the candidate might very well match the description of the Antichrist as found in the book of Revelation.

When did this happen? When did Christians become some of the world's greatest haters? When did Christianity lose that over-the-top love and under-the-bridge hope for which the early Christians were most famous? What happened to "They'll know we are Christians by our love"? Why do today's Christians love so badly?

"Wait a minute," you say. "That's an isolated case. Every religious tradition has its negative, lunatic fringe. No religious tradition can be judged by its worst expressions." You're absolutely correct. In fact, the founder of Methodism John Wesley said back in the eighteenth century that the "grand stumbling block" to the credibility of the gospel was "the lives of Christians."[15]

But here's former Senator Alan Simpson, himself a devout disciple, who, when someone is getting too nosy and noisy, asks: "Who gave you your Jesus shoes?" When did rudeness become "Jesus shoes"? Since when did walking the Jesus talk mean to be judgmental, be abrasive, be loud? When one accepts Christ as Savior, why is one's first compulsion to immediately start "taking stands" for Jesus against this and against that?

Who did give you your Jesus shoes?

More than anything else, missional art #1 is coming to terms with the image of Christ. What is your image of who Jesus is? Who is this Christ child that came into our world one day long ago, and every day thereafter?

You'll read this many times before you're done with *AquaChurch 2.0*, but change agents must comprehend this above all else: Metaphors are the very stuff of which the mind is made. Metaphors shape biology. Our metaphors alter our body's molecules and microbes. You don't "get" a body. You construct your body. Your metaphors structure your body. And you have a choice of what metaphors to build your life around.

Change your metaphor, and the molecular architecture of your body changes with it. Change your metaphors, and the architecture of your soul is altered. When you think differently, you act differently. The Bible teaches that as you think in your heart, so are you (Prov. 23:7). Images possess generative, conceptional powers that can change the world.

Jesus rearranges the molecules in the body. Jesus turns our beings inside out and upside down. The body is the "temple of the Spirit." Your body is riddled with the sacred. Your body is suffused with divinity—the wild, vibrant energies of the sacred. And when you let that energy of the Spirit work within you, your mind, your body, and your world will change.

The World's Greatest Lover

I used to think that the best definition of the gospel was this one: "Jesus ate good food with bad people." Then I got the gospel into four words: "Be there with all." I now have a two-word distillation of the gospel: Jesus loves. These two words say everything about who Jesus is and why he visited planet Earth. But you have to go through a lot of layers to get to the real essence of who Jesus is.

> Nothing is free but love.[16]
>
> —Last line in Nadya Aisenberg's poem "The Home Museum"

What is Jesus all about? Think about who he is to you as you read the following list:

To the imprisoned, Jesus is THE KEY TO FREEDOM, the DOOR OF SALVATION.

To the sick, Jesus is THE GREAT PHYSICIAN.

To the naked, Jesus is THE LILY OF THE VALLEY, more adorned than all of Solomon's raiments.

To the attacked, Jesus is ADVOCATE and REDEEMER from the law.

To the addicted, Jesus is SUPPLIER OF EVERY NEED.

To the debtor, Jesus is the PAYER OF OUR DEBT, our EARNEST.

To the lonely, THE COMFORTER HAS COME.

To the drowning, Jesus is an ANCHOR and GREEN PASTURES.

To the homeless, Jesus is the CORNERSTONE to that MANSION, just over the hilltop.

To the depressed, Jesus is THE SUN OF RIGHTEOUSNESS, THE ROSE OF SHARON.

To the educationally harassed, Jesus is THE ALPHA AND OMEGA.

To the lost, Jesus is the NORTH STAR, the BRIGHT AND MORNING STAR, the DAY STAR.

To the wanderer, Jesus is THE WAY.

To the dead, Jesus is THE LIFE.

To the seeker, Jesus is THE TRUTH.

To the hungry, Jesus is THE BREAD OF LIFE, THE BAGEL OF THE DAY.

To the thirsty, Jesus is the CUP OF HEAVEN, the VINE that can turn water into WINE.

Jesus is all of the above, to all of the above. But to the world, to everyone everywhere, Jesus is THE WORLD'S GREATEST LOVER.

> Jesus shall reign where'er the sun
> Doth his successive journeys run;
> His kingdom stretch from shore to shore
> Till moons shall wax and wane no more.[17]
>
> —Isaac Watts

Who is Jesus? The World's Greatest Lover. You can't outlove the Lord.

Who am I? I AM the one Jesus loves.

Who are you? YOU ARE the one Jesus loves.

Who is I AM? I AM is LOVE.

It's time to take Christianity back. Every Christmas I get out my handwritten bumper-sticker: "Forget putting Christ back into Christmas. Put Christ back into Christianity." Christians are called to be the greatest lovers in the world. It's time the church launched a new kind of arms race. You can be right and be doing right things. But if your "rightness" is not enveloped in an overwhelming embrace of love, your "rightness" is wrong. Love is eternity based. The more you give, the more there is to go around.

Disciples of Jesus are called to love with a love that is "from God and of God and toward God." Or in the words of the ancient liturgy, "to know

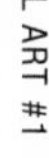

God, to love Him and serve Him in this world, and to be happy with Him for ever in the next." We don't merely love love. Augustine said of himself before he was converted: "*Amabam amare*" or "I loved to love" or "I love falling in love" or "I love being in love." If Augustine was into the love experience, people today are into the love of experience. But real love is not the love experience or the experience of love (which is really the experience of oneself). Instead, it is the experience of God through self-displacing love for another.

Bright Lights

Lives totally fixed on Christ become Christ-bearers for others. This missional art is not something one does once and that's it. Charting the course of one's life by the coordinates of Christ is a daily exercise. Furthermore, leadership that has mastered this art reminds people why they became disciples of Jesus in the first place. A leader reminds people of their first love. A leader helps people remember the first time they heard the music.

In other words, leaders don't point to their own star. They point to the North Star.[18] Leaders don't cast long shadows. Leaders cast stars. In the military service there emerged an expression: Good soldiers wait until they see the whites of their eyes. In the service of Christ, good leadership is waiting until you see the lights of their eyes.

People today want to see stars. Don't believe me? Check out ebay.com. There you'll find available an amazing array of star memorabilia. What is lighting up people's lives? Can you see the light in their eyes? Are their eyes lit up with the fire of the Spirit? Does an occasional twinkle of star add quality to their existence?

How do you know if a vision is catching on with others? How can you tell if other people "have the vision"? Look in their eyes. Are they shining? Are they sun-ripened? Is there star power? Are they guilty of absurd bouts of optimism? Are they starry-eyed? Do their fingers touch the stars?

Then the vision is finding a home.

O happy band of pilgrims
If onward ye will tread
With Jesus as your fellow
To Jesus as your Head! …
O happy band of pilgrims,
Look upward to the skies,
Where such a light affliction
Shall win so great a prize.[19]
—John Mason Neale

In a lifetime of following the North Star there will be many roles that will come your way and catch you unawares—"fool," "myth maker," "blunderer," "ghost," "ghoul," "martyr," "scapegoat." But there is no role so important as this one—pointing others toward the "Morning Star." In an era when today's "bright lights," in both senses of that term, are supplied by the media, not the church or the academy, there is more reason than ever before for disciples to reclaim the ministry of the "Morning Star."

The historian my teachers cut their teeth on, and therefore, the historian drilled and filled into me, was Charles A. Beard. He was once asked by one of his students whether he might be able to put the lessons he had garnered over a lifetime of historical study into a few brief maxims. Beard compiled and offered these four brief sentences:

a. Whom the gods would destroy they first make mad with power.
b. The mills of God grind slowly, yet they grind exceedingly fine.
c. The bee fertilizes the flower it robs.
d. When it is dark enough you can see the stars.[20]

It is time now for the stars to come out.

In *The Trespasser*, by D. H. Lawrence, Helena and Siegmund are lying in the sand, waiting for the sun to rise. "Each was looking at a low, large star which hung straight in front of them, dripping its brilliance in a thin streamlet of light along the sea almost to their feet. It was a star-path fine and clear, trembling in its brilliance, but certain upon the water." To Siegmund it seemed like a lantern hanging at a gate to light someone home, and he wondered what would he find if he followed the "thread of the star track."[21]

> Arise, shine, for your light has come, and the glory of the Lord rises upon you.
>
> —Isaiah 60:1

People are desperate to follow the "thread of the star track." But first the morning stars must appear. Robert Louis Stevenson, who was very ill as a child, recorded a childhood incident in his diary. He was seated by a window at nightfall, watching a lamplighter light the street lights below. His nurse came into the room and asked him what he was doing. "I'm watching a man make holes in the darkness," he replied. The world is watching for lamplighting individuals and communities who will punch holes in the darkness.

> The Wesley brothers, John and Charles, called the medieval mystics "LIGHTS SET IN DARK PLACES."

Morning Stars are lights who allow God to set them in dark places. Gospel singer Amy Grant is one such Morning Star. I shall never forget an Amy Grant concert at King's Island in Cincinnati in the midst of the controversy that swirled around her during the summer of 1986 for "crossing over" into the secular market. Many Christians laid into Amy Grant, outraged that people could tune to any rock radio station in the nation and hear her sing about her love for Jesus.

At the concert Grant told about songs she was working on and how her tour was going. But then it became very quiet, and out of the silence she confessed to feeling great pain over all the abuse and derision from her sisters and brothers in Christ. She then visibly straightened up and spoke of her resolve not to listen to it. And then came out these words, so powerful I wrote them down on the spot.

> Some people think I should stand in the light and give my witness. But I believe God has called me to stand in the dark, and there give off my light. I know there is danger in the dark, but God's Word has told that I'm all right as long as I don't lose sight of the light.

John's gospel is known as the "I am/You are" gospel because of the richness of its metaphors for ministry like salt, leaven, and light. Jesus did not call us to be the light of the church. We are not called to be the light of the light. We are called to be the light of the world, following in the path of the "true light," the "light of life" (John 8:12). "For you were once darkness," Paul wrote to the Ephesians, "but now you are light in the Lord. Live as children of light" (Eph. 5:8–9). Where light is there will be beauty, truth, and goodness.

> I was doomed to go to hell by the time I was 7. I had been told that if you smoke cigarettes and drink beer, you're going to hell. And by 7, I was gone.[22]
>
> —Former Methodist Willie Nelson

A rabbi is said to have once asked his students: "When can we know that the night has ended and the day begun?"

"Is it the moment," suggested one student, "when you can tell the difference between a sheep and a dog?"

"No," said the rabbi.

"Is it," asked another, "when you can see the difference between a fig tree and an olive tree?"

"Not that either," said the rabbi.

"Then when is it?" the students asked.

The rabbi answered: "It is the moment when you can look at a face never seen before and recognize the stranger as a brother or sister. Until that moment, no matter how bright the day, it is still the night."

God wants us to be salt, leaven, and light. Salt was such an important symbol in the early church that when someone was baptized, a pinch of salt

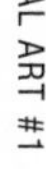

was placed on the new believer's tongue. Purified in Christ, we are called to be a purifying agent in the world.

Leaven was given as an image not that we might be the leaven of the leaven, or even to produce more leaven. The church as leaven exists to be an everlasting, ever-leavening agent that can turn dough into bread for a hungry world.

Light illumines the darkness. If there's darkness, the blame should be attached where it belongs; not to the world that is dark but to the church, which is failing to provide the light.

Stop for a moment. If that last sentence didn't hit you like a brick, read it again. Then think silently about each of the statements below:

- If there's spiritual blandness, the blame should be placed where it belongs; not on the world that's so bland and boring, but on the church, which has been given a gospel that adds spice to life but is placing the world on a salt-free diet.
- If there's rottenness, the blame should be placed where it belongs; not on the world that's rotting, but on the church, which isn't salting it enough to stop it from going bad.
- If there's unfed hunger out there, the blame should be placed where it belongs; not on those who are gobbling up counterfeit spiritualities and fast-food pieties, but on the leaven that isn't getting into the dough to make bread for a hungry world.

As a child in the 1950s, I heard a story at a holiness revival meeting in New York. It seems a certain missionary, home on leave, was shopping for a globe of the world to take back to her mission station. The clerk showed her a reasonably priced globe and another one with a lightbulb inside. "This is nicer," the clerk said, pointing to the illuminated globe, "but of course, a lighted world costs more."

What has lighting our world cost you lately?

> All things have become light, never again to set; and the setting has believed in the rising. This is the new creation.[23]
>
> —Clement of Alexandria (third century)

The psalmist observed how "The heavens declare the glory of God; the skies proclaim the work of his hands" (Ps. 19:1). Is the firmament showing God's handiwork through you and through your church? Or are the people passing through the gates of deep darkness and peering into more deep darkness?

AQUACHURCH #1
ECCLESIA

Houston, Texas

www.ecclesiahouston.org[24]

Ecclesia describes themselves as a Holistic Missional Christian Community.

- *Holistic*: They believe that the gospel impacts every area of a person's life and culture. They reject unfounded categories that divide the world into uniquely sacred or purely secular. God is redeeming all of creation through Jesus.
- *Missional*: They believe that the church exists for the world and not for herself—she is to introduce and usher in the kingdom of God into every part of this world.
- *Christian*: They embrace the teachings and divinity of Jesus Christ as well as his unique role as the means of salvation from sin for all who believe. They embrace the Scripture as God's primary instrument by which he introduces this message to the world.
- *Community*: They believe that salvation brings people together as a reflection of a triune God: Father, Son, and Spirit. Saved from sin by faith through grace, the people of God are able to live in unity as was intended by God in the beginning.

CAPTAIN'S LOGBOOK

PERSONAL LOG

Use these ideas to stimulate your thinking about how the principles of this chapter could affect your ministry. Consider sharing these ideas with other church leaders.

1 Conduct an honest appraisal of your "personal coordinates and orientation" toward Christ the North Star. Don't think about how hard you work or what results you've achieved. Think about Christ in terms of priority.

- In all honesty, how are you doing in your relationship with Jesus Christ?
- How are you "ordering" your private life to ensure that your relationship with Jesus Christ is foremost and growing?
- What do you need to do to make sure you're setting your course by the North Star, Jesus? Write down your answer to this question, and keep it where you'll be reminded of it often.

2 Everybody seems to be a fan of something. What are you a "fan" of? Check out www.fanclube.net or www.musicfanclubs.org, and visit some fan clubs online. Note the eerie intensity of their enthusiasm about every detail of their celebrity's life or their sports team's record. Consider the following questions:

- Why doesn't the church do better at giving people something worthy of their devotion?
- How is being a "fan" different from being a "disciple"?

3 Look up and read the words to the following hymns: "O Morning Star," and "Jesus, Keep Me Near the Cross." If you like to sing, sing one of the songs aloud. Then think about following questions in relation to the songs:

- What does Jesus offer the people of today's culture?
- How can you best present Jesus to that culture?

4 Meditate on this early sermon from Melito, bishop of Sardis (died c. 190). Melito's *Homily on the Pasch* has been called "one of the most beautiful meditations ever written on the work of Christ."[25]

> Understand, therefore, beloved,
> how it is new and old,
> eternal and temporary,
> perishable and imperishable,
> mortal and immortal, this mystery of the Pascha:
> For, as a Son born,
> and as a lamb led,
> and as a sheep slain,
> and as a man buried,
> he rose from the dead as God, being by nature God and Man.
> For he is all things:
> inasmuch as he judges, Law;
> inasmuch as he teaches, Word;
> inasmuch as he saves, Grace;
> inasmuch as he begets, Father;
> inasmuch as he is begotten, Son;
> inasmuch as he suffers, Sheep;
> inasmuch as he is buried, Man;
> inasmuch as he is raised, God.
> This is Jesus the Christ,
> to whom be glory for ever and ever. Amen.[26]
> —Melito of Sardis (second century)

5 Think about this statement from page 46: "Christian leaders are not customer-centric but Christo-centric. Their focus is not 'what the customer wants,' but 'what Christ wants.'" Carefully analyze what this means in relation to what was said on page 38 about the mystery of the gospel:

"It is always the same (content), and it is always changing (containers)." Consider:

- What's the difference between being "customer-centric" and making sure the message of Christ is in containers today's non-Christians will pick up?
- What is it that Christ wants you to do?

To help sort that out, get out your concordance and do a New Testament word study of the word *follow*.

6 It is crucial that the reader recognize the importance of the chronometer or ship's clock to the navigator of the ship (p. 47). Ask yourself:

- What would this parallel in my church?
- Who do I call or what process do I use to discern "what time it is" in my local church?
- What time is it in my church?

7 Think about the story of the person who received hate e-mails in response to his support of a political candidate (p. 50).

Consider:

- How does this happening highlight the problem of "contents and containers" that we mentioned earlier?
- How would you answer this question: "When did Christians become some of the world's greatest haters?"
- What must your church do to shed the image of "the world's greatest haters" and work toward becoming known as "the world's greatest lovers"? Write down your thoughts on this question.

8 Think about this claim: "Far too much current preaching is moralistic. It is exhortation to do, or be something. The good news is not primarily a summons to effort. That way lies despair. The gospel is an announcement of an unspeakable Gift whom men [and women] are to receive: 'Behold, I stand at the door, and knock.'"[27]

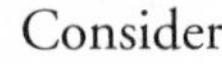

Consider:

- Do you agree with this claim? Why or why not?
- Is this true of your preaching?

Ship's Log

Use these activities with your church leadership to help them understand and own the principles of this chapter and how they relate to your church's ministry.

1 Ask your leaders to assess the following: "Say 'I'm a Christian' to these pilgrims, and they flee for their lives. Say 'I'm a disciple of Jesus,' and they gather round to hear more" (p. 49). Ask:

- What evidence do you see of the accuracy of this statement?
- How can we as local church leaders address this issue in our church? in our community?

2 Make your meeting room as dark as you can. Turn on a bright flashlight, and slowly wave it around the room for about a minute without saying anything. Then turn on the lights, and wave the flashlight around the room for another one-half minute. Then ask:

- How is this light like Jesus, our North Star?
- What is different about the shining light in the darkness and in the light?
- Why is it sometimes difficult to keep our focus on Jesus?

Read John 8:12. Ask:

- How does this passage relate to what we've just experienced?
- The flashlight had the most effect when the room was dark. What does that say about our ministry?

3 Discuss from a biblical perspective this quote from Tom Robbins' *Jitterbug Perfume*: "Should you fail to pilot your own ship, don't be surprised at what inappropriate port you find yourself docked."[28]

Read together Matthew 6:24; Hebrews 12:1–2; and any other passages people think of that apply. Ask:

- If we don't pilot our ship, who will? Explain.
- What inappropriate ports might we be headed toward?

4 Have leaders name songs that testify to the love of Christ, such as, "The Love of God Is Greater Far," and "Jesus Loves Me, This I Know." Ask:

- How is our church telling the message of those songs?
- How is our church demonstrating the message of those songs?
- What "containers" do people in our culture use to deliver their messages?
- How do the "containers" our church uses compare to those in use in our culture?
- What "containers" might we consider to better deliver God's message to our community?

5 Read the following assertion by Michael Riddell: "We have succeeded in separating Christ from people, so that they imagine he is the icon of good and respectable people, and has little relevance to their own sordid and tangled lives. Jesus who lived and died as a 'friend of sinners' has been blasphemously translated into the enemy and judge of sinners. The grace and forgiveness which he offered has been swallowed up by self-righteous and prudish moral crusading. The healing love of God is once more locked up in sanctuaries and ceremonies."[29]

Form pairs, and have each pair develop a defense of the church to Riddell's charge. After five minutes, have pairs present their defenses. Then discuss:

- Are any of these defenses legitimate? Why or why not?
- What have been the motives of the church in going the direction we've gone?
- What changes should happen within our congregation to get us sailing the right direction?

6 Refer back to question 6 from the Personal Log section. Ask your leaders to answer the same questions as they relate to your church. Listen carefully to their answers, and plan a strategy for refining your time-discerning, decision-making process of getting ministry accomplished in your church.

MISSIONAL ART #2

STUDYING OUR COMPASS: THE BIBLE

The moving Moon went up the sky,
And no where did abide:
Softly she was going up,
And a star or two beside.[1]
—Samuel Taylor Coleridge

No navigator goes anywhere without a compass. No sailor would set out to sea without a compass. The compass is absolutely as essential as you can get. Without it, you can't expect to get anywhere. Except lost.

Ferdinand Magellan, often celebrated as one of the best navigators in history, led the first circumnavigation of the globe. On board Magellan's five ships were 35 compass needles.

A compass is a strip of magnetized steel, which, when balanced on a pin point and free to swing in any direction, eventually comes to rest with one end pointing north—the end that is then painted red or black.

God has given spiritual navigators a compass: the Scriptures. The Scriptures point us to Christ. They enable us to locate the North Star. They are not Christ. They are not what we worship. But the compass points us to our life work—following Christ.

> The Scriptures are the manger in which Christ is laid.
>
> —Martin Luther

The compass of the Scriptures is the key instrument for any student of the Spirit. In times of peril at sea, sailors were even known to rope the compass around their necks, a literal lifeline should they capsize or be thrown overboard. Even liberals know they cannot do without the text of Scripture. At the same time they don't know what to do with it.

> P. T. Forsyth was right (though I usually admit this only to my Baptist friends): The real successor to the apostles was not the episcopate but the New Testament.[2]

The Scriptures direct us to certain places amid uncertain times. If ever there were a desert island book, the Bible is the one. You especially need a compass when darkness sets in and the North Star is hidden. The compass keeps you on course.

In some ways a twenty-first-century leader is no different from a modern leader, a medieval leader, or an apostolic leader: A leader is known by the company he or she keeps. Howard Hendricks defines the leader as "a person with a magnet in his heart and a compass in his head."[3] The magnet in the heart is Christ; the compass in the head and hand is the Bible.

> We are asleep over charts at running windows
> We are asleep with compasses in our hands.[4]
>
> —Poet W. S. Merwin

Digesting the Scriptures

Philosopher Emmanuel Levinas once defined the Bible as "a volume inhabited by a people." But he quickly added that it was "also a volume that has nourished that people, almost in the literal sense of the term, like the prophet who, in Ezekiel 3, swallows a scroll."[5] Ezekiel was handed a written scroll, and God said, "Eat what is before you, eat this scroll; then go and speak to the house of Israel" (Ezek. 3:1). Eugene Peterson's *Eat This Book* (2006) catches the power of this image for the way the Scriptures are to be internalized until they become part of every cell of our body.[6]

To learn this second missional art, we as navigators must so give ourselves over to the Word of God that it re-speaks in us. Our first-stop assignment, as the angel instructed St. John on Patmos, is to so swallow the Word that it passes through our system—our liver, our kidneys, our intestines, our brain—and becomes a part of who we are until the compass is literally "in the head" if not "in the body."

> The apostle Paul believed that when the Word of God becomes a part of who you are, "you are a letter from Christ, the result of our ministry, written not with ink but with the Spirit of the living God, not on tablets of stone but on tablets of human hearts" (2 Cor. 3:3).

God speaks to humans through the human. All divine revelation is culturally mediated. This means that the Bible must be metabolized through the passions and polemics of the culture in which it will be lived out. Too much of "biblical Christianity" is being mediated by an outworn, lovelorn modernity. Presenting the Bible to our culture involves attaining and synthesizing the best information and resources we can find, as well as tracking cultural changes and tacking to stay on course.

Back to Basics

Vince Lombardi, the legendary Green Bay Packers head coach, was a fanatic for fundamentals. After a game in which the Packers lost to an ill-deserving team, Lombardi called his team together and roared, "Okay, we go back to

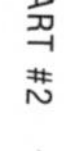

the basics." Then, holding a football high enough for all to see, he continued to yell, "Gentlemen, this is a football."

For the church, it's now back to blocking and tackling basics. To a world that thinks it's quoting Shakespeare when it quotes the Bible; to a world in which the Bible has become an unknown book; to a world that picks up the Bible when it goes spoiling for a fight; to a church that gives restaurant menus and TV guides closer readings than it does Scripture: to this world and to this church it's time to hold up the Bible and say:

People, this is a Bible.

People, this is a life compass.

People, this is what helps you find the North Star.

Off course? Lost your bearings? Drifting in a dark sea? People, this is how you find life's bearings.

The compass, strict and sure, is what enables us to locate our lives in relation to the Star of Bethlehem. The compass is what shapes and fashions our lives into the likeness of Christ.

> Why does this huge, sprawling, tactless book sit there inscrutably in the middle of our cultural heritage … frustrating all efforts to walk around it?[7]
>
> —Canadian literary critic Northrop Frye

The great C. H. Spurgeon, a preacher who reached out and grabbed the guts of the people of his day, once said that the Christian bloodline ought to be a Bibline.[8] Missional art #2 entails mastery of this Bibline bloodline. Novelist Joyce Carol Oates writes of a character's grandmother: "We are linked together by blood, and blood is memory without language."[9] Christians are linked together by the blood memory of the Bible that circulates through the body of Christ.

There is nothing more exciting in life than to find your sense of direction. Why is it that when we open God's Word we expect to be bored? It is theologically incorrect to talk of making the Word "come alive." It already is.

We're the ones who have tried to kill it. We've sucked the blood right out of the Bibline. We've drained it dry with boredom, banality, and mediocrity.

"Breathe on Me, Breath of God" is a song the soul should sing every time one opens the Scriptures. To study and learn the Scriptures is to inhale the energies of the Spirit. We inhale the breath of God. We exhale the breath of life: biblical stories. Through modulating exhaled breath, humans fashion stories, stories to build lives upon. When the stories of Scripture become "our" stories, when biblical images and metaphors become "our" images and metaphors, when we structure "our" lives around the cornerstone Jesus story, a new architecture for our souls is constructed.

Of Ruts and Rivers

Donna Markova distinguishes between a "rut story" and a "river story." Rut stories keep us stuck in old tracks and trajectories. They limit us, lock us in place, and harm the soul. The organizing stories that built modernity and dominated Western culture for the last five hundred years have collapsed. Think about it. Less than one generation ago, fully one-fifth of the world's population lived under the organizing story of communism, which has gasped its final breath right before our eyes.

Think about it. The mind-without-a-soul/body-without-a-soul organizing story of Enlightenment rationalism has exploded in our face. If rational intelligence is our highest value, then computers are the pinnacle of creation. The ruts are giving way to rivers.

River stories move us forward.[10] River stories add life-giving software (accumulated memories and learning) to the brain's hardware (billions of neurons). The greatest river story in history is the story of Jesus of Nazareth, who taught that God's Spirit moving in the human soul is life's highest value.

Sara Maitland has defined theology as …
"(1) the art of telling stories about the divine and
"(2) the art of listening to those stories."[11]

Church Overboard

Jesus is the Morning Star, the "Sun of Righteousness." The Bible is like the moon. Its glory is a reflected glory. An eclipse occurs when the moon moves into a position of direct alignment with the earth and the sun. When that happens, the moon hides the sun. In some of our churches, the Sun is in eclipse, blocked by the moon. The Word made word has eclipsed the Word made flesh.

> We live by a small trickle of electricity from the sun.[12]
>
> —Biochemist/Nobel laureate Albert Szent-Gyorgyi

When the sun is partly visible behind the moon, it is called a partial eclipse. A total solar eclipse occurs when the new moon passes directly between the sun and the earth. When the moon totally obscures the bright sun, daytime turns to darkness. Large segments of the Christian church today are living in various stages of eclipse—with the light of Christ obscured by all sorts of interferences. Just as the magnetism of the moon draws the tides, so the magnetism of the Scriptures draws people into more flowing and intimate relationships with the Sun, the Morning Star. An eclipse blocks that magnetic pull.

> When you're true to the compass, you have the freedom of the seas.
>
> —Anonymous

The phrase "O.B." (OH BEE), usually yelled, is an abbreviation for "overboard." Someone overboard is the most dreaded emergency at sea. There are a couple of places within the church where "Gone Overboard" needs to be declared. Jesus himself was forced to yell "O.B." at various times in his ministry. Here's one example:

> You diligently study the Scriptures because you think that by them you possess eternal life. These are the Scriptures that testify about me, yet you refuse to come to me to have life.
>
> —John 5:39–40

Let's look at where we should be yelling, "Oh Bee!"

Oh Bee #1

The soul goes overboard when the Scriptures, which point to Jesus, begin pointing to themselves. The witness of the Bible is not to get people to believe the Bible but to believe God. It does not say "Believe in the Bible, and you will be saved," but "Believe in the Lord Jesus, and you will be saved—you and your household" (Acts 16:31).

The prince of Grenada, an heir to the Spanish crown, was sentenced to life in solitary confinement in Madrid's ancient prison. The dreadful, dirty, and dreary nature of the place earned it the name "The Place of the Skull." Everyone knew that once you were in, you would never come out alive. The prince was given one book to read the entire time … the Bible.

With only one book to read, he read it over hundreds and hundreds of times. The book became his constant companion. After thirty-three years of imprisonment, he died. When they came to clean out his cell, they found some notes he had written using nails to mark the soft stone of the prison walls. The notations were of this sort: Psalm 118:8 is the middle verse of the Bible; Ezra 7:21 contains all the letters of the alphabet except the letter J; the ninth verse of the eighth chapter of Esther is the longest verse in the Bible, no word or name of more than six syllables can be found in the Bible.

This individual spent thirty-three years of his life studying what some have described as the greatest book of all time. Yet he could only glean trivia. From all we know, he never made any religious or spiritual commitment to Christ. He simply became an expert at Bible trivia.

When knowing facts about God, Jesus Christ, and the Bible takes precedence over a living relationship with Christ, the Sun goes into eclipse. When knowledge about Christianity becomes more important than entrusting one's life to Christ and being changed from the inside out, the church is in eclipse.

> There is something terribly wrong when we argue about the Bible more and enjoy it less.[13]
>
> —Clark H. Pinnock

When "life" anagrams itself into "file" in the lessons of Scripture, we make the words of Jesus a substitute for an experience of Jesus. Psychiatrist R. D. Laing put it like this: "When we look into the brain, we do not see the sky, we see only brain."[14] We don't discover the God of relationship by examining the laws and mechanisms of the universe. Nor do we discover the Way, the Truth, and the Life by memorizing verses and mastering facts. Are we reading the Bible in such a way that it brings us alive to relationships with Christ, even a God experience? Are we reading the Bible in such a way that Christ—his love, his joy, his grace, his peace—is being formed in us?

The words of God cannot be separated from an experience of God. Once they are, the Bible becomes an idol. I am a fundamentalist, not of the word but of the image: I am a fundamentalist about the image of God in Jesus the Christ.

> Those dreadful hammers! I hear the clink of them at the end of every cadence of the Bible verses.[15]
>
> —John Ruskin

Oh Bee #2

The living word fights for breath amid our smotherings of the Scripture as litmus test, magic wand, and the ultimate "peep show." And much of

the biblical argument today is conducted at the level of "'Tis … 'Tain't … 'Tis … 'Tain't."

In Nazi-hunter Simon Wiesenthal's thesis about the six components that make genocide possible, "Bureaucracy" comes right after "Hatred" and "Dictatorship."[16]

There are still three words that send customers right up the wall—three words salespeople are now instructed never to use in relationships with clients: "That's Our Policy."

Three equivalent words drive today's hearer up the wall when debating moral and ethical issues: "The Bible says." People know how bureaucracies of church, state, and corporation—which are in love with labels and have lost track of people—filter what "The Bible says" into forms favorable to themselves. What postmoderns yearn to hear is "What Jesus Says" and "What is Jesus Doing?" And even, "What do you do as a disciple of Christ?"

But I have to live
where the black Bibles
are walls of granite,
where the heads are bowed
over eternal fire.[17]
—Scottish poet Iain Crichton Smith

Jesus used the Scriptures to draw people into a deeper relationship with and experience of God, not as a word-whipping or take-no-prisoners attack on people who disagreed with him. So much of our toting and quoting of Scripture is laced with enough corrosive acid to eat out a marble baptismal font. If Jesus had to draw lines, it was only in something as permanent as sand. And the lines he drew verbally were connecting lines, not dividing lines.

Love God, and do what you will.[18]

—Augustine, Bishop of Hippo

Oh Bee #3

For centuries mariners used stars and other heavenly bodies for navigation. Today we are doing the same through Google Earth and GPS (Global Positioning System), which can tell anyone on planet Earth their location and altitude to within thirty feet of anywhere. The stars are now twenty-four satellites that circle the earth in precisely determined orbits every twelve hours. The starlight is now radio waves that can't be blocked by clouds. The sextant is now computer chips, miniaturized radio receivers, and atomic clocks that keep time to within millionths of a second over an entire year. The compass is now the fiber gyroscope or one of the other GNSS systems,[19] but one of many twenty-first-century technologies for navigational guidance.

The texts and traditions of our faith point us to Christ. But the Scriptures always involve a different form of technology.

Well into the twenty-first century, the church remains a bastion of Gutenberg culture. In some circles, to be a Christian has become synonymous with being against electronic media, the primary language of our emerging culture. In a Google culture that is visually oriented, it is an abnegation of duty not to use an EPIC interface (Experiential, Participatory, Image-rich, Connective) to reach people with the gospel.[20] The church's inability to speak biblical truth to this Google world is a symptom of a limp mind, lazy mission, and lack of historical perspective on mission.

How long has the Bible been a book? Well, in one sense for 1,500 years. The book made its appearance in the fourth century, not the fifteenth. But the Bible began as oral tradition. It quickly became a scroll. Christianity itself arose in history during a sea change from scroll to codex, a paradigm shift comparable only to the one today from print to screen and from nuts and bolts to silicon chips. Scrolls were difficult—all that rolling and unrolling just to find one line. So by the time of Jesus, some scribes actually began cutting scrolls into "pages" and binding the pages along one of their long sides with a decorative protective cover. This is what was called a "codex," and the Chinese came up with the same idea at about the same time.

> Christians were the first—and now perhaps we can say it happened a century earlier than we thought—to make the crucial transition from writing on a scroll to writing on a codex—that is, what we now call a book.[21]
>
> —A. E. Harvey

Jesus mastered the dominant media forms of his day. From his reading the scroll in Luke 4 (most likely the Septuagint), we know he could read, which only a small percentage of first-century people could do. We know that Jesus could speak Greek. We also know that he could write. How do we know this?

1) He conversed with Pilate and the centurion, conversations possible only if Jesus spoke Greek (Greek was the official common language in Galilee as well as the language of home).

2) He had disciples with Greek names (Philip and Nathanael, bicultural names).

3) Jesus' occupation was as a builder, and as such he worked extensively with Gentiles.

4) Jesus wrote in the sand.[22]

The world of books was begun by medieval monks, not printers. But again these were manuscript books, not print books; parchment books, not paper books. It could take a monk an entire lifetime to make one manuscript book that was written on vellum, bound in blind-stamped calf over wooden boards, with brass clasps and catches.

Most often, the Bible circulated in multiple manuscript books. Not until the thirteenth century did one-volume Bibles exist. But the real answer to how long has the Bible been a portable book is five hundred years. The core technology of the Protestant Reformation was the book. Protestant Reformers claimed the printing press as their medium of choice.

Protestant churchmen were accused as early as a generation after the invention of the printing press of turning an entire European culture into the "people of the book." Printed books may have been one of Western Europe's first mass-produced objects.

How long have Christians used mass communication technologies? The core technology of the Puritan Revolution was the innovation of the newspaper. The core technology of the Methodist Revolution was a host of mass print technologies.[23] Nineteenth-century evangelicals were awed by the power of mass publication to touch the human soul and were committed to using it. But their response to new media forces and forms was shaped by five key features, according to the pioneering research of historian David Paul Nord:[24]

(1) While they embraced new technologies, at the same time (2) they stood in fear of them and understood their dreadful power to lead people astray and to produce "vile, licentious literature"; (3) new genres of cheap, popular literature were dangerous, but could be used with care for the glory of God;[25] (4) the tracts and simple narratives were means to the larger end of getting the largest number of people to move their reading from evil literature to great literature, including the greatest literature of all—the Bible; (5) they were determined to get the latest technology to the poorest backcountry regions of the country.[26]

Some have always objected to various technological forms of the Scriptures. Dissenters have appeared in the days of scroll, codex, manuscript book, and mass printing. When photography appeared on the scene, they said that it reflected an age of surfaces and would make us into shallow, surface people. But the opposition to print was especially divisive.

Johannes Trithemius, abbot of Sponheim, denounced printed books in 1492: "If writing is put on to parchment it can last for a thousand years, but how long will printing something on paper last? At the most a paper book could last for two hundred years."[27]

Never before the invention of the printing press did a technology so divide Christians as it did in the sixteenth century. That is until today and the technologies of electronic culture.

The technology that fueled the Protestant Reformation was the printing press, and the new delivery system for learning and faith development was the book. The technologies that are fueling today's ReOrientation are GRIN (Genetics, Robotics, Information Technology, and Nanotechnology), and the new delivery system for learning and faith development is the Internet. Soon there will never be a time we will NOT be connected to the Internet.

This does not mean an end to print culture. A British poll on the reading habits of contemporary Englanders reveals that half the population reads a book at least once a month (nonfiction is the most popular category), and that 30 percent of the people "feel they have a book in them" (only 2 percent have gotten it out).[28] What the dominance of screen culture over print culture means is that, in the words of Alvin Kernan, author of *The Death of Literature*, reading books "is ceasing to be the primary way of knowing something in our society."[29]

Compasses are now computers, cameras, multispectral scanners, satellites, and the Global Positioning System. Smartphones, iPhones all now come with GPS. For some Christians, to be handed the possibility of making the Scriptures come alive in all media forms—print, audio, video, mp3—feels like being handed a poisoned chalice. But we must take advantage of every communication tool to deliver God's Word to today's population. The missional art of the compass involves making God's Word a GPS resource on the Internet, where all the media forms of the past are converging to deepen and intensify basic patterns of relationship and communication.

TNT

In the future, satellite systems will be the navigator's primary means of fixing position. But electronic devices and satellite systems will not always be available. Computers "go down." We will always need the print compass of a book Bible to take with us wherever we go.

South African minister John W. De Gruchy tells of passing through a security gate at Heathrow Airport.

> My hand luggage emitted the ominous sound which alerts police to the presence of a hidden weapon. Having been taken aside by a police officer, my luggage was searched, and eventually the officer confronted me with the offending article. It was a Bible with a metal zip. My immediate reaction was to protest: "that's only a Bible," to which the officer with some theological insight replied: "Maybe, but the Bible can be a very dangerous book!"[30]

Especially when we take it seriously.

My Bible has TNT engraved on the leather. This scroll is a stick of dynamite. This codex can explode old habits. This book can blast base fixations and detonate new devotions. This Web site can release enough energy to move any mountain and mend any life. If I hear one more time a Christian sigh, "The church just can't compete with Hollywood,"[31] I'm going to twist someone's tongue.

Hollywood is the one that can't compete with the Holy. Nothing on earth can compete with the power of God to enliven and enlighten.

"Amanda" was a six-year-old Sunday school student, the daughter of a county sheriff. On "Presentation Sunday" at her local church in Boulder, Colorado, she was given her very own Bible. During coffee time in the fellowship hall, a member of the church congratulated her and asked if he could see her Bible.

"OK. But don't open it."

"Don't open it? But why shouldn't I open it?"

"You'll let God out."[32]

Open the Scriptures.

Let God out.

AQUACHURCH #2
GINGHAMSBURG CHURCH

Tipp City, Ohio
ginghamsburg.org

As an AquaChurch concerned about reaching today's culture, Ginghamsburg recognizes the felt need of trying to maximize life and the desire for something more. Even though people may add activities to their lives, the inner hunger still goes unfulfilled. Ginghamsburg understands that Jesus Christ is the One who can fill that hunger, and seeks to provide that opportunity to a Google world. In seeking to bring God's Word—Jesus Christ—to today's culture, Ginghamsburg Church:

- Offers powerful, weekly God-experiences in multiple, unique settings. This includes Saturday, Sunday, and Monday services, each with a unique feel.
- Recognizes that not everyone has the same worship experience, and has offered a variety of settings to foster that venture.
- Has an ingenious Web site that is informative and descriptive regarding the various missions and visions for the community.
- Has over twenty ministries, including CyberMinistry, whose mission is to web empower the church to expand its ministry impact locally and around the world. As technology grows and changes the CyberMinistry plans to remain on the cutting edge to utilize these capabilities to do the work of Jesus Christ in new and innovative ways.
- Acknowledges that despite advances in technology, there is still a need for true connection. This is why they have developed a ministry of cell groups and even online communities to meet that goal.

CAPTAIN'S LOGBOOK

PERSONAL LOG

Use these ideas to stimulate your thinking about how the principles of this chapter could affect your ministry. Consider sharing these ideas with other church leaders.

1 Theologian John Baillie once remarked, "The New Testament does not say, 'You shall know the rules, and by them you shall be bound,' but, 'You shall know the truth, and the truth shall make you free.'" Ask yourself:

- Which half of the above statement is most representative of my ministry?
- Which best fits my personal life?

2 Two sailors are washed off the deck of a fishing vessel in a storm. One is able to grab a rope and hang on. The other is not. Think about the following questions:

- How are the Scriptures like that rope?
- How are you like the sailor clinging to the rope?
- Who can you think of who is like the sailor who couldn't catch the rope?
- What must you do to hold fast to the rope?
- What forces are trying to pull your fingers from that lifeline?

3 Melissa Southrey of Absecon, New Jersey, describes each of us as a "walking Bible." Another description of Christians says we are moons: The only brightness of the moon comes from the reflected glory of the Sun. Read 2 Corinthians 3:2–3, 17–18. On a piece of paper, draw a Bible with legs, or a moon. On that drawing, write your response to the appropriate questions below:

- What are the strong passages of your "walking Bible"?
- How does the light reflecting from you affect those you come in contact with?
- If you are a "moon" or a letter of Christ, what glory of the Son are you reflecting?

4 To navigate on the open sea, using the North Star and a compass, what must one know? How does your situation compare to being out on the open sea? How can your Bible guide you as a compass guides a sea captain?

5 What feelings hit you when you think about reading your Bible? Are they feelings of preparation ("I need to study so I can prepare my sermon outline!"), perspiration ("I am tired of trying to make sense out of this old book!"), or inspiration ("I am always moved by what this book says to me!")? Spend a few moments reading the Bible from a totally inspirational point of view. Read with a spontaneity that breeds not just head-filling information, but heart-filling transformation. Ask yourself—when was the last time God spoke a clear and compelling message to me? What was the message? Did I heed it as well as hear it?

6 Think about the following statement: "God speaks to humans through the human. All divine revelation is culturally mediated" (p. 67).

- How do you react to this statement?
- When have you felt genuinely affirmed in your "culturally mediating" process of teaching from the Scriptures? Who affirmed you? Why did it seem genuine?
- How does this statement make you feel about your role as teacher of the Word?

7 Every teacher of the Scriptures needs to hear the indictment of the ages regarding what we've done to God's Word: "We've drained it dry with boredom, banality, and mediocrity" (p. 69). Why do you think our handling of the Word of God has brought this disappointing analysis?

- How can we recover the energy and relevance of God's Word?
- Read 1 Corinthians 4:1–2, and ask yourself the following:

  Have I proved myself faithful of the trust given me?

  How can I be a better "steward" of God's mystery?

8 The Bible is the compass God has given us to guide our way even when times get rough. Bob Benson puts it this way: "The Bible does not deny the reality of suffering and evil. Neither of them is excluded from its pages in either the stories of the heroes and heroines or in the stories of those who seem to be only tragic victims. But in the face of all the mishaps and misfortunes that have come along to befall the human race, the Bible continues to affirm that he will get us

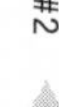

home."[33] Reflect on God's faithfulness. Remember his consistency in your life. Then breathe a prayer of gratitude and realize … he will get you home!

Ship's Log

Use these activities with your church leadership to help them understand and own the principles of this chapter and how they relate to your church's ministry.

1 "In Australia we use the term 'white-anting.' It derives its meaning from the Australian white ant, which has a fondness for wood fibre. White ants will eat their way through the interior of wooden framing in a building, completely hollowing it out. The surface of the timber seems perfectly intact, and there is no obvious evidence of the ants' activity. No evidence, that is, until the entire building collapses. The Christian church in the West has been 'white-anted.' On the surface it appears intact. But the heart of the church has been eaten away, and the whole edifice stands in danger of imminent collapse."[34]

- How accurate do you believe this assessment is? Explain.
- Do you think this assessment applies to our church? Why or why not?
- What actions should we take to avoid the kind of collapse described here?

2 In global positioning systems aboard ships, there is a "Man Overboard" button. When you push this button, the system automatically records the coordinates of your location so that you can return and find whatever or whomever you lost and where you lost it. With your leaders, develop a list of "Man Overboard button" Scriptures we can push to lock our location in place and remind us who we are. Once you've developed the list, choose two or three to be guiding principles for leading your church.

3 Walk through the "OH BEE" sections of this chapter (pp. 71–77), looking at the various forms the Bible has taken. Then form groups of three or four people, and tell groups they're part of a Google Gutenberg Bible Project. They're to develop a Web Bible. Give groups about ten minutes to sketch out what it would be like. Then have groups report. After the reports, ask:

- How well would these attempts at a Web Bible connect with non-Christians out there?
- How would Christians relate to this Web Bible?
- What insights has this exercise given us for our church's ministry?

4 Rich Everett, one-time manager of interactive communications for Chrysler Corporation, says there are four steps to landing a customer:

a) Tell—Tell about the product.

b) Sell—Explain why someone should buy it.

c) Link—"Link" interested parties into a showroom.

d) Think—Give them enough information to "think" about whether they are going to buy it or not.[35]

Have leaders form pairs and discuss:

- How might these four steps be helpful in getting people into the "showroom" of the Bible?
- How might we incorporate variations of these steps into the ministry of our church?

Be sure to have pairs report their insights to the group.

5 Howard Hendricks says a leader is "a person with a magnet in his heart and a compass in his head" (p. 66). Poet W. S. Merwin says, "We are asleep with compasses in our hands" (p. 66).

Analyze the synthesis of these two quotes with your leaders:

- If the magnet in the heart is Christ and the compass in the head and hand is the Bible, in what way are we asleep with the Bible in our hands?
- What brought about this lethargy of the soul?
- What can we do in these times and in our church to awaken the Word of God that is living and active and sharper than a double-edged sword? (See Hebrews 4:12.)

6 Evaluate the truth of the following statement: "The church's inability to speak biblical truth to this Google world is a symptom of a limp mind, lazy mission, and lack of historical perspective on mission" (p. 74).

- Is this true for our church? Explain.

- How can our church translate the truth of the printed word into a visually oriented format?

7 Ask your leaders the following question, and have them write down their answers before discussing them: How true is the statement that "the technologies that are fueling today's ReOrientation are GRIN (Genetics, Robotics, Information Technology, and Nanotechnology), and the new delivery system for learning and faith development is the Internet" (p. 77)? After everyone has written an answer, have leaders tell what they wrote and why. Then discuss:

- How should our church use computer technology and the Internet?
- How can our church make God's Word a GPS (Global Positioning System) resource for the world?

After your discussion, carefully define steps your church may want to take to participate in this new delivery system for the future.

8 Before leaders arrive, plan a course involving several turns for your leaders to walk around your church. Record the directions in terms of compass headings and number of steps taken, but don't leave any kind of markings on the course or mark any landmarks on the directions. For example, you might begin with "Starting from the doorway of our meeting room, take seventeen steps due north. Then walk twelve steps east." Continue the course until leaders get back to your meeting room.

Photocopy your directions for your leaders. To add interest, reverse the directions for about half of the leaders. Provide a compass and directions for each leader, and start them out on thirty-second intervals. When all have returned to your room, discuss the following questions:

- What was it like using a compass to guide you?
- How was this experience similar to using the Bible to guide us in life? in our ministries?
- How can we rely more fully on God's Word as our compass to guide the ministry of our church?

MISSIONAL ART #3

CASTING THE ANCHOR: TRADITION

Drop anchor into God.[1]

—Joyce Huggett,

British author/missionary in Cyprus

English cultural anthropologist Nigel Barley sums up the enterprise known as "fieldwork" on the last page of his *Adventures in a Mud Hut*. It's in the form of an exchange that aptly summarizes what it's like for the church to voyage the seascapes of twenty-first-century culture.

> "Ah, you're back."
> "Yes."
> "Was it boring?"
> "Yes."
> "Did you get very sick?"
> "Yes."
> "Did you bring back notes you can't make head or tail of and forget to ask all the important questions?"
> "Yes."
> "When are you going back?"[2]

All Noahs, Peters, and other would-be leaders must now become anthropologists. The as-good-as-dead Industrial Age cultural paradigm has been replaced by a new culture that requires the fieldwork skills of an anthropologist, the dedication of a missionary, the patience of a saint, the learning curve of a child, the cunning of a spy, the stamina of an athlete, and the resolve of a Coast Guard sailor.

Christ is the Lord of all ages past, present, and to come—call it 21-C (twenty-first century), 3M (Third Millennium), PC (Pacific Century), Post-modernity, Google-world, or what you will. The Polish Pope John Paul II established the Pontifical Council for Culture in 1982 because of his conviction that "the destiny of the world" hinges on "the Church's dialogue with the cultures of our time." Admitting the impossibility of contextless theology—"there is an organic and constitutive link existing between Christianity and culture"—Pope John Paul insisted that "the synthesis between culture and faith is not just a demand of culture, but also of faith. *A faith which does not become culture is a faith which has not been fully received, not thoroughly thought through, not fully lived out.*"[3]

Faith is embedded in specific cultures.
Faith is shaped by forces and commitments
that are beyond one's choosing or control.

The phrase "until I return" is often used to translate the Greek in John 21:22–23. Implicit in the Greek phrase *heos erchomai*, however, is more the meaning, "while I am coming." Jesus is saying less "stay behind until I return" than "stay behind *while I am returning*." We mistake Jesus' intention when we look only to some culminating moment and not also look around us for the ways in which Christ is returning all the time. The gospels are so adept at presenting this rhythm of past, present, future (for example, Jesus' "A time is coming and has now come" [John 4:23; 5:25]) that it can easily escape our attention.

On Christmas Day the Sweet children have learned that no presents can even be handled much less opened without first the reading of the Christmas story. I will never forget one Christmas morning at 6:00 a.m., when eight-year-old Thane marched into the bedroom, plopped in a chair, and demanded of two sleepy parents, "What gospel are you reading out of this year?"

"Luke, I think. Why?" I managed to reply.

"How long does its Christmas story go?" Thane countered.

From the other side of the bed, a voice interjected, "It's still going on."

Every introduction to biology requires students to learn a refrain: "ontology recapitulates phylogeny." What this means is that all new growth and development must first pass through all the previous developmental stages. To live faithfully in the twenty-first century, we must live out of the full two-thousand-year history of the Christian church and not lobotomize the last nineteen centuries to get back to the first century. God did not put us through the past two thousand years for no reason. God did not put us through the Enlightenment's Age of Reason for no reason.

What we now share in common as Christians has not always been commonly shared by our Christian ancestors. We view God and life through theological lenses that have been ground in a two-thousand-year process. When we become Christians, we participate in a faith that a community has been living long before we arrived. How I live my life has been shaped by a thought community that long precedes me. I have been spiritually instructed by twenty centuries of Christian thought and practice. I have been an apprentice to Martin Luther and John Calvin, John and Charles Wesley, Charles G. and Elizabeth Atkinson Finney, Ida Mae Boggs, Mabel Boggs Sweet, and …

The Christmas story is still being told.

> The only alternative to tradition is bad tradition.[4]
>
> —Church historian Jaroslav Pelikan (1923–2006)

Hauling the Anchor

One of the earliest images of the church in Christian art, as we have seen, is that of a boat. The image of the church as boat, and of tradition as anchor, has adorned our holy spaces ever since the church's first days. Sometimes the anchor image has been combined with the cross to form an unforgettable symbol of Truth and truth together. If Jesus is the Truth (capital T), and the Scriptures contain the truth, then the traditions of the church expand and enhance our experience of both.

Throughout the church, warnings abound that we stay "anchored" to "doctrinal moorings" as we enter these choppy waters of what may be Christianity's first "perfect storm." One can hear these calls from outside the church as well. Futurist Faith Popcorn's book *Clicking* outlines sixteen twenty-first-century trends, one of which she calls "anchoring" and defines as "spiritual exploration in which we ground ourselves by looking back at the past—to prepare for the millennium and beyond."[5]

The use of the same "anchoring" language gives one pause. Isn't the place for the church on the high seas? A boat is always in forward motion. Is not "anchoring" the exact opposite way to launch a ship? How can the church move into the future when it is "anchored"?

If one exegetes the biblical image of "anchor," one of the key texts that immediately surfaces is Hebrews 6:18–19, where "hope" is said to be like an "anchor" that is "offered to us." We are instructed to move ahead in safety and confidence by casting our anchor forward and then "grasping the hope set before us" (NEB). Now here is a strange image: that of casting an anchor into the future and winching one's way forward by holding on to the past for dear life.

> Geared to the Times.
> Anchored to the Rock.[6]
> —Billy Graham's first slogan

The biblical image is clearly one of casting an anchor ahead, not behind, and then pulling oneself forward. At a conference just outside of Cape Cod, Massachusetts, a naval officer from the Second World War helped me exegete this image when he told how the battleships he was on survived terrible hurricanes in Chesapeake Bay. It was in similar fashion sailors in the eighteenth and nineteenth centuries wormed their ships through tight places or dangerous spots.

It seems that when storms or turbulent seas threatened a ship that was docked in harbor, a crew of some eight or nine sailors would be sent out in a motor launch or "whale boat." Their mission was to haul the ship's anchor onto planks set across the stern of the launch. Motoring out to sea in the midst of the storm as far as the chain would take them, the anchor would then be let down and the ship winched forward into deeper water on the anchor chain.[7]

In other kinds of wind one casts the anchor forward for other reasons: to establish a pivot point from which to cast off, set sail, and stay untangled from other boats, booms, docks, rocks, and other hazards.

> In the legend of the Welsh Prince Madoc's discovery of America, his ship got stuck in Chesapeake Bay. After trying unsuccessfully to free the vessel, the crew asked Prince Madoc what to do. He responded, "kedge on our anchor." So they rowed out as far as they could with an anchor, dropped it into the sea, and then winched their way toward it.[8]

This ancient sailing practice of using the anchor to pull a ship along, called "kedging," is what I mean by the AncientFuture methodology of moving backward into the future.[9] The AncientFuture Mariner inculturates the gospel in every time and clime, especially when the ecclesiastical ship is docked in harbor and a storm is brewing at sea. It works equally as well when just the opposite is the case, and one must find a way to move with no wind. To get back out on the high seas, the church must work its way forward by "kedging off"—dropping an anchor (a symbol of tradition) into the future. Even into the midst of force-ten gales, the church must pull itself by that anchor into the future. Until "there [is] no longer any sea" (Rev. 21:1), we will need in every age to cast the anchor of tradition into the future and then winch our way forward. Like the lowly worm, spider, and clam, the church locomotes by throwing an anchor of tradition ahead into the future and pulling itself to it.

Yoked foresight and hindsight yield insight. The future is always found in the past. This NewAncients methodology seeks to make the past current. It does not mean retiring the old, discarding scarred antiques, or launching the fashionable. The key to relevancy is more constancy than recency. The blend of the venerable with the vogue, the well preserved with the pregnant, is our only security amid the uncertainties of the future. A flash in the pan spews forth the spirit of the times. But a woman or man of the hour brings to a boil the spirit of the times mixed with the ancient of days.

The more "conservative" one becomes—in the truest sense of the word *conservative*—the more cutting-edge is one's ministry. God's dream is not a church that is "good as new," but "good as old." "Good as old" is better than "good as new." The problem with the church today is not that it is "too traditional," but that it is not traditional enough. It has held the future to a frozen version of the past, ignoring much of tradition. It has reduced the rich, full tradition of the Christian faith into a bounded set of rituals, formulas, or principles. Liberals call them "stands"; conservatives call them "fundamentals."

Twenty-first-century mariners are rearview visionaries. Without ancestors in the faith, no Christian can be quite a Christian. Without the humus of Clement of Alexandria, Augustine, Aquinas, Hildegard of Bingen, Luther, Calvin, the Wesleys, and Edwards, how can Christians take root and blossom? True leaders offer the future what the saints of the past have lived and died to defend. Looking at our faith history, we can distinguish genuine newness from nowness.

Modern society was a culture that consumed its own past. In contrast, twenty-first-century pilgrims honor the bones of the dead and make those bones live (Ezek. 37). "Moses took the bones of Joseph with him," reads Exodus 13:19. Moses didn't leave without taking his past with him. Those bones were the symbol of the Hebrews' history, prompting them in their struggle to remember, equipping them in their war against forgetting.

Poet/graphic designer William Blake admonished his readers to "Drive your cart and your plow over the bones of the dead."[10]

We must not go anywhere without carrying the bones and stones of memory with us: the memory of our past, the memory of our ancestors, and the memory of our holy places. Those bones and stones are the memory of the future, the imagination of the past. They're at the heart of our worship.

Do not move an ancient boundary stone
set up by your forefathers.
—Proverbs 22:28

Outside of an AncientFuture Faith, twenty-first-century pilgrims are spiritually ill-tuned. French composer Saint-Saens adhered to classical principles of music while at the same time functioning as a formal innovator of surprising resourcefulness. In the same way, the Rime of the AncientFuture Mariner brings together tradition and newness, institution and inauguration, innovation and consolidation.

Inculturating Christ

The fifty-fifth anniversary of H. Richard Niebuhr's classic *Christ and Culture* (1953) has come and gone. In spite of Niebuhr's massive contributions, the church needs a theology of culture today even more desperately than when Niebuhr's book was written.

From my vantage point as a historian, the church can choose one of four ways to respond to culture, including the emerging culture.[11] From my vantage point as a theologian, the church's choice will profoundly influence its unity of spirit and its living out of the purpose for which Jesus lived and died and rose again. Each of the four modes of relating Christ and culture is a variation on the real "Lord's Prayer," the prayer of Jesus himself just before he left to cross the Kidron valley to the garden where he would be betrayed (John 17).

As he addresses God, Jesus first admits "My prayer is not that you take them out of the world" (John 17:15) but then immediately acknowledges that his disciples "are not of the world" (John 17:16). The true path through culture lies somewhere in between. We are called, in Jesus' words, to be in the world. Not of the world. But not out of it either.

Jesus laid out a triangulation methodology of orienteering through cultures.

We need to hear Jesus say that again. The church as the body of Christ is called to triangulate: to be in the world, not of it ("My kingdom is not of this world" [John 18:36]), but not out of it of it either ("My prayer is not that you take them out of the world"). Through the centuries the church has repeatedly gotten into trouble by getting too cozy with any one part of Jesus' "in-not-of-but-not-out-of-it-either" triangular orienteering.

> He was in the world, and though the world was made through him, the world did not recognize him.
>
> —John 1:10

What will be the church's response this time?

1. Anticultural Response?

This attitude, where the church sets itself up in opposition to the prevailing culture, takes to extremes the mandate that we are not of this world. The anticultural bias has been present in the church since the first solitaires sought God among desert caves and sands.

> There will always be a niche for museum churches. Some people even like to live in a museum. Visit Colonial Williamsburg, and keep count as you walk down the well-preserved colonial streets of how many front doors have the metal plaque on them which reads "Private Residence."

Communal attempts at anticulturalism are quite visible today. The 150,000 Old Order Amish who live in the United States and Canada reject "modern" clothing and conveniences such as indoor plumbing, electricity, and automobiles. In Judaism the Hasids and Lubovitchers offer similar visual reminders that the late twentieth century, much less the twenty-first century, isn't for everybody.

Both of these traditions embody much that is missing from contemporary life (such as community, sustainable lifestyles, and deep spirituality). But unless one lives completely cut off from all other human contact, it is virtually impossible to be a successful anticulturalist. You have to live in the world somewhere. The gospel must be "enfleshed" in some culture. Even the Amish have embraced some culture—that of the early nineteenth-century German settlers known as the Pennsylvania Dutch. Try as they might, they cannot escape the 5 million tourists—350 for each member of the community—who annually flock to Lancaster County, Pennsylvania, lured in part by an "Amish Web Site" supplied by the tourist industry but maintained by the Amish themselves. The Hasids live in the Poland of the 1870s. Everyone must live somewhere in history, in some culture, whether past or present. No one can opt out of history.

Nowhere does the Bible say that Christians must look like they fell off a covered wagon. And when Christians do look that way, they have compromised themselves with a specific culture. I saw an Amish son in Ohio working on a personal battery-powered computer while riding with his father in a horse-drawn carriage. Many Amish now have cell phones which they "charge up" at friendly neighbors' outlets.

The anticultural image of the future is of an idealized past. Jesus calls us to live out of the past, not to live in it or to disengage it from the present and future. The past is a wonderful place to visit, but we are not called to live there. Indeed, how many of us would really want to live there? How many of us could have lived there? How many of us would have died there?

As with all endangered civilizations, we must protect faiths that live in another time; they face a stark future and must be protected from outside influences. But to emulate them is to go the way of the dodo. To feed off the faith and corpses of our predecessors without growing our own is to engage in spiritual necrophilia.

Like the top of a mountain that provides a great view of what has been and what might be but is no place to live, the past must not be dehistoricized or abstracted from the real world. Stay on the mountain, and you don't hear the robin's song or the loon's haunting cry; you don't see the fields of clover or smell the fragrance of flowers. To live, one must go down and enter the world. One must "enflesh" the world for it to be claimed by God.

2. Incultural Response?

This attitude is at the opposite end of the spectrum. Here the church is so anxious to fit in to the world that it becomes merely an extension of the culture and has lost any distinguishing particularity as a culture of its own. The church becomes of the world: "The world is too much with us."

Everyone knows these "golden retriever" churches. If the culture throws a stick, "golden retriever" churches go bounding after it, slobbering and eager to please. Even those who happily own these indiscriminately accepting animals bemoan the fact that if a burglar broke in, the dog would just hold the flashlight for him. Too many inculturated churches are holding too many flashlights for too many burglarizing forces and figures.

Some forms of inculturation assume the congruence of church and culture. It is assumed that the primary symbols of the church and of the culture are identical. The church sees itself in some way as representative of the culture at large and prides itself on its shaping, transforming role. In this inculturation, civil religion and faith religion become one and the same. Churches in nations where the two grew up together often exhibit the most radical forms of inculturation.

Other forms of inculturation involve identification with a specific subculture—whether ideological, professional, or geographical. These churches become so painfully "politically correct" that any attempt to articulate a transcultural value judgment, a moral absolute, or a biblical truth is quickly shuttled away to a committee or task force (a representatively correct one, of course) instead of witnessed to the world.

The church is to identify with the world's needs, but not its desires. As St. Augustine pointed out, "We move spiritually not by our feet, but by our desires." When our desires are shaped by the culture and not by the Spirit, we become children of the times, not children of the Spirit. The "new spirit" promised by the Scriptures becomes a "now" spirit. We are to be "at home" but not "at peace" with God's chosen place and time for us. There is a basic incompatibility between the church and whatever time in which it lives.

> Demas, because he loved this world, has deserted me.
>
> —Paul, 2 Timothy 4:10

3. Countercultural Response?

As the name predicts, these churches and theologians have their roots in the sixties. In fact, the typical countercultural church is probably heavily populated by "boomers"—children of the sixties who, according to Wade Clark Roof's work, are deeply divided between "traditionalists" (54 percent) and "counterculturalists" (46 percent).[12]

The countercultural church tries to take seriously Jesus' dictum that his disciples are not of this world. Thus the church as a countercultural culture offers the world an alternate way of living and a reading of the culture that cuts against some grains. But while the countercultural church is not of the world and is in the world—though it resents having to be there—it is most often out of it in an academically fashionable or politically "in" way. To be in the world means to be with the cultural and intellectual circles of the day, but never of them.

To distinguish itself from the rest of the world, the countercultural church describes itself with aggressively isolationist language. Instead of wearing odd clothes or using horse-drawn surreys, church members use their vocabulary to cordon themselves off from the world. They pontificate such profound half-truths as "let the church be the church," or "reaching out without dumbing down." And as Stanley Hauerwas and William Willimon state it, "the first task of the church is not to make the world more just, but to make the world the world."[13] They speak of the church as an "outpost," "beachhead," or "colony," and designate true Christians as "resident aliens" or "anachronisms" or "old/young fogies." The countercultural church can even come down with a worse case of "remnantitus" than the anticultural church.[14]

The problem with the countercultural model is that it creates an artificial wall between Christians and the world God loves—a love so deep and wide that God sent Jesus to die for it. Jesus did not ask God to take us out of the world. In fact, Jesus' opposition to the temple-based religion of his day, which led more than anything to his condemnation and death, was precisely because he opposed the temple cult's concept of holiness as separation.[15] We are not somehow grandly "above" the political, economic, scientific, technological, or artistic influences of our times. The countercultural church tries to find theological rationale for purposively and proudly remaining out of it.

The church is not so much a refuge from the world as a rescue shop and redemption center in it and for it. "God did not send his Son into the world to condemn the world, but to save the world through him" (John 3:17).

> If I cannot imagine the apostle Paul as a pugnacious guest on *Nightline*, or citing a character's anguished struggles with Roman Catholicism on *Homicide*, then my apostle Paul—and my sense of the Christian's cultural mandate—is too small.[16]
>
> —Episcopalian/editor Douglas L. LeBlanc

4. Incarnational Response?

Perhaps even better would be the term "intercultural." The aim of the incarnational church is a contextualization process first demonstrated in Jesus' own incarnation. When Jesus dressed, he did not dress in a generic, culture-neutral way or put on clothing that set him apart from everyone else of his day. He dressed himself in the customary garb of the day where he lived. He spoke the language of the day in which he lived. He fully inhabited the cultural space of the first century.

The doctrine of the incarnation validates this world on its own terms. If our Savior joins us where we are, not where we ought to be, what excuse do we have to not join people where they are while insisting on where they ought to be? If Jesus descended into hell and founded his church at the very "gates of hell," what hells need we fear? Incarnation is not inculturation or acculturation. It begins with Christ, and then moves to a cultural context, not the other way around.

> Lesslie Newbigin rightly insists that the gospel only retains "its proper strangeness, its power to question us … when we are faithful to its universal suprarational, supranational, supracultural nature."[17]

Jesus himself set forth cultural principles for his disciples to follow and demonstrated the incarnational method at work: Jesus told the seventy, "When you enter a town and are welcomed, eat what is set before you" (Luke 10:8). Earlier, when Jesus sent out his disciples, he gave them the freedom to stay—"search for some worthy person … and stay at his house until you leave" (Matt. 10:11).

Paul was only following in his master's footsteps when he admonished the church to contextualize the gospel in the culture: "I have become all things to all men so that by all possible means I might save some" (1 Cor. 9:22). No wonder that by New Testament times, the church had become inculturated …

at Rome, at Ephesus, at Corinth, at Antioch. The church was fast becoming a global assembly of grassroots fellowships.[18]

The incarnational Christian realizes that the gospel travels through time not in some ideal form, but from one inculturated form to another. In the words of one theologian, the "fiction" of a "'pure' and 'naked' Christianity" has done much damage.[19] What missiologists call "the culturally indigenous church" is the aim of the incarnational church.

Max Stackhouse makes a distinction between the "textuality" of the church—its faithfulness to the gospel—and its "contextuality"—its faithfulness to the world in which it finds itself.[20] That distinction is absolutely critical. If Michael Carrithers is right when he argues that the crucial human attribute is adaptiveness (plasticity),[21] then what makes us truly human is our ability to change our ways in response to new social situations.

God reaches all peoples and all ages through culture.[22] There is no such thing as an unmediated gospel. The incarnational model uses the knowledge, the ignorance, the strengths, and weaknesses of the indigenous culture to contextualize Christ for its age.

> All theologies, then, are necessarily local theologies, ineluctably contextualized, indigenized, on the way to full inculturation. There is no such thing as Christian faith by itself (*fides qua*), existing pure and unalloyed in the depth of one's heart, in some prelinguistic or alinguistic state.[23]
>
> —Vietnamese theologian Peter C. Phan

The great preachers of the past were those who belonged so deeply to their time that they could speak to their times. Where did we get this notion that to get under the skin of one's age is to incur disrespect and disdain? Why has *Zeitgeist* ("Spirit of the Age") become such a bad word? We don't want to participate in the spirit of twenty-first-century culture? We don't want to "discern the times"? Our primary ecclesiastical problem is also a historical problem: a church out of place in time. We can't stand outside our time and transcend our time unless we first stand in our time.

To be sure, incarnational churches must clearly and cleanly distinguish between content and container, between "who they are" and "how they function." The incarnational model takes into account the coordinates of its time but creates a new spirit of the time. It doesn't just catch the spirit of the age; it helps create a new spirit. It is in touch with the culture, but not in tune with it. The issue for the incarnational Christian is not whether the gospel will be inculturated in this Google culture, but how the gospel will be inculturated; not whether our social context shapes the experience of the gospel, but how and when.

> Don't copy the behavior and customs of this world, but be a new and different person with a fresh newness in all you do and think.
>
> —Romans 12:2 TLB

To avoid becoming an obedient lapdog or a rebellious hippie, leadership that is missional, relational, and incarnational must learn to distinguish between that which aids in the transmission of the gospel and that which is merely contemporary static.[24] A missional, relational, and incarnational church gladly uses all the technological advances of culture to help it witness more effectively to a technological world. The only authentic inculturation is "inculturation from below," in which "below" includes whatever is on the streets, from the poor and oppressed to popular culture.

Twenty-first-century spirituality, as well as intellectual and artistic endeavors, must come to terms with popular culture.[25] To a culture where "any place can be a church, any song a prayer, and any person, a priest"[26] (as one Gen Xer put it), popular culture becomes even more important as spirituality is self-assembled.

Missiologists like Andrew Walls and Aylward Shorter have done the most to argue for the inculturation of the gospel.[27] William Reiser defines inculturation as "the process of a deep, sympathetic adaptation to and appropriation of a local cultural setting in which the Church finds itself, in a way that does not compromise its faith."[28] The best definition, however, comes out of an African context:

> The inculturation of the Church is the integration of the Christian experience of a local Church into the culture of its people, in such a way that this experience not only expresses itself in elements of this culture, but becomes a force that animates, orients and innovates this culture so as to create a new unity and communion, not only within the culture in question but also as an enrichment of the Church universal.[29]

How does the church continually inculturate itself without losing the integrity of the gospel?[30] Through this AncientFuture "anchoring." An understanding of "the anchor" is the best biblical guide, principle, and metaphor to help us live out this AncientFuture Faith in whatever age God has chosen us to live.

AncientFuture Orienteering

AncientFuture orienteering is the retrieval of traditions from the past and their re-appropriation into twenty-first-century settings of ministry. It is not a nostalgic capitulation of the present to some romanticized "golden age." Rather it is a "recapitulation" (Irenaeus)[31] or "retrieval" (David Tracy)[32] of our two-thousand-year past into our twenty-first-century future. It is a recovery of the past and its appropriation into new contexts, or what some Asian theologians call "repeat without repetition."

We're going to explore three orienteering stages to this "retrieval": trust, transplantation, and turbocharging ("reintegration").

1. Trust the Tradition

First, one must trust the tradition, and trust it enough to carry it into an uncertain future. One looks to historical resources for assistance in coming to terms with the future. Luther's debate with Erasmus over free will and salvation, for example, is one every believer ought to know by heart. With this kind of trust, one honors the ancestors and holds oneself accountable to them. For example, I hope that one day John Wesley will take delight in my ministry.

Trust combines exegesis with ethnology as one tracks the transcultural truths of the faith. The AncientFuture Christian lives out of the past, not in it. That initial cast of the anchor is critical. Just as in fishing for trout, the chances of really hooking on to something significant diminish with each cast. In fact, after seven casts that come up empty, one should consider moving to another place in the stream of the future, or using another anchor.

> As church consultant Bill Easum puts it, Christians need to be "rooted but not root-bound."

One of the biggest problems in this first step is discerning the difference between "tradition" and "bad habits." A helpful metaphor in making the distinction is that of scaffolding. When we construct a church building we use scaffolding. But when the church is completed, we take down the scaffolding. How ridiculous it would seem if ten, twenty, or thirty years later the scaffolding was still up. Unfortunately, a lot of churches refuse to take the scaffolding down, clinging to it as if it were the church. They have confused the "scaffolding" of institutions with the "tradition" of the saints.

2. Transplant the Tradition

Second, one must transplant the tradition so that the familiar is given new meaning and power. Once one trusts tradition enough to discover it again for the first time, one then delivers that tradition in a way that the tradition has never seen before. Every fresh outpouring of the Spirit reinvents the past, and in so doing honors it and betrays it at one and the same time.

Notice, the word chosen here is *transplant*, not *transform*. When one transforms something, one changes its essence. Transplantation is transferring transcultural truths into a new cultural context. The work of contextualization is translation, not transformation.

Just as Jesus recasts the human race,[33] so we are to recast the gospel for every culture and community. Jesus took the old Scriptures of Israel and recast them in a new light; we take the new teachings of Jesus and reinterpret them in light of the old Scriptures of Israel and recast them within the context in which God has placed us.

This is what it means to be "disciplined" disciples: to transplant the gospel in the community and neighborhood we're in.

3. Turbocharge the Tradition

Third, once the tradition has been trusted and transplanted, it is our mission to turbocharge it for a new day, to find a way of bringing it back that fastens it on the memory and imagination. The act of turbocharging harkens back to the past while heralding the future at work.

Let's look at a concrete example of how AncientFuture orienteering works. The Gutenberg to Google shift, the transition from representation to participation, requires a transition from performance modes to participatory modes of worship. How would this work? The Google world needs to be offered an opportunity to make decisions, choices, and commitments in worship.

1) Trust the Tradition: Our forebears often said "Amen," "Praise the Lord," "Hallelujah," even "Glory" in worship. If the preacher needed encouragement to get going, they said "Preach it, brother." If they didn't like what the preacher was saying, they muttered "Well …"

How likely are we to get people to "Say Amen, Somebody?" Not very. But is there some way that we could make worship more participatory by getting them to say something? People need to feel free to say something. What might they say?

2) Transplant the Tradition: Is there any word that people today are saying that might mean the same thing as "Amen?" Hasn't "YES!" become almost a mantra of Google culture?

But let's get out our compass and sextant to see if we are in dubious waters. My computer word search of "Yes" leads me to 2 Corinthians 1, starting with verse 18.[34]

> As God is true, the language in which we address you is not an ambiguous blend of Yes and No. The Son of God, Christ Jesus, … was never a blend of Yes and No. With him it was, and is, Yes. He is the Yes pronounced upon God's promises, every one of them. That is why, when we give glory to God, it is through Christ Jesus that we say, "Amen." (NEB)

Can the translation be more direct? Jesus is the "Yes" of God, to which we say: "Amen."

3) Turbocharge the Tradition: When you come to introduce this low-level form of participation in worship, you will need some surplus energy to combat the inertia of saying nothing. In this turbocharge phase, we often learn the most from our kids. Watch how they say "Yes." Did you notice that added gesture of the clenched fist and arm that pulls in as the word is proclaimed: YES!

AncientFuture orienteering at work.

And all God's people said, … YES!

Anchor's Aweigh!

When archaeologists were finally allowed to dig in what some call Christianity's holiest site, the Church of the Holy Sepulchre in Jerusalem, they were astounded to discover on a wall beneath the church a red and black graffiti of a boat, with the Latin words under it "DOMINE IVIMUS"—"Lord, we went," the "beginnings" thought in Psalm 122, the psalm of pilgrimage.[35]

When will we go? An AncientFuture church enters uncharted waters by casting the anchor of tradition ahead of us.

Or in the words of the unofficial Coast Guard motto, which take us to our next missional art for spiritual navigation: "We have to go out; we don't have to come back."

Multi-site
www.lifechurch.tv

LifeChurch.tv is an AquaChurch that reenergizes traditions of the church and community to provide true connection amid today's culture. LifeChurch.tv is a multi-site ministry that transcends metropolitan regions. Each week through satellite broadcasts, LifeChurch.tv enables each of their twelve locations to be connected as one. Their mission is to lead people to become fully devoted followers of Christ. Their commitment to AncientFuture marining is seen in the way they connect traditional methods and ideas with a contemporary medium. They accomplish this through:

- Global worship to God and an experience of a powerful and relevant message, which teaches primarily from the Bible.
- A talented live band that has a style consistent with today's culture in order to provide worship that connects.
- Being passionate about sharing the love of Christ by caring for each other and positively impacting their communities.
- Adoption of a traditional set of "essential beliefs." Each of these point back to their mission and are united through "charity."

- Offering a global Internet campus that offers true community and a live interactive worship experience.

CAPTAIN'S LOGBOOK

PERSONAL LOG

Use these ideas to stimulate your thinking about how the principles of this chapter could affect your ministry. Consider sharing these ideas with other church leaders.

1 How do you tell the difference between a spiritual anchor and a barnacle? Consider the following questions:

- What traditions within your church have become barnacles?
- What traditions are truly anchors?
- How might you begin scraping off some of the barnacles and relying on the true anchors?

2 Think carefully about the transitions that are occurring or have recently occurred around you: in your personal life, in your household, in your church, in your area, in our culture, in our world. Rank the top three for yourself, and then for the people in your church, and then for the people in your community. Reflect on the following question: How could you use the anchor of tradition to move forward amid the turbulence?

3 Read the Aaronic blessing (Num. 6:24–26). Think of times that blessing would be appropriate today. Use it to start (or end) a leaders' meeting. Use it to bless your congregation. Find someone to sing a musical rendition of it. Say it to your children. Make it a "family blessing" that you tuck your children in with at night.

4 Think about how a sea anchor is used in the deep sea: Often it is thrown off the bow of the ship just to dangle deep in the water in the midst of a storm.

Consider:

- How does this use of an anchor keep the ship headed in the right direction?
- How does this use of an anchor protect the ship and its cargo?
- How is this like reaching back to tradition in times of turmoil?

5 Consider the importance of tradition to your faith experience. Spend a moment defining and redefining what tradition means to you, both good and bad. List traditions that you've seen as negative. Then list ones you've seen as positive. Perhaps even listen to the song "Tradition" from the musical *Fiddler on the Roof*. Now think of a tradition that has had a positive spiritual impact on your life. How has it been helpful? What tradition in your life has lost its impact and needs to be transplanted or turbocharged?

6 As much as we study 1 Corinthians 9:22 ("I have become all things to all men so that by all possible means I might save some") and talk about "the culturally indigenous church," congregations seem to have a hard time doing what we study and talk about. Many have tried to make their ministries more culture-conscious, only to fail. For example, a church I know of put in thousands of hours and thousands of dollars trying to initiate and maintain a seeker-sensitive Saturday night service. After six months, fewer than a dozen "seekers" had attended, and none had made faith commitments. Also, the warmth of a "me and my three" view of the church family—in which ministry to those outside the church is largely ignored—can be extremely inviting to an overworked pastor. In addition to all that, we face the question of how tradition fits into the picture. So how does one develop an AncientFuture ministry that really connects God's Word with today's culture? Spend an hour reflecting on this chapter, studying God's Word, and praying about this issue. Assess your church's ministry within its culture as well as your leadership in the effort to have an impact on your culture.

7 As you think of tangible ways to prod your church toward a more biblically balanced theology of culture, be sure to rely on the three orienteering stages to "retrieval" of past traditions: trust, transplantation, and turbocharging. Do the "in-the-trenches" work of carefully identifying practical goals that will help you trust, transplant, and ultimately turbocharge your faith traditions so that they will make an impact on your culture in fresh and life-transforming ways. List one tradition and work through the three stages right now, using the "Amen!" and "Yes!" example (pp. 102–3) as a model. Write down a plan for implementing that turbocharged tradition within a month.

Ship's Log

Use these activities with your church leadership to help them understand and own the principles of this chapter and how they relate to your church's ministry.

1 Give everyone something with which to write. Tell leaders to draw something representing a fond memory of a family tradition. After they've begun drawing, stop them, and say, "I'd like you to use crayons for your drawing instead." Distribute crayons. After they begin drawing again, stop them, and say, "Fold your paper in half and draw only on one side." Allow people to finish their drawings and allow them to present what they've drawn. Then ask:

- How did it feel when I kept changing the instructions on you?
- How is this like what happens in our culture?
- What transitions is our culture undergoing right now that affect the ministry of our church?

2 Think about advertisements you've seen recently that connect with something from the past. Name some of them, and allow leaders to name others. Then ask:

- What is the appeal of this AncientFuture advertising?
- What AncientFuture strong points does our church have to offer today's culture?

3 There are a lot of different kinds of "anchors" that one can cast out, depending on the weather conditions. We must be able to distinguish different kinds of weather and winds if we are to choose the appropriate anchor. We must be able to discern the different winds of change to know what parts of the tradition to use in our orienteering. How do we learn how to read culture? Form groups of three or four, and have each group brainstorm five ways to learn to read culture. Then bring everyone back together and share your lists. Pick at least two to begin working on this month.

4 Historian Jaroslav Pelikan distinguishes between tradition and traditionalism in the following way: "Tradition is the living faith of the dead; traditionalism is the dead faith of the living."[36] Discuss:

- What are some prominent "traditionalisms" we see in churches today?
- What "traditionalisms" may be killing our church's living faith?
- What traditions are worth developing to encourage living faith?

5 "I love Calvin a little; Luther more; the Moravians, Mr. Law, and Mr. Whitefield far more than either. I have many reasons likewise to esteem and love Mr. Hutton. But I love truth more than all." John Wesley wrote these words to Elizabeth Hutton in 1744.[37] Discuss the following questions in pairs or small groups:

- To what extent does our following of certain theologians and spiritual writers obstruct our vision of "Truth"?
- Do our ministries show that we love truth more than all?
- Do our lives show that we love truth more than all?

6 Set out dictionaries and other helpful resources. Have your leaders use the resources to define "faith" and "culture." Encourage people to look for differences and similarities between the two. Have leaders report what they've found, and then read Hebrews 12. Discuss:

- Can faith really be faith without infiltrating the culture around it? Explain.
- Why do churches tend to lose the "culture-infiltrating" part of their faith?
- How is our church doing in infiltrating the culture around us with our faith?
- How can we become better "infiltrators"?

- What practical, relevant connections are we making each week that help people understand how to apply faith to their daily life culture?

Consider assigning leaders to watch for and tabulate such connections throughout a week of your church's ministry. Then evaluate what changes you need to make.

7 English clergyman Geoffrey Anketall Studdert-Kennedy wrote, "God gave his children memory that in life's garden there might be June Roses in December."[38] Have leaders read Psalm 111. Ask:

- What effects do memories have on our faith?
- When has God provided or done something for you that you look back on as faith-enhancing? Explain.
- What events in the history of our church could be faith-strengthening if everyone knew about them?
- How could we use those events to encourage AncientFuture faith among our people?

8 John 17 is sometimes called the "High Priestly Prayer." Have everyone read it silently. Ask:

- Why is this prayer called Jesus' "High Priestly Prayer"?
- What does this prayer teach us about relating to our surrounding culture?

Have everyone skim through the "Inculturating Christ" section of this chapter (pp. 91–100). Discuss:

- Do you agree with the "in-not-of-but-not-out-of-it-either" assessment of our ideal relationship with culture? Why or why not?
- Which of the four attitudes toward culture most clearly identifies our church?
- Whichever it is, how can we improve on our inculturation of our faith into our community?

MISSIONAL ART #4

WALKING THE GANGPLANK: RISK TAKING

Unless you have sent one out,
it's no use to wait for
your ship to come in.
—Belgian proverb

Every journey begins with initiative, lots of risk, and a leap of some kind. In early water transport, boats were made of bundles of reeds, bound logs, inflated goatskins, open-mouthed pots. Regardless of what material the ship is made of, you can't "board" any ship without taking risks—either leaping from land to ship across an expanse of water, or negotiating some sort of gangplank, that narrow ramp by which you board or leave larger ships.

"Boarding" was one of Martin Luther's favorite definitions of faith. The person who doesn't have faith, he said, "is like someone who has to cross the sea, but is so frightened that he does not trust the ship. And so he stays where he is, and is never saved, because he will not get on board and cross over."[1] The test of faith is "getting on board."

From Zero to One

We are born to be risk takers. Every child is a risk taker. With every step toddlers take risks. A baby's first step is the biggest risk of all. Parents do right making a big deal about a child's "first step." For the distance from zero to one is greater than the distance from one to any other number. Once you achieve "one," you have momentum—a momentum so great that it carries first-time walkers forward at a run, not walk. Once you achieve "one," you also have a model, and models are important because, in Bertrand Russell's witty phrasing, models have all the advantages of theft over honest toil. Once a child takes that first step, it's batten down the hatches.

To learn how to go from zero to one—from nothing to something—to overcome inertia with initiative, is to develop one of life's most constructive "crossover" skills.

On binary computers, the difference between zero and one is the difference between on and off. It's no different in the church. The difference between an "on" church and an "off" church is the difference between zero and one.

> Stability itself is nothing else than a more sluggish motion.[2]
>
> —French philosopher Michel de Montaigne

Inertia is another word for "sin." Business theorists Gary Hamel and C. K. Prahalad describe an experiment with monkeys that illustrates the "problem of sin" known as inertia:

> Four monkeys were put into a room. In the center of the room was a tall pole with a bunch of bananas suspended from the top. One particularly hungry monkey eagerly scampered up the pole, intent on retrieving a banana. Just as he reached out to grasp the banana, he was hit with a torrent of cold water from an overhead shower. With a squeal, the monkey abandoned its quest and retreated down the pole. Each monkey attempted, in turn, to secure the banana. Each received an equally chilly shower, and each scampered down without the prize. After repeated drenchings, the monkeys finally gave up on the bananas.

> With the primates thus conditioned, one of the original four was removed from the experiment and a new monkey added. No sooner had this new, innocent monkey started up the pole than his (or her) companions reached up and yanked the surprised creature back down the pole. The monkey got the message—don't climb the pole. After a few such aborted attempts, but without ever having received a cold shower, the new monkey stopped trying to get the bananas. One by one, each of the original monkeys was replaced. Each new monkey learned the same lesson. Don't climb the pole. None of the new monkeys ever made it to the top of the pole. None even got so far as a cold shower. Not one understood precisely why pole climbing was discouraged, but they all respected the well-established precedent. Even after the shower was removed, no monkey ventured up the pole.[3]

Spiritual apathy is one of the deadliest of the "seven deadly sins" because it involves the lack of energy to start afresh, to launch into the deep, to be open to change.

> It's the start that stops most people.
>
> —Anonymous

Every organization needs zero-to-one people, risk takers who can take the lead in the introduction of a new order of things. In fact, zero-to-one people (also known as make-things-happen people) are the most valuable people in any group. One of the most important people you can have on your team or staff is the person who makes two words out of that one word *inaction*.

The Brass Neck

In Scotland, there is a phrase: "He has a brass neck." It means that someone has so much self-confidence that he is willing to stick his neck out. People with "brass necks" are capable of sticking their necks into places that are risky, places where they could get their heads chopped off. Children are born with brass necks. All biological systems—like children—work not so much by trial and error, but by trial and success. Emerging generations explore life not by first looking under the hood and seeing what kind of horsepower and firepower they have, but by taking off and experiencing it.

I shall never forget the day our eight-year-old son, Thane, came in from outside agitated and aroused. "Look at my new skateboard," he exclaimed. "It's got a scar on it."

"I'm sorry, Thane," I replied with concern. "Maybe we can rub it out."

"What do you mean? Why would you do that? I want scars on my skateboard."

Sensing that I was about to learn something significant, I asked: "What do skateboard scars mean to you, Thane?"

"A scar means you're getting better, Dad. So the more scars on your skateboard, the better off you are. I know someone at school who had so many scars his board broke!"

Kids learn by doing. They wear their scars as badges of honor. A beat board is a beautiful board.

Rubbermaid usually ends up rated the "Most Admired Corporation in America." Their tacit motto is one of "You don't like those products? I got others." Rubbermaid introduces one new product a day, one in ten of which is a total failure.[4] One study of 2,036 scientists throughout history "found that the most respected produced not only more great works, but also more 'bad' ones. They produced. Period."[5]

> Error is the heroic form of finding one's way—
> a purposeful wandering toward truth,
> a pilgrimage in which the heart's longing is guide.[6]
> —Poet Jorie Graham

Some years back Joyce Carol Oates published a treatise on the relationship

of failure to fine literature. She recalled the time T. S. Eliot was interviewed by a university audience: "When it was observed to T. S. Eliot that most critics are failed writers, Eliot replied: 'But so are most writers.'"[7]

They all had their share of failures. But they kept producing. The worship team at Ginghamsburg United Methodist Church (Ohio) risks it all every Sunday. Every worship experience is built on a willingness to lose it all the next week for the sake of the gospel. For example, one Sunday when it was time for the call to worship, the pastor stood up from the front row, said he'd had a rough week, and asked the congregation to call him to worship. Then he sat back down. Several awkward minutes passed before people began standing and reading aloud favorite or worshipful passages of Scripture. The people's call to worship—a risky venture—resulted in a powerful, life-lifting experience. The church's flaws are the admissions costs of its ambitions for God and the gospel.

> There is something vulgar in all success.
> The greatest men fail—or seem to the world to have failed.[8]
> —Oscar Wilde

The Risk of Safety

It seems that the more distance life puts between us and childhood, the more rubbery our necks. The older we are, the harder it is for us to take those first leaps of faith, to engage in trial and success. It's almost as if to be an adult is to become hard-wired to avoid risks.

Jesus didn't go for the brass ring. He went for the brass neck. Perhaps that's why Jesus said that only those with the faith of a child will enter the kingdom of heaven (Mark 10:15). No risks? No new sounds, no new sights, no new thoughts. Only zero-to-one-people can bulldoze their way through life's roadblocks to change, conversion, and transformation. Perhaps that's why Jesus reacted so strongly against the bureaucracies of his day. Avoidance of risk is a sacred principle in bureaucratic cultures.

There is nothing more difficult to take in hand, more perilous to conduct, or more uncertain in success, than to take the lead in the introduction of a new order of things. Because the innovator has for enemies all those who have done well under the old conditions, and lukewarm defenders in those who man do well in the new.[9]

—Machiavelli, 1516

To be a leader is to walk gangplanks, to have a brass neck. There can be no Midas touch without a brass neck. There can be no successes without trials. Only those who risk going too far, T. S. Eliot cautioned, can possibly find out how far one can go.

What causes many churches to become places of lowered expectations and diminished dreams? Rubber-neck leadership. What contributes to our molten mediocrity that covers every move we make (or don't make) and covers up our cowardice? Rubber-neck leadership. The church of Jesus Christ has become a church of rubber-neck recreants. We either refuse to stick our necks out for good and the gospel, or we spend our time rubber-necking—onlooking and bystanding on life's shipping lanes, where floating objects and foul-weather misfortunes lie in lurk and where overturned vessels give silent testimony to the cruel complexities of nature.

We are making choices to become risk-free, fail-safe ships that spend entire tours of duty hugging harbors. Our ancestors' zeal for God has given way to another kind of zeal: a zeal to seek immunity from life's prosecutions. We are more concerned about the question "what are your securities?" than the question "what are your ministries?" Our pews are occupied by people who want to be moved, but who don't want to move. It is not just a few people who are bedridden all of their lives—we are becoming a church of, for, and by the bedridden and beached.

The biggest risk of all is to embrace the future. It's a lot easier to live in the past. The church's low risk tolerance and fear of postmodern, post-Christian cultural situations is debilitating to the church's witness. This

unholy predicament that the church finds itself in today—fear-ridden, safety-fixated, immunity-seeking, risk-averse in a high-risk culture—can be reversed only if the church abandons its risk-free approach to ministry and mission and rediscovers the gangplank. The good news is that our cultural phobia is both treatable and preventable.

> When you pass through the waters, I will be with you.
>
> —Isaiah 43:2

"Take Care" trips easily off our lips as a way of wishing people Godspeed. The church's more native farewell is "Take Risks."[10] The sad truth is that "Take Care" strategies create harbor cultures.

Entrepreneurial Risk

On the other hand, "Take Risks" strategies create high-seas cultures. A high-seas culture is an enterprise culture, as the burgeoning number of college majors in "entrepreneurial studies" attests. The word *entrepreneur* comes from the French meaning "to undertake." An "entrepreneur" is someone who undertakes new and risky ventures with initiative, industry, integrity, and identity. A church for the high seas must become an enterprise culture. A "Take Risks" church that knows how to use the gangplank lives out a more entrepreneurial, failure-embracing approach to ministry than a "Take Care" church.

> Entrepreneurs are people who do
> what they aren't quite sure how to do.

The danger for the church today lies with armor and brakes. The benefits lie with risk and speed. For the church to become an enterprise culture and place a high premium on entrepreneurship, it must cease crushing the imaginative and energetic self-starters in its midst. "Take Risks" churches are unafraid of failure. When every decision has to be right, people get paralyzed and immobilized. That's why "Take Risks" leaders are "Take Charge" leaders.

An entrepreneurial spirit in the church is more important today than ever. Why? Twenty-first-century culture is a TEOTWAWKI culture. TEOTWAWKI stands for "The End of the World as We Know It." It's not simply that the five-hundred-year reign of the modern world is over and a postmodern world is being born. Twenty-first-century culture is at best indifferent, at worst hostile to Christianity. The establishment of the Christian church in Western culture ("Christendom") is dead. What is more, the church itself is dying in the West. Buddhism and Islam are this country's fastest growing faiths. The TEOTWAWKI culture of the twenty-first century is a foreign country for most churches.

Martin Luther King Jr. talked about people's need to be divinely dissatisfied.[11] Our churches need to be "divinely dissatisfied" with the way things are and divinely driven to create some new realities. How many policies and practices have outlived the world for which they were created? How many bananas are there for the picking if only we will risk climbing the pole-like trunk?

Our Model Risk Taker

Jesus was spiritually daring. He gave us a model for how to handle TEOTWAWKI transitions in what scholar Beatrice Bruteau calls "The Holy Thursday Revolution." By his foot-washing gesture, which was a "shocking reversal of the proper roles of the Rabbi and his disciples, or servants,"[12] Jesus called into clear consciousness the dead and destructive nature of the old paradigm.

The second great event of "Holy Thursday" was Jesus' anticipatory presentation of a new model of "holy communion" between humans—and between humans and God. He materialized his new vision of the "communion paradigm" in the form of food, which he passed out along with new

metaphors, images, and thoughts, which he then trusted his friends and followers to develop and practice.[13] Jesus risked trusting his greatest message to the hands and feet and mouths of novices—followers who didn't really understand who he was until after his earthly work was over.

A TEOTWAWKI culture mandates four core entrepreneurial competencies. Let's look at what makes up those competencies.

1. Out-of-the-Boat Conceptions

How good are you at thinking "out of the boat"? Give yourself a test.

Which of the following numbers is the most different from the others?

1) One

2) Thirteen

3) Thirty-one

Which number did you choose? If you're like most people, you concentrated on the spelled-out numbers of "one," "thirteen," and "thirty-one." And you probably said, "one." But who told you to ignore the notational numbers 1), 2), and 3)? If you included them—as a child might have done—then you easily would have picked the number 2 because it is the only even number and has neither a 1 nor a 3 in it (as all the other numbers do). In the words of the designer of this quiz, "Because we're so used to seeing the numbers behind the parenthesis as 'not part of the problem' (serving only to enumerate the elements that are part of the problem), it is very difficult to break this assumption and view them as an essential element in the correct solution."[14]

Jesus was a master at making people think "outside the box" and getting people to climb "out of the boat." In the Scriptures, Jesus is pictured sometimes in the boat with his disciples, even sleeping inside the boat. But at other times Jesus stood out of the boat, calling his disciples to join him, not to abandon the boat but to rock the boat.

Remember how the religious leaders opposed Jesus? What got Jesus in such trouble? He associated with people outside the boat: the "ritually unclean," those defined by the religious establishment as "unholy" and "unworthy" and "disreputable." Clearly he did not look to the world as "the enemy." In fact, Jesus stood in the midst of the world and invited his disciples to join him there. This is the powerful symbol behind his calling Peter to join him out of the boat, onto the water. We don't have to go through life kicking up stones or stubbing our toes. Jesus enables us to go through life walking on water. Peter risked leaving the safety of the boat and stepped out onto the water (Matt. 14:22–33). For one shining moment he lived "by faith," not "by sight" (2 Cor. 5:7).

> Do not go where the path may be.
> Go instead where there is no path, and leave a trail.
> —Ralph Waldo Emerson

Like he did in the first century, Jesus is now in the twenty-first century standing outside the boat. He seems more active now in the world (out of the boat) than in the church (in the boat). The notion that God is working in the church and not working in the world is preposterous—to disconnect from the world is to disconnect from the Spirit's workings in the world. Unfortunately, a lot of Christians don't give God the freedom to be God, to do whatever God wants to do, to be no respecter of persons or traditions, to work outside the church as much as in the church.

In a Boeing 747, the inertial navigation system is often called "Fred." It is "Fred's" job to tell where the plane is—and if where the plane is doesn't match the flight plan already filed, a correction is made. How does "Fred" calculate where the plane is? By looking outward at the world—not by looking inward. Our calling is to be in mission where God is at work. God can be as much at work in the world as in the church (some would argue more so). Biblical faith does not isolate us from the world, but pushes us into the world and presses us into service in the world. Perhaps the church needs a new theology of what it means to be a "friend of sinners."

2. Small-Waves Mastery

You don't have to make big waves to make change. The smallest ripple can make the biggest waves in Google culture. Small waves are potential tsunamis. Small inputs can have massive consequences. The power of small waves is manifest on the Internet; one single computer can create a tidal wave. In a Google world, a little goes a long way.

> Small companies, right down to the individual,
> can beat big bureaucratic companies ten out of ten times.
> Therefore, unless the big companies reconstitute
> themselves as a collection of small companies,
> they will just continue to go out of business.[15]
>
> —John Naisbitt

You can change the world. Small companies are changing and re-creating the global economy. In fact, the majority of U.S. exports are created by companies with less than two dozen employees.[16] Small players are dominating the twenty-first-century global economy, which should make the small-membership church reconsider its futures.

> Dare to be wise; get started. The man who puts off
> The time to start living is like the hayseed
> Who wants to cross the river and so he sits there
> Waiting for the river to run out of water.
> And the river flows by, and it flows forever.[17]
>
> —Horace

Someone put together a series of "one vote" decisions that underline the power of one:

- In 1645, one vote gave Oliver Cromwell control of England.
- In 1649, one vote caused Charles I of England to be executed.

- In 1776, one vote gave America the English language instead of German.
- In 1845, one vote brought Texas into the Union.
- In 1868, one vote saved President Andrew Johnson from impeachment.
- In 1875, one vote changed France from a monarchy to a republic.
- In 1876, one vote gave Rutherford B. Hayes the presidency of the United States.
- In 1923, one vote gave Adolf Hitler leadership of the Nazi Party.
- In 1941, one vote put the draft into effect.
- In 1960, one vote per precinct in four states gave John F. Kennedy the presidency of the United States.

3. Speed Theorizing

In chaotic as well as in democratic systems like postmodernity, everything is in perpetual motion. A Google world requires leaders who can display rapid response and readily adapting skills, who do not view speed as dangerous, who do not see speed in and of itself an apocalyptic calamity.

"Speed" is a key strategy for success in the future. Organizational structures that are flexible, flippable, and fast are equations for success. It may be a football world in terms of mentoring—which we'll see later—but it's a basketball world in terms of momentum and pace.

Get off the last shot. Even if you miss, it's better to have missed the basket than not to have gotten off the shot.

> You miss 100 percent of the shots you never take.
>
> —Hockey great Wayne Gretzky

4. Surprise "Just-in-Time" Design

The organic, feeling-our-way-forward nature of the future means more than that our organizational structures need to be mobile, pliable, flexible.[18]

Expect spontaneity and serendipity in everyday life. Design your life journey not through planning but through preparedness. We are living in a world of "disharmonious conjunctions," the organizing principle of a chaos world. Nothing can be planned.

> No woman in my time will be prime minister.[19]
>
> —Margaret Thatcher's 1969 prophecy

"They Should Have Seen It Coming" was the headline in Mississippi's *Hattiesburg American* on the bankruptcy of Dionne Warwick's "The Psychic Friends Network." If even the psychics can't "see it coming," what hope do we have of building a design strategy based on prediction, control, and planning? "But wait," you say, "I like to plan ahead." Hear Proverbs: "In his heart a man plans his course, but the Lord determines his steps" (Prov. 16:9).

We must shift from program and planning modes of movement to preparedness modes[20] of locomotion. In twenty-first-century culture, budgets work no better than diets. Who was it who first said, "Every time I get ends to meet, someone moves the other end"? Don't diet; change your life strategy. Don't budget; change your life strategy.

James Martin was once described by *Computerworld* magazine as "the computer industry's most widely read author ... and foremost authority on the social and commercial impact of computers." In his book on the "new business revolution," Martin argues that long-range planning is pointless because change is now so fast that nothing can be planned for. He says that in the future, more things will be designed "just in time."[21] For this reason Intel's initial business plan was one page; Sun's initial business plan was three times longer—three pages.

"Just in time" is what our preacher ancestors used to call "Prepared Unpreparedness."[22] Our ancestors had a strong sense of "Providence" in which they believed that God was doing something great with them at that moment. They believed they were actors in the great drama God was acting out in history. They didn't know what would happen tomorrow or where they would go next. But they knew their job was to "act" when called upon by God. Hence their motto of "prepared unpreparedness."

Preparedness does not mean short-term, near-future thinking, which is blind to global signals and changes. But preparedness does mean putting God in the captain's seat and giving up one's control over the journey. Can you give up where you want to go, as Paul did when God sent him to Macedonia? Can you give up your plans, as Philip did when God sent him to Gaza, and there he met the Ethiopian eunuch?

> The Clairvoyance Society of Greater London will not meet today due to unforeseen circumstances.
>
> —Notice in the *Financial Times*

Here is a primary test of whether you are living missional art #4: Do you sometimes go in directions you do not wish to go? It's the John 21:18 test: Sometimes God is taking you in directions "where you do not want to go." Are you finding yourself doing some things you do not wish to do and going where you don't want to go? Be prepared for the unexpected. You serve an unpredictable Lord in an unpredictable culture.

> The lowly mussel has a lot to teach us about change and stasis. This mollusk has to make only one major existential decision in life, and that's where it's going to settle down. After making that decision, the mussel cements its head against a rock and stays put for the rest of its life. I've discovered that many people are like that: they're so resistant to change that they might as well be cemented in place. If leaders share that trait—if they suffer from what we might call the "mussel syndrome"—the results can be devastating for their organizations.[23]
>
> —Manfred Kets de Vries

Playing It Safe While Taking Risks

We all risk a lot of things. Almost every minute we take risks.

For example, at school and at work, we risk the food they are serving in the cafeteria every day. A little boy listened carefully as the teacher made the morning announcements to the class. And when he heard the teacher say, "Today is Groundhog Day," he muttered, "Boy, am I glad I brought my lunch."

Chaos theory tells us that order comes about in the cosmos because of disorder. Until one acquiesces in insecurity and allows things to become uncertain, there can be no higher elevations of surety and stability.[24] In other words, our security is in insecurity; our safety in the very act of risking itself.

Safety at sea involves playing it safe and taking risks simultaneously. Safety first does not mean risk-free. You can be "safe" and "risky" at the same time.

- There is nothing that you do that is risk-free. Nothing.
- There is nothing that you eat that is risk-free. Nothing.
- There is nobody that you know who is risk-free. Nobody.

Even the U.S. Supreme Court decided in 1981 that "safe" does not mean "risk-free."[25] Loan officers, life insurance companies, and lovers already know that every person is a "risk." All premiums in life are "risk-based." A universe of love is a universe of risk.

Safety involves more than flares, emergency procedures, always wearing safety harnesses or lifeline security wires that prevent people from falling overboard, or knowing by heart Defoe's "Directions for Sea-men" or the Coast Guard "Rules." Safety at sea is an outlook and lifestyle. A safety stance means skirting trouble rather than getting out of trouble when you are up the stick. Before any journey, the risks must be calculated and an intricate, delicate risk-balance of positives and negatives confronted. No one can predict what dangers and unlikelihoods the journey will bring.

There are dangers out there, from sharks to collisions to explosions to "man overboard" to bad weather. In popular Hebraic piety, Satan was most fierce in three occasions: when you walk along on a road, when you sleep alone in a dark house, and when you sail on the high seas.

On great seas one needs life rafts and emergency kits (grab bags) and PFDs (personal flotation devices). Part of the challenge of Perfect Storm leadership is learning to stay alive. A dead (defrocked, dismissed, burnt out) leader doesn't lead anybody.

> "I want you to remember," says General George S. Patton at the opening of the 1970 film *Patton*, "that no [soldier] ever won a war by dying for his country."

Read Romans 16, which Robert Dale calls "Paul's risk takers' hall of fame." Here are some of the people and households Paul bet his ministry on:

- Phoebe, "a servant of the church" (v. 1)
- Priscilla and Aquila, who "risked their lives for me" (v. 4)
- Epaenetus, "the first convert to Christ in the province of Asia" (v. 5)
- Mary, "who worked very hard for you" (v. 6)
- Adronicus and Junius, "who have been in prison with me" (v. 7)
- Ampliantus, "whom I love in the Lord" (v. 8)
- Urbanus, "fellow worker in Christ" (v. 9)[26]

Due Diligence

A safety consciousness means measuring risk and managing risk, which implies and includes asking five questions. Due diligence requires the charting of a risk profile. Or in the language of golf, what's the "risk reward"? Here are the top five "risk reward" questions on any risk profile chart.

Risk Reward Question 1

What are you prepared to give up or take on to reach your destination?

Things near and dear to us may need to go by the wayside. The Franklin expedition to the Arctic in 1845 set out with "a 1,200-volume library,

a hand-organ that played fifty tunes, and formal china and sterling silver flatware"—all of which had to be discarded before the end was in sight.[27]

But we also may need to take with us things we don't like if we are to play it safe on our high-risk journey.

> Sauerkraut. That was the watchword on Captain James Cook's triumphant second voyage, which set sail in 1772. By adding generous portions of the German staple to the diet of his English crew (some of whom foolishly turned up their noses at it), the great circumnavigator kicked scurvy overboard. Not only is sauerkraut's chief ingredient, cabbage, loaded with vitamin C but the fine-cut cabbage must be salted and allowed to ferment until sour to be worthy of the name. Practically pickled in brine, sauerkraut keeps forever aboard ship—or at least as long as the duration of a voyage around the world. Cook made it his oceangoing vegetable, and sauerkraut went on saving sailors' lives until lemon juice and, later, limes replaced it in the provisions of the Royal Navy.[28]

Risk Reward Question 2

What are the possible outcomes, what are the chances of each outcome happening, and what are the consequences of each outcome?

> Sometimes the lapses and losses are forgivable, even admirable, because they result from attempting too much.

There is a vast difference between "risk taking" and "gambling." This is where the scenario-model of preparedness comes in handy and is the reason "what if" software modeling is widely available. The church must hope for the best while anticipating worst-case scenarios. What's the worst that could happen?

If you aren't living on the edge,
you're taking up too much room.
—Anonymous

One of the most profound insights ever written about journeying comes from Thornton Wilder's pen. The worst is not to be in the midst of an adventure and be saying to yourself, "Oh, now I've got myself into an awful mess; I wish I were sitting quietly at home." You know you are really in trouble and experiencing life's worst "when you sit quietly at home wishing you were out having lots of adventures."[29] Suffering and striving can be good for us. Tough times bring out our best and summon our peak performances.

Risk Reward Question 3

What are my backups? What are my emergency procedures?

In the Google world, redundancy is more a positive than a pejorative word. We need parallel systems for backup and flexibility in contingencies for start-ups.

Risk Reward Question 4

Who has been there before me that I can learn from?

The soul needs travel guides. The art of mentoring is one of the most significant art forms of the twenty-first century. This is the one area where football has something to teach us: Not only are coaches everywhere (offensive, defensive, personal position coaches, personal trainers, team coaches), but each person is multiply coached.

Joshua mentored with Moses for more than forty years, and his success in taking the Israelites into the land of Canaan and bringing down the walls of Jericho could not have been done without this mentoring.

The difference between a hero and a coward
is one step sideways.
—Actor Gene Hackman

Risk Reward Question 5

Who has the right of way?

This is the easiest of the questions to answer, and the quickest way to prevent collisions. The answer to the question "Who has the right of way?" is always the same: the other vessel.

> When the soul owns herself sincerely to be nought
> The whole of heaven flows in as freely as a thought.[30]
>
> —Coventry Patmore

Benjamin Zander is the world-renowned conductor of the Boston Philharmonic Orchestra. He calls the first rule of leadership "Rule Number Six" and illustrates it with the story of two prime ministers, sitting in a room, discussing affairs of state.

> Suddenly a man bursts through the door, screaming and shouting. The prime minister who's hosting the meeting says to the man, "Peter, please remember Rule Number Six." Peter is immediately restored to calm. He apologizes, bows, and walks out. About twenty minutes later, a woman comes flying in. She's beside herself. The prime minister says, "Maria, please remember Rule Number Six." Maria apologizes and walks out.
>
> The visiting prime minister can't contain his curiosity: "My dear colleague, what is this Rule Number Six?" The other prime minister says, "Very simple: Don't take yourself so [expletive] seriously." The visitor replies, "That's a nice rule. What, may I ask, are the other rules?" The prime minister answers, "There aren't any."

Zander continually reminds himself of this right-of-way question. He places a blank sheet of paper on the stand of every musician at every rehearsal.

That paper is an invitation to the players to say how effective he is being at making them the best that they can be.[31]

Even after all due diligence has been exercised and these five questions have been answered in practice as well as in theory, one must still face the possibility that God is calling us to stand against the tide. Poet D. J. Enright calls this the best sentence Norman Mailer ever wrote: "There was probably no impotence in all the world like knowing you were right and the wave of the world was wrong, and yet the wave came on."[32]

What is the worst thing that can happen to me? Not to lose my life. But to not be where Jesus is.

Enter At Your Own Risk

Those who go beneath the surface do so at their peril.[33]

—Oscar Wilde

The church must not romanticize risk taking. Sometimes you win. Sometimes you lay down your life. Sometimes you are forced to walk the gangplank into the deep. You and I can read the Bible in English today because William Tyndale walked the gangplank of martyrdom. Leaders can't expect to have beliefs and not pay a price for those beliefs. You can't buy a deeper walk with God. But you have to pay for it. In fact, "bear witness" literally means to suffer, as the word *martyr* first meant "witness."

Bizet's *Carmen* was scorned at its first screening. So was Beethoven's Fifth Symphony. Jesus was rejected and despised and ultimately walked the gangplank himself. What makes us so special that we deserve being spared similar treatments?

The Harry Emerson Fosdick classic *The Meaning of Service* (1920) uses

an analogy from the Holy Land to convey our creation as people who gain life by losing it, who find safety in risk.

> The Sea of Galilee and the Dead Sea are made of the same water. It flows down, clear and cool, from the heights of Hermon and the roots of the cedars of Lebanon. The Sea of Galilee makes beauty of [this water], for the Sea of Galilee has an outlet. It gets to give. It gathers in its riches that it may pour them out again to fertilize the Jordan plain. But the Dead Sea with the same water makes horror. For the Dead Sea has no outlet. It gets to keep.[34]

Carved in wood over the door of a church in Ohio are these words: "Enter at your own risk."

God is doing a new thing.

Take Risks, church.

Retrieve life by risking it, Jesus said.

Besides, that very plank that you used to get on board can also become the very thing that saves you from drowning after a shipwreck.

> Be not afraid to trust God completely. As you go down the long corridor, you may find that He has preceded you and locked many doors that you would have entered in vain. But be sure that beyond these there is one that He has left unlocked. Open it and enter, and you will find yourself face to face with a bend of the river of opportunity, broader and deeper than anything you had dared to imagine in your sunniest dreams. Launch forth on it, for it leads to the open sea.[35]
>
> —F. B. Meyer

AQUACHURCH #4
THE CHURCH OF GETHSEMANE

Brooklyn, New York
www.thechurchofgethsemane.org

The Church of Gethsemane is an AquaChurch founded by men and women of diverse backgrounds who have been incarcerated. It is a church that specializes in changed lives, embracing Jesus' admonition to "visit those in prison" with an outward focus that embodies the full meaning of "walking the gangplank." As a prison ministry, The Church of Gethsemane seeks both justice for the world and the empowerment of the gospel in everyday existence. No one is turned away from this church. All are welcome. Gethsemane thrives on diversity and a sense of inclusiveness. Their mission is to create a missional community that comforts and challenges, struggles and sustains, heals and liberates. They do this by:

- Welcoming all into their congregation, with no provisos.
- Allowing all members to have an equal opportunity to serve as ordained leaders in the church.
- Understanding that each child as well as adult is part of the church family, and participates in sharing the responsibility for caring for the whole community.
- Incarnating the history of their name as a place where Jesus went to be strengthened in a time of despair; those who worship at Gethsemane are creating a place for strengthening.
- Believing that together, they can do as Jesus did: transform a cup of suffering into a cup of strengthening for one another and for the world.

CAPTAIN'S LOGBOOK

PERSONAL LOG

Use these ideas to stimulate your thinking about how the principles of this chapter could affect your ministry. Consider sharing these ideas with other church leaders.

1 Do a personal risk inventory of your life this past week. When confronted with a new reality, did you immediately pass blame? Did you seek a "safe" solution? Were you willing to risk failure to see a better result? Write down at least four times you faced something new and how you responded. Also write how you could have responded better.

2 John Harrison invented a chronometer that would stay accurate on board ship and thus could be relied on to measure longitude. Instead of accolades, he received all sorts of opposition from the scientific establishment. The powers that be refused to give up their old ways of measuring longitude by the stars. Sound familiar in the church? Sound familiar in your life?

Consider:

- Why is the church of Jesus Christ, the church that is primed to proclaim a Lord and Savior who "makes all things new," so opposed to the new when it does come?
- How can you be more open to new things that the Lord might bring into your ministry?

For the whole gripping story of Harrison's life, see the illustrated edition of *Longitude: The True Story of a Lone Genius Who Solved the Greatest Scientific Problem of His Time* by Dava Sobel (Penguin, 1996).

3 Refusing to follow Jesus until you first experience what will happen to you if you do follow him is like refusing to get wet until you learn how to swim. Leaders must be willing to make mistakes, to go off course. But leaders must also be willing to stand correction. Being in error and correcting errors go together.

Think about the following questions:

- What is keeping you personally from risking for the kingdom?
- What possible errors frighten you most?
- How might you correct your course if it ends up in error?
- What really do you have to lose?

4 Do a Bible study of Acts 16. Write down every risk that someone took for the cause of God's kingdom. Answer the following questions:

- What good things happened as a result of the risks?
- What bad things happened as a result of the risks?
- What good happened from the bad that happened?
- Were the dangers worth the risks? Explain.

5 Think back through your knowledge of the Bible and contemplate this question: How is the Bible the story of a God who continually risks everything? Jot down examples of how God staked everything on less-than-perfect people.

6 Rate your own personal practice of risk taking on a scale of one to ten (one being the lowest and ten the highest level of risk taking). Ask yourself:

- What accounts for this rating?
- Do I need to work to lower or raise it?
- Does my risk-taking level match the expectations of my church?
- What would Jesus do?

7 Consider this statement: "It seems that the more distance life puts between us and childhood, the more rubbery our necks" (p. 115). Consider:

- Do you think this is true in your life? Why or why not?
- What experiences have softened your resolve to either lessen or intensify your risk taking? Be very specific.
- What would you do differently if you had a "do-over"?

8 Think about this Ralph Waldo Emerson quote: "Do not go where the path may be. Go instead where there is no path, and leave a trail." Does it cause you to be nostalgic? Does it sound more like you in your youth than it does now? On a piece of paper, draw where you think God would like your trail to lead in the next year. Include uncharted territories you'd have to enter, obstacles you'd face, and pitfalls you'd want to avoid. Then pray over what you've drawn, asking for God's help in leaving the beaten path to follow him.

Ship's Log

Use these activities with your church leadership to help them understand and own the principles of this chapter and how they relate to your church's ministry.

1 Have your leaders chronicle a day in their lives from the standpoint of risks. Have them write down all the risks they took—even those taken without a thought at the time. To get started, read the following: "The danger inherent in having an annual X-ray is equivalent to the danger of flying one thousand miles in an airplane, driving fifty miles by car, riding ten miles on a bicycle, eating forty tablespoonfuls of peanut butter, spending two days in New York City, or smoking one and one-half cigarettes."

After leaders have completed their chronicles, give them an opportunity to share. Then have them form groups of four and score each other's risk taking on a scale of one to ten (one being the lowest and ten being the highest). Then discuss:

- Do you agree with how your group rated your risk taking?
- Are you happy with your risk rating?
- How does our willingness to risk affect our church?
- What risks do we need to consider to make our church more effective in reaching our community?

2 Marketers distinguish five types of response to change:

a) Experimenters—People who like change, enjoy playing with new ideas, aren't afraid of failure, and will take risks, even if appearing outrageous.

b) Early adaptors—Adventurous people who catch on quickly to new ideas and customs, but who don't want to be seen as too far out of step with others. They constantly worry about the "one oddness too many" phenomenon my wife warns me about.

c) Front-runners—Once a new idea or custom starts to catch on and become acceptable, these people take it up quickly. They enjoy being "in the know" and "in style." Their motto could be "Never Do Anything for the First Time."

d) Late adaptors—The cautious types who won't adopt or adapt to change until it has been around a long time. Only when it is safe will they change, hence these will be virtually the last ones to get an iPhone or Wii.

e) Slow movers—People innately suspicious of any change, and adjust either slowly or not at all. Either they become part of a museum culture or are the absolute last to adapt. They're still wary of computers.

Have your leaders pretend they are the town council in an 1890 meeting called to decide whether to buy some electricity or to stay off the grid. Discuss the following questions:

- What would worry us about this new thing?
- How likely would we be to vote in favor of it? Explain.
- Which of the categories above would we fit into? Which one would God want us to be in?
- How is this electricity example similar to any decision we're facing in our church?
- What do we need to do to bring our church along in following God's leading?

3 Is anyone more expert at risk management than parents? Invite some experienced parents from your church to discuss "risk management" with your leaders. Be sure to consider how the principles of parenting a child are similar to and different from leading a church. Ask the parents to give you any suggestions they have for leading your church in the future.

4 Discuss the following quote from New Zealand theologian/novelist Michael Riddell: "When we know that we are safe in Christ, we are free to go wherever we want and mix with whoever we find, and do it without fear. Our orientation will be one of mission: concerned not with isolating and protecting our inner purity, but with finding ways to make the Christ who is within us accessible to others."[36]

- How does a concern with protecting our inner purity sometimes keep us from reaching our community?
- How can a mission orientation take away the fear of risk?
- How can our church better "make the Christ who is within us accessible to others"?

5 Robert Dale argues that entrepreneurs are characterized by (1) a passion to see results; (2) a sense that all failures are temporary; (3) endurance—the will to keep on keeping on (but knows when to hold and when to fold, as Kenny Rogers would put it); and (4) an outsider's mind-set.

How entrepreneurial are you really? Consider Robert Dale's "Entrepreneur's Checklist."

a) Do I believe in my own competencies?
b) Do I believe in my ministry opportunity?
c) Am I willing to work sacrificially?
d) Can I see and enter open doors of possibility?
e) Can I make decisions and act on them?
f) Am I able to lead by example?

Discuss how the entrepreneurial spirit applies to the church.

6 Look up the dictionary definition for "inertia." Discuss:

- How can inertia be equated with "sin" (p. 112)?
- What is it about local churches and human beings that tend to resist change?
- Why is that first step toward change so important in the church?
- What is the first step we should take toward more effective ministry?

7 Think about the discussion of the skateboarder and the Rubbermaid corporation, whose motto could be "You don't like those ideas/products? I got others" (p. 114).

- Why do you think the church is so afraid of failure?
- How do you respond to the admonition that the church should be more open to failure?
- What possible success do you see in your church's future that is worth risking failure over?

8 Read the insightful book *The God Who Risks: A Theology of Providence* by John Sanders.[37] Then discuss with your leaders Sanders' thesis that God can be in control of anything without constantly controlling everything. Ask:

- What is the basis on which we take risks?
- How does Sanders' view affect the way one looks at risk?
- What risks might Sanders suggest we take action on?

MISSIONAL ART #5

LISTENING FOR SONAR: VIBRATIONS

When through the deep waters
I call thee to go.[1]
—From "How Firm a Foundation" (1787)

It had been a long wait. For three months, weather and bureaucrats had blocked the voyage. The time of year was still not ideal to cross the Atlantic, but when administrative clearance was granted, the Wesley brothers boarded. On December 10, 1735, some 225 passengers weighed anchor on the *Simmonds* and set sail for America.[2]

The Oxford "methodist" system of John and Charles Wesley required a rigorous "discipline" of prayers, readings, exhortations, fasts, self-scrutinies, and "good works." Part of this discipline included keeping a detailed journal that doubled as a daily diary and a spiritual logbook. Thanks to this journaling, we know exactly how these "methodist" passengers spent their days on this long, arduous sea journey.

Each day began at 4:00 a.m. with spiritual exercises. These aerobics of the soul didn't let up, except for two meals (supper having been scrapped because of miscalculated rations), until about nine or ten in the evening. When not involved in private or public devotions, the "methodists" were busy exhorting and counseling those who sought spiritual guidance.

Wesley's busy schedule kept his mind off the creaky, leaky, rickety boat that trapped the "methodists" as they slowly made their way to Savannah, Georgia. Sometimes Wesley's journal reads more like a weather report than a spiritual diary. The delay in setting sail had put the ship in the path of a series of severe winter storms. Again and again the *Simmonds* was beaten and tossed by life-threatening weather. Every vile wind, every violent wave, every day or night of bad weather was meticulously cataloged by the waterlogged Wesley.

What bothered Wesley most was how the very real threat of a shipwreck reduced his faith to shivering shards. On January 17, 1736, Wesley recorded how a great wave burst clear down into the lower cabin where he, his brother Charles, James Oglethorpe, and others sat praying with an ill passenger. John found himself sheltered by a convenient bureau from that sudden deluge, but when he was confronted by the instant prospect of being swept overboard into the sea, he was "afraid to die."

A few days later (January 24), as yet another storm pounded the ship, John rather foolishly ventured on deck. Immediately an enormous wave "came with a full, smooth tide over the side of the ship." Wesley went completely under and admitted he did not expect to lift his head again "till the sea should give up her dead." Though unhurt, Wesley once again found himself cringing in the face of death as he asked himself, "How is it that thou hast no faith? being still unwilling to die."

What made Wesley's spiritual dilemma even worse was the presence onboard of a small band of Moravian Christians who showed no fear whatever betide. With a newly ignited faith and under the spiritual leadership of young Count Zinzendorf, these twenty-six men, women, and children kept to themselves. Yet their composed and confident faith affected everything aboard the ship—including Wesley's daily regimen. For three hours a day John studied the German language so that he might more completely understand this community of faith.

It troubled Wesley that these Moravians were not suitably impressed with his intimidating spiritual regimen. Wesley divulged some days later that the Moravians quickly saw through his busyness. They deemed it yet another attempt to stack the divine account-books and earn through merit

that definitive gift of salvation. Not until two years later, however, did Wesley concede that his Moravian shipmates had showed him the "more excellent way" of the Reformation mantra "justification by faith."

On Sunday, January 25, the fierce storm that had nearly swept Wesley out to sea the day before continued to besiege and batter the poorly caulked ship. All day the "methodists" huddled below deck. That evening John slithered his way down the ship's rolling corridor and slid in among the Moravians for their Sunday evening service. The small band was already joyfully singing one of the hymns John admired for its sweet assurance and quiet power.[3]

As the Moravians sang, the storm suddenly walloped the ship with an enormous wave. As Wesley described it, this one liquid battering ram "split the mainsail in pieces; covered the ship, and poured in between the decks, as if the great deep had already swallowed us up." The ship sounded as though it were being torn apart, promising a cold and imminent death for all aboard. The panicked screams and shouts of the English passengers filled the companionways. But in the small cabin where the Moravians and John Wesley were gathered, the magnificent hymn continued without breaking a beat. The Moravian Christians sang on without so much as a shudder, holding hands to keep their balance as they sang the great hymns of the faith.

Astounded and envious of this complete trust in the providence of God, John Wesley confronted one of these simple believers after the winds had calmed and the waves abated. Wesley's journal records the exchange:

> "Was you not afraid?" He answered, "I thank God, no." I asked, "But were not your women and children afraid?" He replied mildly, "No; our women and children are not afraid to die."

It was a transforming moment for Wesley. Though Oxford trained, spiritually rigorous, theologically sophisticated, and musically gifted, he couldn't say that. He was afraid to die. But in the Moravian community, even the faith of little children had attained a level of maturity that enabled them to look into death's face without flinching.

Wesley learned two things from this sea episode. First, living in the light made singing in the rain possible. Second, the best way to go through a storm is to sing.

> While there's music, there's hope.[4]
>
> —Wilfrid Mellers

Ice

In the writing of Dante, the deepest pit in hell is a place of ice, a place more horrible than fire.

The ship *Endurance*, trapped in the Weddell Sea in the early 1900s, was literally being crushed by Antarctic ice packs, crinkled up as if to be thrown away like a tissue. Sir Ernest Shackleton had no choice. Either the ship's crew had to abandon ship or be pulverized into an antarctic pulp.

When they divided up and climbed aboard their new home, three small lifeboats, each crew member was allowed to take off the crumbling ship up to two pounds of personal possessions. Shackleton allowed only one exception. He granted permission for one sailor to take his banjo in addition to his two pounds. Shackleton believed that music could supply the crew with a "vital mental tonic"[5] that would not only barber up their spirits but maybe even save their lives. Sure enough, one of the ways they kept sane through months-long open-boat sea-bobbings between heaven and hell was to sing to one another sea chanteys—"Captain Stormalong," "A Sailor's Alphabet"—along with songs of hearth and church.[6]

All Ears

There are many "arts." It takes multiple "arts" to approach "truth," just as it takes multiple gospels to approach "The Truth." But of all the "arts," the one that comes closest to expressing all the others is music.

Leadership is a sound event, a vibrational phenomenon.

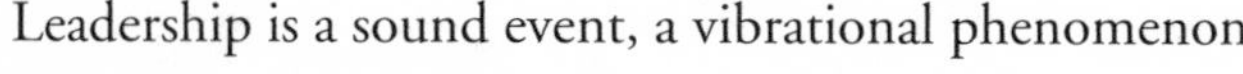

The second millennium was brought to a close by leaders who kept in their sights "visionaries." New degree initiatives (BA and MBA) were endowed by business magnates for whom "vision" was a byword for leadership competence. Airport bookstalls were kept stocked by writers for whom "vision" was the sexiest of twenty-first-century leadership notions. Few concepts racked up more frequent-flier mileage during the past fifty years than "vision." In fact, it seems sometimes as if the only sense operating in the church today is vision: sounds and smells, tastes and touches are trampled under in the vision quest. If vision was the concept of the century last, vibration is the discourse of discovery for the century now. The twenty-first century revolves around vibration. Electronic culture is an aural culture (witness the billion-dollar phone sex industry). These are the days of aural abundance to the degree where sound marks are becoming trademarks, with distinct aural brands (trademarked sounds of pings, sproings, and boings) on the Internet. Our body is becoming one big EAR. Music consumption now plays such a role in how we define ourselves and construct our personal histories and spiritual identities that people now go "church surfing" (fleeing some, joining others) primarily on a vibrational basis.[7]

Only when the visual is joined to vibrational can postmoderns feel what they see. And part of the postmodern identity is a throwback to more primitive societies where feeling what you're seeing is at the heart of life itself.[8] How does one best transmit feelings? How can one best transmit thoughts? Through words? Through pictures? Or through sounds?

> It's not that music is too vague for words;
> "it's too precise for words."[9]
> —Felix Mendelssohn

Feelings and thoughts are most powerfully imparted through the vibrations of sound. In fact, music is so powerful in iPod culture that, in composer Brian Ferneyhough's words, it is difficult not to feel like a "puppet on a string" when it comes to the power of music to shape one's thoughts and emotions.[10]

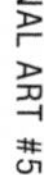

That's why in 1998 Pope John Paul II brought out a musical disc, entirely in Latin, of him saying the rosary and singing hymns. What rituals do you know that don't involve music? The heart of ritual is the alignment of vibration with vision—visible soundtracks, if you will.

Not insignificantly, the liturgy of the church is seen as Christianity's first theology. Martin Luther made a liturgical suggestion that sometimes a hymn or hymns be substituted for various segments of the litany on occasion because "[Music] drives away the Devil and makes people cheerful; one forgets all anger, unchasteness, pride, and other vices. I place music next to theology and give it the highest praise.... I would not change my little knowledge of music for a great deal.... Experience proves that next to the Word of God only music deserves to be extolled as the mistress and governess of the feelings of the human heart."[11]

Reformer John Calvin so respected music's command over the whole person and its involvement of the whole congregation emotionally that he advocated strict controls over its use: "We might be moved to restrict the use of music to make it serve only what is respectable and never use it for unbridled dissipations.... There is hardly anything in the world that has greater power to bend the morals of men this way or that, as Plato has wisely observed. And for this reason we must be all the more diligent to control music in such a way that it will serve us for good and in no way harm us."[12]

Other leaders appreciated the powers of music and feared them as well. Augustine recommended abolishing music in liturgy, since its potential for good was only surpassed by its potential for ill: "I realize that when they are sung these sacred words stir my mind to greater religious fervor and kindle in me a more ardent flame of piety than they would if they were not sung.... But I ought not to allow my mind to be paralyzed by the gratification of my senses, which often lead it astray. For the senses are not content to take second place. Simply because I allow them their due, as adjuncts to reason, they attempt to take precedence and forge ahead of it, with the result that I sometimes sin in this way."[13]

What is the number one export of USAmerica? Music and images. People around the world are right to fear the spread of one culture's music. Russian "village writers" like the popular Siberian writer Valentin Rasputin oppose Western influences and especially denounce rock music, which he calls "spiritual AIDS."[14] A musical victory is a greater cultural and spiritual triumph than a military victory.

What God Has Joined ...

Vibration and vision belong together. They have common interests. Leaders need to exercise both of them at once. But vibration comes before vision. It is more important to hear what you see than to see what you see.

It isn't the early bird that gets the worm. It's the listening bird that gets the worm. When worms hear footsteps, they make a "slurp" sound. Robins pluck their worms more from sound than from sight. While earthworms are deaf, it is the worms' sense of vibration that gets them in trouble. When Charles Darwin—this might be his most endearing feature—placed a container of earthworms atop a piano and banged out one note at a time, the worms "instantly retreated into their burrows in response to the vibrations."[15]

Leaders are born to give vision. But vision comes from vibration, seeing from hearing. Most important is to hear into sight. In the biblical witness—at Creation, at the burning bush, at Mount Sinai, at Pentecost, for example—sound becomes sight. Scientists tell us that noise from the cymbals crashing at Creation still echoes across the universe. The Bible begins with the Spirit "vibrating" over the waters. The Bible ends with an invitation to come to the waters and sing.

> Mortals, join the mighty chorus
> Which the morning stars began.[16]
> —Henry Van Dyke (1907)

For leaders, it is never too often to be reminded of this verse—or to remind others of it: "Faith comes from hearing" (Rom. 10:17). When Jesus said in Matthew 6:22 "If your eye is sound, your whole body will be full of light," I like to think that the "sound eye" is more than just my play on words. Followers of Jesus have vision that is voice-activated. They hear a vision before they see a vision. Our faith is not well and our leadership not wholesome when there is no coming together of the vibrational and the visional, the inner and the outer, the invisible and the visible, the ear and the eye. Leadership is the furrowing of paths in which vibration and vision slot into one another. Leadership is a seeing ear, a hearing eye.

An old film about the laws of sound shows a handful of iron filings placed on a thin sheet of metal. A musical tone was played near the sheet. Suddenly the filings arranged themselves in the form of a snowflake. Sound became sight, as vibrations took physical shape. Another tone was sounded, and the filings changed their formation, this time into a star.

Every note sounded created its own physical form. The invisible became visible. Sound became sight.

Remote Sensing

"Sonar" refers to listening devices onboard ship that conduct "remote sensing" to sketch underwater topography.[17] For example, the depth finder executes "echo soundings." It listens for the sounds bounced off the bottom to determine the depth below the hull. In channel navigation, "soundings" are essential to avoid "shoals," shallow water where the boat will run aground, or "strands" and sandbars where the boat might become stranded. Early riverboats took primitive "soundings" with a weighted line periodically thrown over the bow.[18]

Sound travels faster and longer in water than on land. A whale can hear another whale halfway around the world. But whether in water or on land, sound is more commanding than sight. The eye can distinguish lights flashing at a fifteenth and a sixteenth of a second. The ear can distinguish clicks separated by only two- or three-thousandths of a second. God gave us more advanced physical competencies for hearing than for seeing.

The role of music in influencing emotions and behavior is only beginning

to be understood. In USAmerica, seven out of ten calls are put on hold. The average person spends an estimated sixty hours a year in telephone purgatory. Does music make people more willing to wait longer? Absolutely! Twenty minutes longer.[19] Why do Gregorian chants have such uncommon power? They recharge the soul.[20]

The ear is not merely an organ for hearing. The middle ear transmits sound to the brain's cortex in the form of an energy charge, which then is distributed throughout the body, toning up the whole system and imparting greater dynamism.[21]

Since the middle ear contains more "receivers" for high-frequency sounds than for low-frequency sounds, high frequencies have the greater charging effect. Indeed, prolonged exposure to low frequencies can be physically and mentally draining. From "Om" to lullabies, from Gregorian chants to modern choral works, certain songs bring a serenity and power beyond words.

> Music washes away from the soul
> the dust of everyday living.
> —Leopold Stokowski

What clamors to be said, although too few are saying it, is that the heart of "matter" is not matter but "vibration." We now know from complexity scientists and superstring physicists that to understand the essence of matter we must first dematerialize our thinking. We have also learned from John Bell (1964) and Alain Aspect (1982) that to comprehend what matter is we must embrace the nonlocal connectedness of quantum physics. In fact, the interconnectedness of the structures of the universe, which is technically known as the physics of nonlocality, has been described as "the greatest discovery of all science."[22]

How could the church have missed "the greatest discovery of all science"? The only thing that makes sense when everything is interrelated is this answer to the question of "What is matter?" Matter is fundamentally—as superstring physics puts it—"vibrating threads of energy."[23] Did you hear what was just said? Did you grasp the spiritual implications of such a statement?

The fundamental realities of the universe are spiritual, not physical; invisible, not visible.

In theological terms, when God created you and me, God created us to be one-of-a-kind, incomparable songs. In the Scriptures, sound is a mark of divine revelation. Each one of us is sounded forth as an original inspiration from God. Everything has a voice. People today want to hear those voices and discover their own song, again.

> There is no greater agony
> than bearing an untold story inside you.[24]
> —Maya Angelou

Leadership as Music Making

Discipleship in the Christian tradition focuses on three elements: teaching, healing, and preaching. Music has an impact on teaching and learning. Whether it's taking music lessons or listening to Mozart, music benefits learning. Even when music is little more than auditory wallpaper, music helps us absorb and maintain information. How did the monks memorize large chunks of Scripture? How did people throughout history learn their theology and doctrine? How did you learn your ABCs? How did you learn the books of the New Testament? Music is the highest learner-based form of learning.

Music also has an effect on healing. Ted Gideonse has sampled the stories chronicling the medicinal power of music:

> 1) Daily doses of Mozart or Mendelssohn brighten the mood of stroke victims;
>
> 2) Music boosts immune function in children;
>
> 3) Premature babies who hear lullabies in the hospital go home earlier;

4) After trying both, eight patients recovering from open-heart surgery chose a regimen of twenty minutes of low-frequency humming over a morphine drip. Also, their hospital stays decreased by four days over those who were drugged.[25]

Music is the highest model for leadership. We are sought by rhythm, caught by melody, and taught by harmony.[26] Rhythm beckons us into relationship, melody unites us into relationship, and harmony tutors us into relationship.

1. Rhythm

Rhythm is not something one creates or "makes" but is something that is already there and comes to get us, hence the hand-clapping and toe-tapping. Rhythm provokes a response and draws the hearer into a relationship. Because "the ear is born open to every sound," contends Capuchin theologian Edward Foley, "the ear is the metaphor for human beings born open to engagement, not just with sounds, but with the people who produce them. Consequently the ear could be considered a physiological metaphor for relationship."[27]

The essence of leadership is sending out vibrations of truth that hunt people down and invite them to join the song. The God of Abraham and Sarah, Priscilla and Aquila is a relational God. The deep, rich rhythms of God's heart beat within us, seeking us out and beckoning us into relationship. We are unfinished and unfulfilled until we resonate with those rhythms stalking deep within us.

"We played pipes to you," Jesus said.

God "sounds" the "call." And when God "calls," a response is required.

"Why did you not dance?" Jesus demanded.

> Twilight is the crack between the worlds.[28]
>
> —Don Juan

Jesus tunes us to the rhythms of the spiritual world just as the sun tunes us to the rhythms of the physical world. The master gland in our body, the

pituitary gland, is directly affected by the sun. So too are our hormonal systems. So too our sleeping patterns. So too our emotional states, which plunge into darkness without sufficient light (seasonal affective disorder).

Ditto the soul and the Sun of Righteousness. The human soul is as much a "sunflower" (so called because the flower turns to the sun as it makes its way across the sky) as the human body.

Leaders are imperfect tuning forks of the eternal, sounding forth as best we can the vibrations of Jesus the Christ—God's Perfect Pitch—which beckon all into a relationship with God.

> I had been my whole life a bell, and never knew it
> until at that moment I was lifted and struck.[29]
>
> —Annie Dillard

2. Melody

Melody belongs in partnership with rhythm, as rhythm-melody vibrations help people place themselves in time and place the time in memory. If rhythm beckons us into relationship, melody unites us into relationship and brings to life the music of that relationship.

A melody is the disciplined disbursement of the breath of life. Just as in God's house there are many mansions, many melodies can be sung at once in a symphony. No one melody is the symphony. Leaders strike a lyric chord that conveys the breath of God, a God who is known and unknown, hidden and revealed, far distant and up close. This chord invites sympathetic vibrations from those who hear it, and when resonance is reached the melodies become contagious.

Why is music so important in a Google world? By its very nature, all music, even "easy listening" music, is relational and participational. In the words of music theorist Alfred Tomatis, "To listen to someone else singing is to enter into a partnership of vibration. Why? Simply because producing sound makes the outside air vibrate. The listener who is situated within this air space is going to find himself 'sculpted' by the vibrations. To listen to someone playing, singing, or speaking is to let oneself be put in vibration with him."[30] That's why, back at the piano, we're all fundamentalists. Take any scholar or scientist raised in a church setting and put him at the piano singing hymns, and he turns back into a fundamentalist. The cadences keep resonating, the melodies keep playing.

> Trust thyself; every heart vibrates to that iron string. Accept the place the divine providence has found for you, the society of our contemporaries, the connection of events.[31]
>
> —Ralph Waldo Emerson

In the African American song-speech tradition, the best preaching modulates from speech to song. Leadership is dependent on one's skill in "tuning" and "whooping." The former is the singing of words; the latter is the saying of words. Henry Mitchell defines whooping as "the use of a musical tone or chant in preaching" as the preacher, usually toward the end of a sermon, moves from speech to song.[32]

The leadership that comes from making melodies is unifying, not divisive. In the words of Foley, sound events unite "singer with the song, listener with the song, singer with the listener, the listener with other listeners, and even in a new way the listener with her or himself."[33] What melodies linger longer in the air for you? This is the music that is composing your soul and composting your memories.

> Musical training is most important … because rhythm and harmony permeate the innermost element of the soul, affect it more powerfully than anything else, and bring it grace.[34]
>
> —Socrates

If community is that which is created by shared experiences,[35] communities of faith are built from the sound up. Sharing the same mission, eating the same food, and singing the same melodies result in the experience of community.

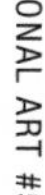

Melodies are the creative scaffoldings that help structure unique church cultures and cohesiveness. Music tells the story of a congregation better than anything else, hence the need for ministers of melody and ministers of poetry. Who are your resident lyricists, your resident poets? Who are your resident composers? Willow Creek's signature song, its through-thick-and-thin theme song born out of crucial times, is "He Is Able." Calvary Chapel's theme song is "Little Country Church."

Each church needs its own theme song, its own melodies that bring to mind ("remind") spiritual truths and experiences.

3. Harmony

During World War II, Christians in Princeton held a prayer meeting to intercede for Jews in Germany. When Albert Einstein heard about it, he left his house at 112 Mercer Street, walked to the prayer meeting, and asked if he might join them. He had brought his violin with him, and wondered if he might "pray" with his instrument.[36]

Are you "praying" with your instrument? What "instrument" are you praying with? Must we all "pray" with the same "instruments"?

The third element of music is harmony. Harmony, like rhythm, is something already there that leaders "hear." Leaders don't so much "compose" or "invent" harmony as "hear" harmony into vibrational and visional form.

People need to vibrate in sync with one another.
People want to sing and dance more,
sit and listen less.

There is too much unison singing in our churches and not enough harmony singing. The gospel of Jesus Christ is a polyphony in which many voices create one music. Worship is a singing school where disciples of Jesus Christ tune their instruments to sing God's praise and "harmonize" their unique melodies in polyphonic form. Singing in harmony involves everyone doing the same thing at the same time but doing it with a difference. In harmony we learn that we all don't have to sing the same beat; we all don't have

to sing the same words; we all don't have to sing the same notes; sometimes we all don't have to be on the same page, but we can all be singing the same love song to Jesus.

Some of our forebears opposed singing in parts precisely because it encouraged the experience of diversity, not uniformity. Theologian John of Salisbury attacked twelfth-century polyphony, where different parts are sung simultaneously. In his view, "Music sullies the Divine Service," for in all "their before-singing and their after-singing, their singing and their counter-singing, their in-between-singing and their ill-advised singing," the service is taken over by the emotions. "The ears are almost completely divested of their critical power, and the intellect, which pleasurableness of so much sweetness has caressed insensate, is impotent to judge the merits of the things heard."[37]

Harmony is absolutely critical for this world of difference not sameness. In fact, God may have hard-wired diversity in the human genetic code. Six-month-old infants prefer listening to musical scales sampled from a variety of cultures than to scales of randomly chosen notes.

One of the most extraordinary moments in the history of Carnegie Hall took place on April 6, 1962. When the concert was about to begin, conductor Leonard Bernstein walked out and surprised everyone with a disclaimer. Before pianist Glenn Gould presented his interpretation of Brahms, Bernstein wanted his audience to know that he personally did not like it. At the same time, he admitted that he respected Gould as a serious musician and found certain portions of Gould's presentation so fresh and arresting it made him question somewhat his own interpretation. Since Gould refused to budge, Bernstein confessed to three solutions: He could assign the conducting to an associate, recruit another artist to perform the Brahms piece, or "submit" his baton to the authority of the artist. By choosing the latter option, Bernstein hoped to model the possibility of something different—harmony amid diversity.[38]

Strike middle C on the piano. The other C's of higher octaves resonate in harmony and can be heard by one whose ear is sensitively trained. That's the essence of leadership: striking harmonics in various octaves of energy depending on the situation. The first harmonic of middle C possesses equal amplitude but different frequencies of expression. Good leaders know when to sound a note that creates a faster or slower sound wave, which means others hear it as a higher- or lower-pitched sound even though it's still the same note and occupies the same tonal position on the scale.

> It is probable that in the artistic hierarchy birds are the greatest musicians existing on our planet.[39]
>
> —Olivier Messiaen

Kist o' Whistles

If vibrations are the building blocks of the universe, it is not surprising that music has occasioned some of the biggest grievances and grudges in the history of the church. Fights over organs, or the "kist o' whistles" battles (as the Scots called the pipe organ), have been replicated over everything from gourd xylophones to guitars.

From the files of Amnesty International comes the story of a Chilean singer who demonstrated the deeper meaning of "dancing in the minefield" (in Annette Kolodny's famously perilous phrase). The singer was imprisoned with thousands of others in the National Stadium in Santiago when the government of Salvador Allende was overthrown by Augusto Pinochet, a career military officer and a ruthless and brutal politician. The singer's name was Victor Juarez. As the singer stood among the frightened and demoralized prisoners, who had been rounded up for unknown reasons, he began a solitary freedom song. A guitar was passed to him. The spirit began to blow. Soon thousands were singing with him this Chilean folk freedom song.

As usual, the authorities were threatened by the power of the spirit moving so freely and blatantly. They seized the young man and took him away.

When the authorities returned Juarez, they dumped him in the midst of the crowd and threw at his feet the guitar, which had been smashed. Not

only had the guitar been destroyed, but all ten of the singer's fingers had been cut off. Horrified, his fellow prisoners drew back. But the young man walked into the moat of empty space they had created, lifted his bloody hands and began to lead in another folk hymn and freedom song. Once more the spirit began to move. The people took up his new song, another Chilean folk hymn.

Predictably, the guards moved in again. This time when they brought him back there was blood trickling from his mouth. They had cut out his tongue. Many wept. Everyone was watching. For a while, the singer lay motionless. Then he stood up and began to sway. Some thought he was fainting. But then they realized his graceful, silent swaying was a dance, a dance to the beat of the song he had led them in earlier, but a song he could no longer sing. Soon they were all swaying silently with him.

When the guards came this time, they wasted no time. They shot him dead in front of all the people. But the spirit continued to blow. The beat went on. Indeed, the beat goes on today in Chile.

When the winds of the Spirit blow, will our churches be ready to move in sympathetic vibration, even to sing? What's keeping you and your church from vibing—fear of the new and unexpected, lack of trust in yourself and your music-making abilities, lack of trust and faith in God?

The last words of the Bible invite us to a sing-along party: "Come." Jesus wants a full house. Will God's house be full? Will you be there? What's keeping you and your church from singing and vibing, that God's house may be full?

> Now unto him that is able to keep you from falling,
> and to present you faultless [and flame flickering]
> before the presence of his glory with exceeding joy,
> to the only wise God, our Saviour, be glory and majesty,
> dominion and power, both now and ever. Amen.
>
> —Jude vv. 24–25 KJV

AQUACHURCH #5
CROSSOVER CHURCH

Tampa, Florida
www.crossoverchurch.org

Pulitzer Prize–winning novelist Margaret Mitchell wrote, "Brilliance is one part talent, two parts wisdom, and three parts passion. Whenever you encounter it in your midst, celebrate it, encourage it, be happy for it." Crossover Church has done just that in the area of vibration in its worship. Crossover has taken the "cross over" by "crossing over" and introducing the gospel to those influenced by Hip-Hop culture. Through this unique innovation, this AquaChurch has caused a vibration of brilliance and passion to reverberate throughout the world as a guide for how to impact today's culture. Crossover Church:

- Uses Hip-Hop music to connect with the hearts and souls of a unique community;
- Shows other churches how to bring their worship to God because of who he is, not because of what we have to offer;
- Champions today's church by providing the tools needed to send the vibrations of worship throughout every aspect of the church;
- Encourages others to consistently seize every opportunity to provide a relevant gospel through the expression of worship;
- Equips churches to participate in a total worship experience, knowing the vibrations of that experience will go to the community beyond the four walls of their church.

CAPTAIN'S LOGBOOK

PERSONAL LOG

Use these ideas to stimulate your thinking about how the principles of this chapter could affect your ministry. Consider sharing these ideas with other church leaders.

1 John Maxwell uses a Moishe Rosen one-sentence mental exercise as an effective tool in dreaming. It simply involves completing two sentences. Complete these two sentences now.

- If I had …
- I would …[40]

If you had anything you wanted—unlimited time, unlimited money, unlimited information, unlimited staff, all the resources you could ask for—what would you do?

Your answer to the second question is your dream.

2 This prayer was written anonymously as a humorous piece for a choir director. But if we really understand missional art #5, isn't there more here than humor?

> Almighty and most merciful Conductor,
> We have erred and strayed from Thy beat like lost sheep;
> We have followed too much the intonations and tempi of our own hearts.
> We have offended against Thy dynamic markings.
> We have left unsung those notes which we ought to have sung,
> And we have sung those notes which we ought not to have sung.
> And there is no support in us.
> But Thou, O Conductor, have mercy upon us, miserable singers;
> Succor the chorally challenged;
> Restore Thou them that need sectionals;

Spare Thou them that have no pencils.
Pardon our mistakes, and have faith that hereafter we will follow
Thy directions and sing together in perfect harmony.[41]

—Anonymous

Consider:

- How does this prayer connect with your life?
- How does this prayer connect with your church? your ministry? your outlook on music?

3 On a radio or CD player, find a radio station that's playing music, or play a CD of your choosing. Take a few moments to listen to the music. Write down what you felt, sensed, and heard. Concentrate on your feelings and reactions. Think about the power of music and its effect on the listener.

- How accurate has your estimation of the power of music been?
- Reflect on the statement "of all the 'arts,' the one that comes closest to expressing all the others is music" (p. 142). How is that statement true?

Remember what you learn from this experience as you plan your worship.

4 Read the following Bible passages: Creation (Gen. 1—2), burning bush (Ex. 3:1—4:17), Mount Sinai (Ex. 19—20), and Pentecost (Acts 2). Consider:

- What is the significance of how "sound becomes sight" (p. 145)?
- How might you use this "sound to sight" concept in future worship experiences?

5 Consider the following statement: "Music is the highest learner-based form of learning" (p. 148).

- How does your church take advantage of this learning tool?
- What role do you take in planning and participating in the music offered in the worship experiences?
- How could you better integrate the ministry of the music with the ministry of the Word?

In the privacy of your study, write down at least three personal, realistic goals for moving your music-making leadership to the next level.

6 Any renewal of your "vibration" ministry will start with a renewal of your understanding of worship. One such place to start would be worship renewal resources by the late Robert Webber such as his *The New Worship* (2007) or *Renew Your Worship* (1997).

7 The dean of evangelical church music, Donald Hustad, writes, "We should expect that new musical styles will appear in periods of renewal and evangelism. This both demonstrates the creativity of the Holy Spirit at these times and offers a fresh message for communicating the gospel.… Musical sounds common to the secular world are effective in pre-evangelizing the uncommitted. Furthermore, this illustrates the incarnational character of the gospel, which uses ordinary human speech and music to communicate the divine message to human beings; in turn, the music and speech may be used by the Holy Spirit to transform ordinary, sinful people into members of the family of God."[42]

Consider:

- What are the implications of this quote for your church's music ministry?
- How does what Paul says in 1 Corinthians 9:22 (NRSV) ("I have become all things to all people, that I might by all means save some") connect with this quote?
- What should be your attitude toward the use of nontraditional music in your church's ministry?

Ship's Log

Use these activities with your church leadership to help them understand and own the principles of this chapter and how they relate to your church's ministry.

1 Members of the Arnstadt Council, employers of J. S. Bach, warned that "If Bach continues to play this way, the organ will be ruined in two years, or most of the congregation will be deaf." People are liking more and more kinds of music, although they have favorites. The favorite? Country Western is the top choice with 65 percent of the people texted in a survey, followed by blues/R&B (63 percent), rock (60 percent), and gospel music (58 percent). A surprising 48 percent liked classical/chamber music, the same percentage as for jazz.[43]

- How do we as leaders sometimes sound like the Arnstadt Council?
- Where do we hear similar soundings in the church today?
- How well do we respond to the music preferences of our people? How well should we respond?

Put together a poll to ascertain the musical preferences of your people. As much as possible, administer the poll to every person who attends your church. Then evaluate the results, and consider how people's preferences are reflected in the current music of your church. Determine what changes you need to make in the types of music used in your worship experiences.

2 Evaluate the following with your leaders: Two surveys by *Christianity Today* reveal that the number of American churches that emphasize nontraditional music more than doubled between 1993 and 1996. The survey also revealed that churches with contemporary praise and worship music showed higher average Sunday morning attendance, and 69 percent of them showed attendance growth between 1992 and 1997.

- How do these statistics fit with what you would have expected?
- How are they different?
- What should be the determining factor in any church's decision to modify music styles?
- What obstacles would we face in modifying our music ministry?
- What benefits might we reap?

3 Study together Colossians 3:16. Focus on the meaning of the phrase "psalms, hymns and spiritual songs."

- What types of songs classify as "spiritual songs"?

- What might the text suggest about variety in music?
- Where do psalms fit into worship?
- How appropriate is the balance of these elements in your worship experiences?

4 Ask one of your leaders to do research on the Internet about "raves." Then have that leader present any findings to your leadership team. Here's a little background: "Rave" music is electronic dance music. "Raves" are all-night, no-rules parties where there is a mix of virtual-reality electronics, techno-music, and theme-dress. The rave phenomenon has hit religious culture in two areas. "Rave Masses" are being conducted in more liturgical settings—the first was conducted at Grace Cathedral in San Francisco in the fall of 1994 with dancing, forty-two video monitors, and flashing images. In more evangelical settings in England and USAmerica, there are "Rave in the Nave" services.

Have your leaders form groups of three or four to discuss the following questions:

- What do you think has spawned this rave phenomenon?
- What might be positive results from Christian raves?
- What can we learn from this phenomenon to enhance the music ministry of our church?

Have groups share their insights with the rest of your leaders.

5 Distribute paper and pens, and ask your leadership team to answer the following two questions in writing:

- What role does music play in your life personally?
- What role does music play in our church corporately?

Have leaders share their answers with the group. Then discuss:

- Why do we have a difficult time putting a finger on music's power?
- How accurate is the statement, "Experience proves that next to the Word of God only music deserves to be extolled as the mistress and governess of the feelings of the human heart" (p. 144)?
- What implications does that statement have for music in the church?

End this discussion by brainstorming suggestions on how your church might better release the inherent power of music. Write down all the ideas you come up with, and then narrow the list to the top five. Work toward sensitively implementing those five ideas within your worship experiences.

6 Read the following statement as a group: "Music tells the story of a congregation better than anything else" (p. 152). Consider together:

- What is the musical identity of our church?
- What one song might stand out from all the rest as the theme of our ministry? Why is that so?
- What might we want to change about the musical identity of our church?

7 Sing together. Have an accompanist come to your meeting, and let leaders choose favorite songs to sing. Encourage leaders to request a variety of song types that are meaningful to them. Spend at least a half-hour singing. If the Spirit seems to be moving, keep going as long as you feel is appropriate. Then ask:

- How was this experience meaningful to you?
- How was this experience like or unlike our regular worship experiences?
- What insights have you gained from this experience that relate to our church's music ministry?

MISSIONAL ART #6

SEEING THROUGH SCOPES: VISION

Where there is no vision, the people perish.

—Old Hebrew proverb

Where there is only vision,
the people have nervous breakdowns.

—New Hebrew proverb

A Three Stooges routine had Larry crying out to Moe, "I can't see! I can't see!" Moe rushed to Larry's aid, asking "Why not? What's wrong?" Larry then smiled and proclaimed, "I got my eyes closed!" Then, of course, Moe bopped Larry on the head.

To get where God is calling you to go, you need to see. Sometimes to get us to see, we need a bop on the head. Other times we need some help to see. Scopes are instruments that aid navigators in "seeing" and give "vision" in situations where otherwise sight would be impossible. In the past, a captain would stand on the bridge of his ship and peer through his "spyglass," a small, hand-held telescope. With the help of that scope, he could keep an eye on what was around him, reading the wind and the sea, so he would know what he and his crew might encounter.

Leaders need keenness of vision. The Bible warns that without vision, there is division. Our ability to "see" and to metaphorize what is seen unites us, gets us somewhere, and releases power in life. A false vision is imprisonment; a true vision is empowerment.

"Visionaries" are not people whose eyesight can peek into the future. Visionaries are those who can peer around them, who can see life for what it is, who can see God for who God is. They are people who can read the "signs of the times," not just the "signs of the future." Visionaries are also those who can heal the wounds of the past by offering new metaphors around which we can shape a new focus for the future.

In the words of that old proverb, "One nail drives out another."

The Vision Thing

Fifty years ago, if you admitted you had a "vision" the people in white coats would come and take you away. Now everyone has a "vision," and those who don't are taken away. You can't run for garbage collector these days without a vision. Every corporation has one. Every individual has one. Every church has one.

Visions in the Bible were gifts of God. They most often were divine revelations to a prophet. Visions were sent by God—not by marketers or consultants or demographers. And at times eyesight was bad and "there were not many visions" (1 Sam. 3:1).

Now, though "the vision thing" reigns, true visions are hard to come by. Philosopher John Ruskin contends, "Thousands can think for one who can see." And again: "The greatest thing a human soul ever does in this world is to see something, and tell what it saw in a plain way." Ruskin was so convinced of the importance of "seeing" that he argued that "to see clearly is poetry, prophecy, and religion—all in one."[1]

Thus also saith the Lord.

One day Philip found Nathanael sitting under a fig tree (John 1:43–51). Philip told Nathanael, "We have found the one Moses wrote about in the Law, and about whom the prophets also wrote—Jesus of Nazareth." Nathanael

replied, "Nazareth! Can anything good come from there?" Philip answered, "Come and see." This is what "visionaries" do—help people to see. To see their times, to see their world, to see themselves, most importantly to see God, and to see for themselves all of the above.

AquaChurch visionaries help people see in a new way and help provide metaphors for their new way of seeing. "If you want to understand the world," insists Pierre Babin, onetime director of the Center for Research and Communication in Lyon, France, "you must change your way of looking at it and the way you perceive its interconnections."[2]

> The transitions from modern to postmodern have altered the functions and foundations of the world in which we live.

Seeing Eyes

In fact, neurologists now tell us that one has to learn to see. Adults who have been blind since childhood, like "Virgil" from Oklahoma who at fifty years of age regained his sight after forty-five years of blindness, can't immediately "see" what they see because they don't have the experience or meaning necessary to interpret the sight.[3] All the nerves and impulses are there. But they are mentally blind. Their habits, their behaviors, are still those of their earlier life; they have "unstable judgment of space and distance."

Jesus' miracle at Bethsaida tips us off to this: The blind man was healed, but at first he only saw "men as trees, walking," the Bible says. Only eventually was his eyesight fully restored, although he was fully healed by Jesus.

In fact, a month after surgery, a seeing Virgil "felt more disabled than he had felt when he was blind, and he had lost the confidence, the ease of moving, that he had possessed then." The physical and emotional impact of the gift of sight can be "almost shocking, explosive."[4] The blessing of this new sense can quickly become a curse.

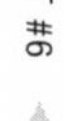

You can't see anything properly when your eyes are blurred with tears.[5]
—C. S. Lewis

One reaction of the body to overload and overstimulation is a shutdown. In some cases there is complete blockage of the new visual world and return to the tactile world. Lots of patients "behave blind" and "refuse to see" even after their sight is restored.

There are plenty of people out there who are "seeing but not seeing" or are walking blindly. More than anything else, faith in Jesus Christ enables us to see and changes the way we see—even when we prefer not to see. Picture this cartoon of a man in an optician's office: His hair is frazzled; his eyes are wild; his legs are all atremble. He says to the doctor, "Doctor, I would like to see things a little less clearly."

How do we begin to navigate ourselves, our church, our structures, our planet in these new waters? The first step is a change of perception. We need to take a new mindwalk, to embark on a new soultrain. We need a new vision, a new way of seeing, and new ways of describing what we see. We need increased powers to comprehend this world as it really is and not as we have been trained to see it from the perspective of modernity.

If eyes were made for seeing, then beauty is its own excuse for being.[6]
—Ralph Waldo Emerson

But beware: No one is stranger than a person who "sees" in a community that is "blind." Pastor Bob Olmstead tells of one busy afternoon driving on a Reno, Nevada, city street when a small, wounded bird wandered out into the highway.

> It huddled on the pavement as the cars whizzed past it and over it, tires somehow missing it. I glimpsed the bird just as the tires

of my car straddled it. At that moment I made a rash decision. I decided to rescue the bird.

I stopped the car, jumped out, and held up my hands to stop traffic. If I could "shoo" the bird over the curb and into the hedge of bushes, it would be safe, at least from traffic. When I approached the bird it scooted away, but it didn't scoot in a straight line. Whether it was too young to fly, whether its wing was injured, I do not know. But every time I bent down and waved my arms the bird would half hop, half fly in a crazy circle and end up back in the middle of the road. I could not catch it and I could not get it to run into the bushes.

By this time I had a considerable amount of traffic backed up. The close drivers were watching me with quizzical or suspicious expressions. Farther back, horns were honking. I kept thinking, "Just another minute and I'll catch the little bird or it will run off into the bushes." So I continued running around in the street, stooped over, flapping my arms, chasing that little feathered thing.

It was only then that I realized the other drivers could not see the bird![7]

Visionaries are like that. Others cannot see what they see. A fear of looking foolish keeps many from following God's vision. But the offense of the cross is something each one of us must take personally.

Metaphorical Missionaries

What "planning" was to the Gutenberg world, "visioning" is to the Google world. We must get rid of the old modernist doctrine that more planning,

more technology, will solve our social problems. Visioning is radically different from "planning." Planners gave maps. Visionaries give metaphors.

Visionaries think in terms of multiple scenarios and "multiple futures." Leaders of the future need what I call complexity vision. The essence of complexity vision is bringing together two processes simultaneously—for example, differentiation and integration. Differentiation is the ability to embrace diversity and uniqueness and to be responsive to the external environment; integration is the ability to achieve harmony and oneness.[8]

Complexity vision is the ability to look at many things at once, the ability to think more than one thought at a time, the ability to abandon old fixations, make new connections, follow your intuitions, and, like Eli Manning in "The Big Pass" (Superbowl XLII) and every other good quarterback, give people a "lead" (even when there is less than a minute left). What you foresee is what you get.

Complexity vision entails a 360-degree sweep of possibilities. "Complex visioning" is the stacking of multiple scenarios at the same time, even opposite scenarios. In other words, "complex visioning" is less an issue of "planning" than "preparedness,"[9] and the essence of preparedness is the constant spinning out of four or five possible scenarios at the same time, each one with its own unique metaphors.

> The best laid schemes o' mice an' men
> Gang aft a-gley,
> An' lea'e us naught but grief an' pain,
> For promised joy![10]
> —Scottish poet Robert Burns

The future belongs to complexity-friendly visionaries who can eyewitness the world with wholesight and foresight and describe what they see with metaphors that can help others to become wholesight eyewitnesses following a whole Christ.

She's a bombshell and a nerd,
a girl-next-door and a geek, a vixen and a dork.
—Super-model Tyra Banks' description
of super-model Rebecca Romijn

Double Vision

The kind of scopes one chooses as an aid to seeing is of utmost importance. In the modern world the preferred scopes were telescopes. Modernity facilitated a monocular, almost cyclopean view of the world—a one-eyed perspective that brought the world to a single point. We must move from a monocular to a binocular view of the world—a two-eyed, bifocal perspective that brings with it a depth perception missing in much of modernity.[11] The need for opening up the second eye is occasioned by the following revelations of a Google world.

A Google World Is Nonlinear and Nondualist

The future never has been linear and never will be. You don't even know what one day will bring forth, much less one year. That's why one-eyed rigidity and squinting inflexibility spell danger in the mind and soul as well as in the earth (earthquakes are the result of brittle and unbending faults). It is dangerous to do linear viewing in a nonlinear world.

You cannot forecast the weather; you cannot forecast an earthquake or a tornado—they are monsters ruled by the principle of nonlinear dynamics. Single-eyed, straight-down-the-middle strategies don't work in a serpentine, nonlinear world.

A Google World Is Uncertain

We live in a post-9/11 world where anything can happen, and happen at once. The unexpected has become the expected. Much in life is beyond our control. Uncertainty must be embraced, not excluded. Until we can harness the capacity to see and hear "out-of-control" as positive, not negative, we will not be able to navigate these chaotic seas. Paradoxically, the more random and dicey the world appears, the more purposeful is the accidental, the more ordered the chaos.

A Google World Is Nonlocal

We are now beginning to discover that atoms, electrons, and photons are connected somehow no matter how distant they are. Everything is "nonlocal." The twenty-first century has said "good-bye" to Einstein's speed limit: light. Nothing is separate from anything else in a world where we can chat and play and interact with anyone from anywhere.

Postmodernity's nonlinearity, nondualism, uncertainty, and nonlocality necessitates that leadership adopt a decentered perspective. It is not so much that opposites meet. Rather, one opposite thing needs another, and sometimes is another.

> And the fire and the rose are one.[12]
>
> —T. S. Eliot

No "Happy" Middles

The middles are not where the action is. There is no such thing as a "happy" middle. The action is on the edge, not the center. There is nothing more deadly in the Christian religion than the middle position. In fact, a move to the center is a move away from Jesus, who is always found on the edges, in the margins, beyond the boxes.

A sixteenth-century legend has Francis de Sales approached by a woman who asks, "Is it a sin to use rouge?" De Sales replies, "Well, some theologians say it's all right; others disagree." The woman, still unsatisfied, presses for a more definitive response. Francis smiles and says, "Why not follow a middle course, and rouge only one cheek?"

There is no middle course. There are now multiple centers. Dramatic

shifts away from the middle can be seen in sources of authority, which are migrating away from middle structures (institutional authority) to end-extremes (personal and planetary authority). In the twenty-first century, there will be two successful economic entities: the mega-brands or the niche specialists; and the powerful huge multinationals or the small, quick entrepreneurs. "The brands that are going to have the most trouble are the ones in the mushy middle."[13]

In the Reformation Era and its successive reforming movements, those faiths that best solved the riddle of the middle succeeded, and those that didn't failed. But these "middle faiths" are in decline today. The ridge of the middle is flattening. Biblical truth is not found in massaging away the contradictions and paradoxes or in trying to mend the "broken middle"[14] but in embracing the divisive tensions and intentions of the world in which we live. The church must bridge the ridge. The church must give up sitting on fences for straddling opposing sides and traversing the borderlands. Truth is not found in the mediocrity of the middle but in the "paradoxical harmony"[15] of a double-edged sword. Orthodoxy is paradoxy.

> How can any people hope to remain unscathed? …
> Can they exist as islands of prosperity in a sea of discontents?[16]
>
> —Historian Paul Kennedy

And/Also, Not Either/Or

In an Age of Connection, every trend generates a counter-trend. Poet W. N. Herbert has a poem that serves as an aphorism of this connectional world: "And not Or."[17]

Can you discover some and/alsos of twenty-first-century culture?[18]

- I have good news and bad news. Which would you like first?
- The double ring of our nation in the past twenty years has been that in the midst of massive downsizings and layoffs, we were also in the midst of a historic hiring boom.

- A Victorian company called "Victoria's Secret" sells the most seductive lingerie imaginable.

> Global Paradox: Growth of Trade Binds Nations, but It Also Can Spur Separatism … A World of 500 Countries?[19]
>
> —Front-page headline in *The Wall Street Journal*

- The greatest challenges in evangelism are the overchurched and the unchurched. The more adults who consider themselves "Christian" say they are "religious," the less likely they are to read the Bible and attend church.[20]
- Doublespeak ("Less is More") is everywhere, from book titles like *Ordinary Miracles* and *Open Secrets* to movies like *Bad Santa* and intellectual constructs like Michel Foucault's concept of "calm violence."[21]
- The two best-selling hair products among baby boomers? In first place, "natural" hair products. In second place, hair coloring.
- Why is it that, just when democracy is triumphing around the world, our American democracy is in trouble?[22]
- The more globalized and industrialized our food system becomes (roughly 10 multinational firms produce half of the 30,000 items in typical U.S. supermarkets), the more interest there is in local foods and the more people are becoming "locavores" (by the way, we used to call "locavores" farmers).[23]

Double Ring/Double Vision

F. Scott Fitzgerald said it best: "The test of a first-rate intelligence is the ability to hold two opposing ideas in the mind at the same time and still retain the ability to function."[24] To paraphrase James M. Cain's classic noir thriller, "The Christian Always Rings Twice."

Some are misreading this as a culture "of two minds," a culture unable to make up its mind one way or the other. But that's a misreading of a culture that is more of "one mind" than we like to think. It's complexly (not simply) a mind that likes to go in different directions at the same time—like the new psychological syndrome recently diagnosed as "shy extrovert."

In fact, it's a mind much like the biblical mind. And as I shall argue in a moment, Christians face in two directions simultaneously.

> It is dangerous to show man too clearly how much alike he is to the beasts without showing him his greatness. It is also dangerous to show him too clearly his greatness without his lowliness. It is still more dangerous to leave him in ignorance of both.[25]
>
> —Blaise Pascal

The essence of the Web may well be its doubleness: It is both collective and individual; language appears orally and written at the same time (it's oral—immediate, contextual, and circumstantial; but it's also written—everything you say or write is archived and lurks somewhere forever).

In a culture where the image or metaphor has replaced the word as the primary coinage of cultural currency, it is no accident that metaphors are themselves a double ring—"two ideas in one phrase," as philosopher Max Black puts it (for example, sweet smile and sharp light). No wonder history's greatest leaders have always been masters of metaphors.

This is not the first time in history there has been this pervasive doubleness and dividedness. Obsessions with double selves, buried lives, secret selves, and private lives characterized Victorian literature and manifested itself in the "double forms" and "split voices" that marked Victorian poetry. Yet this Victorian doubleness was a true split: It was an either-or doubleness, not a both-and doubleness.

For the first time in history a culture can indeed have it both ways. Google culture is less tightrope than trapeze. And the back-and-forth movement can be dizzying. In a world where the "normal distribution curve" is no longer

a "Bell Curve" but a "Well Curve," one has to understand the Double Ring phenomenon to survive.

Double Vision is crucial for strategizing during times of immense change. Double Vision is a diagnostic that can help churches and individuals think about their attitudes, their directions, and their capacities.

Ministry Strategy

The double ring is more than a metaphor; it's a strategy for ministry. Strategy needs to be a verb, not a noun; strategy is something you "do," not something you "have."[26] And what the church "does" strategically is take ministry to the edges, not to the center and then finds best-of-both-worlds solutions. Roper Starch calls these "cool fusion solutions."[27] Or in more theological language, the church must cross the crowded ways of life.

For five hundred years we have been mastering the center/periphery dynamics of the modern era. We now need to master the double-helix dynamics of the postmodern era. We don't have blueprints for how to build bridges that span the boundaries of difference. We don't have lexicons that instruct in the discourse of difference.

What I like to call "aloha theology" ("aloha" means both hello and good-bye) plays both rings simultaneously in a surround sound world. Ministry must strike both rings, must bring together opposites. In the bringing together of opposites, aloha theology is a creative, constructive theology. Paradox is the essence of creativity. When fifty-eight famously creative types were studied (like Picasso, Mozart, and Einstein), the one thing they shared was their ability to bring together opposites as mutually embracing, not mutually exclusive.[28] The creative leader is the one who can think out of both sides of the brain.

> I do not like to get the news, because there has never been an era when so many things have been going right for so many of the wrong persons.[29]
>
> —Ogden Nash

Global outreaches like Habitat for Humanity and Hospice have been more creative than the church. Ministry in a pluralistic world must bring together the opposites; it must embrace and bridge a world that is homeless and well housed, a world that is both dying and healthy, a world that is obese and anorexic at the same time. We must reach a world in which economic health and social health seem to be in inverse proportion.[30] The higher our income, the worse off we feel.

Creative ministry inhabits multiple tracks. It sounds a stereo spirituality instead of a mono or hi-fi spirituality. In dual tracks, each channel pursues its own path and offers up a distinct sound. When they come together, there may be interference, but stereo sound. If the gospel can't be heard in surround sound, it's not the gospel.

For example, don't blend black and white into fence-sitting gray. Instead, bring black and white together into "hot fudge sundaes" or "baked Alaska" or *Seinfeld's* black-and-white cookie. Straddle ebony and ivory in all of their mutual attractions and oppositions, and you get the tremendous energy of Paul Celan's celebrated poem *Todesfuge* (*Death Fugue*).[31]

The Double Ring Top Twenty-Five

Wonder why you feel impaled on two-pronged forks more and more? There's a reason. Listen to the double rings in this little exercise in paradoxalism:

1. More people are becoming rich than ever before, while more people are becoming poor than ever before.[32] The gap is larger now than at any time since the 1930s.[33]

> The problem is not that some of us are getting rich. That's good news. The problem is that most of us are getting nowhere.[34]
>
> —Robert Reich

2. Similarly, there are more African American upper-class Cosbys, Winfreys, Jordans, and Johnsons than ever before. Simultaneously, there are more

black homeless and underclass than ever before.[35] A black child born in Washington, D.C., in 1998 has a lower life expectancy than any child in the Western Hemisphere except those in Haiti. But Washington, D.C., blacks have the highest median income for blacks of anywhere in the nation.[36]

> We're getting the good jobs and the bad jobs,
> but the middle jobs we're losing.[37]
> —Economist David Wyss

3. The less you get paid, the harder you have to work.

4. The companies of the future are the global, consolidated corporations, or small, independent companies.

5. Information Age economies globalize and localize at the same time.

6. People are getting more back to nature, more "unplugged," more "natural," and at the same time more high-tech and computerized ("green" computers). The more we love nature, the more nature goes extinct.[38]

> I'm a high-tech redneck.
> —Country western song

7. More and more people long to belong, while people hate to be lumped and claimed. There are more and more individualized ways of living and more community-based ways of life.[39]

8. The nurturing of creative individuals and super-geniuses has become one of the most important tasks of this emerging culture. Yet at the same time the most powerful force for change in any culture is teamwork.

9. Churches are getting smaller (house churches and cell groups) and larger (megachurches). The majority of church members are in large-membership churches; the majority of pastors are in small-membership churches.[40]

10. The public trusts information, especially if it carries with it scientific status, while the public also believes there are scientific studies to prove just about anything and is becoming more and more skeptical of information.[41]

11. "Hot" and "cool" are standard adjectives of approval. They mean the same thing.[42]

12. Worship is becoming more liturgical and more free-form, more abstract and more realist. The Eastern Orthodox and the Pentecostals have inherited the earth.[43] There is even a new denomination—the "Charismatic Episcopal Church."[44]

13. Televangelists have become gods that control millions of people's lives, while televangelists are held in absolute contempt by millions more.

14. New houses are built bigger and bigger (Hummer Houses, I call them), while families are smaller and smaller.[45]

15. America is becoming more diverse than ever in its racial, ethnic, and religious makeup, but media culture is making us more homogenous than ever before in experiences and expectations across such groups.

> While differing widely in the various little bits we know,
> in our infinite ignorance we are all equal.[46]
> —Karl Popper

16. The demographics of personal-computer use are getting younger … and older. The two most computer-savvy segments of our population are our children and the fastest growing group, those fifty-five and older.

17. People are less and less interested in religious things, while at the same time more and more people are interested in spiritual things. Sixty-five percent of Americans say religion is losing its influence in American life (21 percent say it is increasing), while 62 percent of Americans say religion has been increasing its influence in their lives (16 percent say it is decreasing).[47]

18. In our rhetoric, our politics, and our media, we are a nation of grand moralizers. In the reality of everyday life, we are in one of the most immoral periods of history, and it seems to be getting more immoral, more sleazy, more grimy every day.[48]

19. More and more people insist on speaking their own native languages, while English is becoming an all-world language.[49]

20. We are seeing the greatest restoration of traditional values since just after World War II, and perhaps the greatest time of sexual experimentation in U.S. history.

21. The two holidays when the most money is spent on home decorating[50] are Christmas—celebrating the good things of peace, hope, love, and life—and Halloween, integrating the terrorizing forces of evil and death.

22. The more that people adopt artificial, self-constructed identities ("point-and-click personalities"), the more exalted becomes the function of being authentic, getting real, and expressing one's true self.

23. In the world of global agriculture today, more and more farmers are making a ton of money, while more and more farmers are facing financial catastrophe.

24. The more we snuggle into the sights, sounds, and smells of our electronic nests, and the more we are able to escape the real world that is out there, the more aware we are of other people's pain and concerned with the plight of others.

> This troubled planet is a place of the most violent contrasts. Those that receive the rewards are totally separated from those who shoulder the burdens. It is not a wise leadership.[51]
>
> —Mr. Spock

25. Boomers are more likely than the average American to shop at upscale stores such as Nordstrom, Saks Fifth Avenue, and Eddie Bauer, and they are more likely than the average American to shop at Target and Home Depot.[52]

TOP 10 Paradoxes

Here are the Top 10 paradoxes that will rule our future. These are not empty paradoxes, as some can be. These are full and overflowing paradoxes that disciples of Jesus must master:

1) Do little large.

2) To move up, move down.

3) Learn to fail so you can succeed.

4) Your only control is in being out of control.

5) It's more important to know what you don't know than what you know.

6) The more you think out-of-the-box, the more you need well-built boxes to think.

7) A graying globe requires greening. An aging planet needs to get younger.

8) Only locavores can globalize.

9) When fast replaces vast, go slowly with the holy.

10) Moore's Law makes Murphy's Law all the more relevant.

Surround Sound Disciples

Paradoxy is integral to our identity as disciples of Jesus. Our faith is cross-grained. Isn't the cross the symbol of bringing the two extremes together—the horizontal and the vertical, the human and the divine?

The twenty-first-century world forces us into Trinitarian thinking and Trinitarian theology. When bridges are built, polarities are replaced by trinities.

The Greek philosopher Heraclitus said "Logos" is that which holds contradictions and opposites together. He used the illustration of a stick. Pick up a stick, with both ends unconnected, and the stick is worthless. But find a way to bring the ends together, find a way to connect the opposite poles so that they somehow touch, find a way to build a bridge from one end of the stick to the other, and suddenly the stick becomes either a weapon that can kill the savage beast—a bow—or a musical instrument that can soothe the savage beast—a harp. Heraclitus called that something that connects the ends together "Logos." According to Heraclitus, even opposites, when combined together under the power of the Logos, produce harmony.[53]

From the strain of binding opposites comes harmony.[54]

—Heraclitus

Our logos is Christ, the humanization of God, the triangulation of God the Creator and God the Holy Spirit. We're disciples of Jesus the Christ, the Lion and the Lamb, the Alpha and the Omega, the first and the last, the "Word made flesh" and "we beheld his glory," the one who has come and the one who is coming. Jesus is "omnipotence in bonds" who one minute walks on water, the next minute washes his disciples' feet; one minute is executed on the cross, the next minute rises from the dead. Our Savior reigns … from a cross.

The Bible ends with these terrifying and joyful words: "'Let him who does wrong continue to do wrong; let him who is vile continue to be vile; let him who does right continue to do right; and let him who is holy continue to be holy. Behold, I am coming soon!' … Whoever is thirsty, let him come; and whoever wishes, let him take the free gift of the water of life" (Rev. 22:11–12, 17).

A journalist was assigned the Lebanon beat. Walking the bombed-out streets of Beirut one day, he heard beautiful music coming from a doorway. He wandered toward the source of the music and there saw a lad playing the weirdest-looking flute he had ever seen. When he approached, the lad stopped playing, smiled, and handed him the instrument. It was not until he picked up the flute did the journalist understand. For what this young Lebanese boy had done was to find in some field a discarded rifle, bore holes in the barrel of that rifle, and transform a gun into a flute.

When the world builds bridges that bring the ends together, it makes weapons. When the church builds bridges that bring the ends together, it should make music (but all too often has made the weapon instead). Which will we produce? Instruments of destruction or instruments of healing? Bows or harps? Guns or flutes?

A vision is not about programs or objectives or scenarios or goals. A vision is about hearing eyes. A vision is about releasing energies. A vision is about life-giving spirit. A vision is about the excitement of shared possibilities, together vision rather than tunnel vision. A vision is about seeing in such a way and communicating what you see that other people come to life with new enthusiasm and resolve.

These are the best of times for ministry. These are the worst of times for ministry. Through Logos power, we can live the two together. Through Jesus the Christ, we can live the two together. We can break the walls down. We can build the body up. We can bring the people together. We can bridge the gaps. We can bridge the ridges.

AQUACHURCH #6
VINTAGE FAITH CHURCH

Santa Cruz, California
www.vintagechurch.org

Vintage Faith Church is an AquaChurch that makes a point of seeing what's going on around it and within it—and responding. VFC has both the vision to reconnect and engage the emerging culture of Santa Cruz and the surrounding area, while they also have the ability to recognize and encourage artists from within their community of faith to express themselves visually as the framework for their Web site. Above all, Vintage Faith Church strives to become a community that approaches the teachings of Jesus and Christian spirituality in a fresh way. Vintage Faith leaders and church members have:

- Clearly defined their purpose as becoming a different kind of community in Santa Cruz that truly reflects who Jesus is;
- Recognized that approaches to ministry that used to be effective can often alienate and build mistrust in this culture. As a result, they have the ability to see the need for change;
- Purposefully chosen to rethink church and live out their faith as

missionaries who would communicate Jesus' love in the language of the culture;

- Understood that "church" is not a building, but actually the people of God, who worship him and who are on a mission together as community;
- Covenanted together to not only having an outward mission, but caring and shepherding for the believers of the church: growing them, helping them cultivate community, and teaching them to be theologians.

CAPTAIN'S LOGBOOK

PERSONAL LOG

Use these ideas to stimulate your thinking about how the principles of this chapter could affect your ministry. Consider sharing these ideas with other church leaders.

1 Two men were sent by a shoe manufacturer to a remote country to sell shoes. One wrote back, "I have terrible news. This is a God-forsaken country. Nobody here wears shoes. I'm coming home." The other man wrote, "This is a wonderful country. I am so grateful you sent me to this territory. Nobody here wears shoes. Send me five thousand pairs." Consider:

- What has been your opinion of today's culture?
- Which of these two salesmen have you been most like in thinking of distributing Jesus to today's culture?
- How fully do you agree with the statement that these are "the best of times for ministry … [and] the worst of times for ministry" (p. 181)?
- How does your view of culture need to change?

2 The leading users of educational technology in the United States are home-schoolers, whose numbers have increased faster than anyone predicted.[55] Think about:

- What double ring is evident in this fact?
- What double ring might this fact create within your church?
- How do the views of homeschoolers fit with the view of your church?

3 Read the following thought from baseball manager Casey Stengel: "I made up my mind, but I made it up both ways." Ask yourself:

- When is a "double ring" not a double ring but an excuse for prevarication or procrastination?
- How can I avoid an either/or ministry attitude in this and/also culture?

4 I have a friend who warns me, "You should not expect to be a bridge between two cultures without getting stepped on by both sides."

- Do you agree with this statement?
- Have you experienced this problem?
- How do you deal with the frustrations caused by critics?

5 Consider having someone report on Charles Handy's book *The Age of Paradox* (1994), in which he says, "Paradox I now see to be inevitable, endemic, and perpetual. The more turbulent the times, the more complex the world, the more paradoxes there are. We can, and should, reduce the starkness of some of the contradictions, minimize the inconsistencies, understand the puzzles in the paradoxes, but we cannot make them disappear, or solve them completely, or escape from them. Paradoxes are like the weather, something to be lived with, not solved, the worst aspects mitigated, the best enjoyed and used as clues to the way forward. Paradox has to be accepted, coped with, and made sense of, in life, in work, in the community, and among nations."[56] Or check out Esther de Waal's *Living with Contradiction*, or Jon Tal Murphree's *Divine Paradoxes*, or Watts Wacker and Jim Taylor's *The Visionary's Handbook*, or N. Graham Standish's *Paradoxes for Living*, or Charles Elliot's *Praying through Paradox*, or Cyprian Smith's *The Way of Paradox*, or my favorite, Parker J. Palmer's *The Promise of Paradox*.[57]

- What paradoxes do you struggle with?

- What contradictions are potential problems within your church?
- How does your faith help you deal with contradictions and paradoxes in life?

6 Any discussion of "the vision thing" must recognize that "true visions are hard to come by" (p. 164). Write your own definition of "vision." After writing your definition, think about the following statement: "Our ability to 'see' and to metaphorize what is seen unites us, gets us somewhere, and releases power in life" (p. 164). If you are the "vision-caster" for your church, write down what it is that helps you to recognize, develop, and communicate God's vision for your church. Press yourself to come up with tangible answers to these questions:

- What do you do to keep your "ability to see" clear and believable?
- How do you keep your personal "I-sight" out of your visionary eyesight long enough to trust that you're seeing God's vision and not just your own perspective?

7 When was the last time you "saw" more of God's vision than you were willing to pursue because of fearful circumstances? Identify those circumstances, and ask yourself how you might be able to overcome the motivation crisis of being a "double vision" leader. Remember the admonition: "Beware: No one is stranger than a person who 'sees' in a community that is 'blind'" (p. 166).

8 Try to identify a church in your community that is a conservatory of the past and laboratory of the future. Write down ways you can better harmonize this "ancient/future" tension in your church.

Ship's Log

Use these activities with your church leadership to help them understand and own the principles of this chapter and how they relate to your church's ministry.

1 Discuss the following thoughts with your leaders. Gary Burtless, an economist at Washington's Brookings Institution, argues that "the fundamental characteristic of the new economy" is "the widening disparity in people's earning capacities depending on the level of skills and education they bring to the labor market."[58] Columnist Clarence Page described a trip to the Dominican Republic. He said as he saw the grinding poverty cheek by jowl to breathtaking opulence, he felt he was witnessing America's future.

- What do you see in our culture that supports these viewpoints?
- What can your church do to prevent the future Page describes and invent another one?

2 Consider the following facts:

- The top 10 percent of USAmericans own more assets than the other 90 percent. Five hundred thousand families—one-half of 1 percent of U.S. households—own 40 percent of the nation's wealth.
- "Within a block of my apartment in the heart of New York City, shiny chauffeured stretch limousines with built-in bars and televisions discharge their elegantly coiffed occupants at expensive restaurants while homeless beggars huddle on the sidewalk wrapped in thin blankets to ward off the cold."[59]
- More and more people have multimillion-dollar annual incomes, while approximately 1.3 billion of the world's people struggle in desperation to live on less than one dollar a day.
- The poorest 10 percent of USAmerican families suffered an 11 percent drop in real income between 1973 and 1992; during that time the richest 10 percent enjoyed an 18 percent increase.[60]

Form small groups to discuss the following questions. Then have groups report what they've discussed.

- How is this new economic arrangement a "plantation economy," reminiscent of the pre-Civil War South?
- What does it mean to your church that the "middle" is disappearing, while the rich are getting richer and the poor are getting poorer?
- How well equipped is your church to minister to the poor—and to the rich?
- What can your church do to build bridges to these groups far away from the middle?

3 One big "middle" in the modern era has been denominations. Denominations were middle way between local communities and whole religious traditions. The model of the denominational church was middle brow, middle class, middle income, and middle age. Now the importance of denominations has declined drastically. However, Peter Drucker argues that denominations will stay on the American scene if they shift "from churches serving denominations to denominations serving churches."[61]

Discuss the following questions with your leaders:

- What do you believe is the future of denominations? Why?
- What kinds of changes would Drucker's suggestion make in our denomination?
- How would such changes affect the ministry of our church?

4 With your leaders, study people in the book of Acts to identify who had "a vision." Form pairs, and assign one of the following passages to each pair: Acts 9:10–19; 10:1–8; 16:1–13; 18:1–11; and 26:1–21. Have pairs discuss the following questions and report on their discussion.

- What clues to understanding the ingredients of a God-given vision do you find?
- What has been the "vision" of our church? How is it like or unlike the visions described in Acts?
- Identify what your group sees as God's vision for our church.
- What will it take to see this vision realized in our church?

5 Examine the statement that the "greatest challenges in evangelism are the overchurched and the unchurched" (p. 172). Form two groups, and have one group create a profile of the overchurched person and the other group create a profile of the unchurched person. Distribute poster board and markers, and encourage leaders to draw as well as describe a typical person in their category. Have groups present their profiles, and then ask:

- How many of the people in our community fit one of these profiles?
- How can what we did in creating these profiles help us minister to both of these groups?

After discussion, have leaders return to their groups and identify ways that your church could reach out to these folks in an authentic, relevant manner.

6 Read the "Top 10 Paradoxes" (pp. 178–79) and brainstorm what you consider to be the "Top 3"—the three that have the most immediate application to your ministry. After you have three, form pairs, and assign each pair one or more of the three, making sure you have all ten covered. Have pairs discuss their assigned "Double Ring" and come up with ways that your church can minister to people on both sides of that double ring. Have pairs share what they've suggested, and decide on at least three things to begin implementing within your church in the next month.

MISSIONAL ART #7

TAKING SHORE LEAVE: SABBATH REST

He leads me beside quiet waters....

—Psalm 23:2

Ask any athlete. Even the best-conditioned body can be pushed only so far before it hits "The Wall." Every athlete has hit it. When physiological and biochemical limitations force the body to shut down safely to avoid falling fatally apart, that's called "The Wall."

Aeronautical engineers learned this lesson toward the end of World War II. Wartime mechanical advances had enabled pilots to push their aircraft to breakneck speeds. But as a plane approached 760 mph, it would seemingly become possessed. The fuselage would start to shake like a rat caught in a giant terrier's mouth. The plane's controls would no longer respond. These aircraft were hitting "The Wall."

"The Wall" these pilots were hurtling into was the sound barrier, a force each plane created around itself. As planes flew faster and faster, they flew right into the air pressure waves caused by the aircraft's rapid forward motion. The force of these pressure waves pummeled the aircraft as it drew closer to them. In several tragic cases planes were ripped apart by their own pressure waves.

Aeronautical engineers had to virtually redesign airplanes to enable them to survive breaking the sound barrier. Wings were thinned down to seemingly foolish frailness. Wing location was moved back and fixed at a sharp angle, enabling them to effectively "knife" through the air. An ugly pointy beak replaced the gracefully curved nose of the airplane, allowing the aircraft to literally punch a hole in that sound-wave wall.[1]

Warp Speed and The Wall

The pace and pressure of a twenty-first-century lifestyle has brought us head-on to another all-too-solid wall. Many of us have already slammed into it. The "speed-of-light pace" of Google living is exhilarating but exhausting. Just as a plane moving through air builds up pressure in front of it as its speed increases, so our bodies and souls, the faster our lives speed up and zip by, feel the crush of growing pressure and risk the approach of a deadly, life-shattering, wall-slamming event.

Warp speed can warp the soul. You can't increase life's speed and stress without affecting the body. You can't increase life's pace and pressures without their threatening to shake the soul apart. We say wistfully, "Things will eventually slow down." How? Spontaneously? The only spontaneous slow-down likely in Google culture is through the spontaneous combustion of a breakdown, crackup, cave-in, or burnout.

If anything, things will continue to speed up in a world where there are no more time zones. In the twentieth century, Einstein removed all referents from time. In the twenty-first century, Swatch has invented "Universal Time," an Internet time that makes any place every place in time as well as in space. The impact of such acceleration on the soul is unknown. A nonstop world is an unprecedented world.

Humans aren't machines. Unlike aircraft engineers, we don't have the option of redesigning our basic physical structure to accommodate such massive accelerations. Our only alternative is to redesign our lifestyle, to structurally realign our schedules to program into our daily routines a specific pressure-release valve that can prevent us from breaking apart after hitting The Wall—whether it be the "deadline" wall or the "hit-your-head-against-the" wall.

The missional art of shore leave is not one we have to invent. Only turbocharge. This relief valve has been part of our tradition all along. It's called sabbath-keeping. High modernity preferred therapy over sabbath. Only by relearning the art of sabbath-keeping can spiritual athletes and spiritual navigators hope to keep safe, sane, and spiritually fresh while cruising Google culture's sea-lanes at breathtaking speed.

> Other people have analysts. I have Utah.
>
> —Actor/entrepreneur Robert Redford

The fast lane is not the only lane. Nor is it the only lane that matters. The double ring of missional art #7 is this: The faster the tracks, the more leaders need to learn the art of slowing down, the art of going slow.

Blue Laws

For those of us modern enough to remember traditional forms of shore leave, the whole notion of sabbath-keeping can curdle the spirit. Still in existence on the law books of a few counties, boroughs, and townships are tattered remnants of a sabbath-serious society we call "blue laws." The bulk of these blue laws focused their embargoes on Sundays, singling out the first day of the week for special legislation. These now quaint-sounding regulations sought to squelch any "business-as-usual" behavior on Sundays—dress codes were outlined; prohibitions against selling or drinking liquor were strictly enforced; non-church-related activities were legally prohibited or at least strictly curtailed until later in the afternoon. In the holiness tradition in which I grew up, we were forbidden to shop on Sunday. Period.

As the pace of life quickened in the high modern era, these blue laws began to fade like blue jeans until they were simply worn away. At first many blue laws were ceremoniously removed from the books as the quest for personal freedoms and the right to an unlegislated lifestyle became the magna carta of the sixties and seventies. But many more blue laws simply stayed on the books while they were summarily ignored in real life. Retailers discovered that if they opened their doors on Sunday morning, it was not the wrath of God that descended on them but hoards of shoppers with hours on their hands and dollars in their pockets.

The whole notion of setting aside one day a week to shut down and rev up has become completely foreign. Digital culture has virtually erased the line between work time and leisure time, public selves and private selves. The notion of "sabbath" is so old-fashioned, outmoded, and foreign that my computer spell-check program keeps underlining the lowercase use of the word sabbath in red, questioning the identity of this strange, unknown word.

Liberty

For those of us raised in Sabbath-observant homes, sabbath-keeping was marked mostly by a litany of no-nos. For younger children, no fidgeting, talking, or sleeping during services. No getting good clothes dirty by playing after church. For older kids, no movies, no parties, no dates on the Sabbath day. Although special meals and gathered families are good memories of these enforced days of togetherness, more than a few sabbath-reared children triumphantly latched on to Jesus' observation that "the Sabbath was made for people, people were not made for the sabbath." We recited that verse as we hit the door and bolted for what we believed would be "freedom."

And what "freedoms" we enjoy. "Freedom" to work twenty-hour days. "Freedom" to work seven-day weeks. "Freedom" to take "working vacations," "working breakfasts," "working lunches," "working dinners." "Freedom" to be dog-collared to electronic ball-and-chains so that one can never get away from work. Ask around: Who doesn't check voice messages and e-mail while on vacation? Ask around: Who doesn't check their voice/e-mail before going to bed just in case a client or someone needs us?[2] Technology enslaves at the same time it liberates. In a "Fast Company," fast-food, fast forward world, we need "Slow Food," slow cities, slow sex, and slow church.

Our freedom from the "Sabbath" exacted a high toll. When we lost sabbaths, we lost spiritual well-being. It is not so much that we "keep the sabbath" as that the sabbath keeps us—keeps us whole, keeps us sane, keeps us spiritually alive. Genuine sabbath-keeping is not a series of "you shall nots" but a string of celebrations. Its goal is not to shut you off from the realities of life, but to open you up to living.

Some of the earliest sabbath-keeping formulas stressed the embodiment, if just for a day, of peace and harmony in all of life. Hebrew Sabbath regulations prohibited even killing insects or carrying weapons—extreme injunctions in those times. But they were serious about the Sabbath. Sabbath-keeping enabled a momentary partnership with God in God's creation project.

Sabbath rest is a two-way channel. For those who labor and are weary, sabbath-keeping is an island of repose amid a sea of daily stress and grinding strain. But the embodiment of sabbath-keeping also creates a place for God to find a "resting place" among God's people (2 Chron. 6:41; Isa. 66:1). Sabbath-keeping prepares a nesting site for the Shekinah, the presence of the Life-Giving, Life-Saving, Life-Sustaining God.

> The one great glory of traveling is always redeemed
> by commotion recollected in tranquility.
> —Travel writer Pico Iyer

Even at the height of sabbath-keeping, sailors aboard ship were given dispensation to alter the rigid one-day-in-seven sabbath schedule. Winds and waves take no notice of calendar time or ritual time-outs. The sea does not stop roiling just because night falls. Squalls do not cease their howling simply because it is the seventh day.

For this reason ships' crews celebrate a string of sabbaths together when the ship pulls into port and shore leave is granted. After weeks of twenty-four-hour watchfulness required by shipboard life, is it any wonder that sailors call their time on shore "liberty"? True sabbath-keeping is never stultifying or stifling. It is joyous freedom. It is true liberation from the "business-as-usual" pressures of deadlines and time lines, bottom lines and wait-in-lines.

One of the great freedoms of the future is the freedom to be free: free to rest, play, enjoy family and friends. The art of leadership is the art of helping people find liberty: "It is for freedom that Christ has set us free" (Gal. 5:1).

Declare a Sabbatical

A 24-7-365 lifestyle mandates the art of 24-7-365 sabbaticals. Life in the fish bowl and life in the fast lane require more frequent shore leaves. No wonder corporate America's sabbatical policies are growing at a 10–15 percent annual clip.

Jesus was accused of being a Sabbath-breaker, but the truth was the opposite: Jesus was a master Sabbath-keeper. In Jesus we have a perfect example of how to insert instant sabbaticals into the midst of crushing, chaotic schedules. Jesus spent his public ministry in the fish bowl of the public eye. Crowds followed him, pressed him, hounded him. They kept him up late and woke him early in the morning. But Jesus never hit The Wall. Jesus always knew when it was time to declare a sabbatical—whether for a moment, an hour, a day, or a string of days.

When Jesus felt the strain, when he had to take a break, when he was drained and exhausted, he would simply announce to his disciples, "We're out of here." Or in the more traditional verbiage, "Let us go over to the other side" (Mark 4:35). One of the best examples of Jesus' ability to recess from stress to rest is found in Mark 4:35. Surrounded by a needy, nagging crowd, hemmed in on all sides by the demands of his public ministry, Jesus recognizes that what the situation requires is a fundamental change of pace. He abruptly declares a downtime.

Jesus doesn't promise himself a vacation when things slow down. Jesus doesn't start elaborate planning for a distant getaway. Jesus declares an on-the-spot sabbatical. And he begins his sabbatical with dispatch. The Greek employed in Mark 4:36, *aphiemi*, is typically rendered as simply "leaving the crowd behind ..." But the word could also be translated to read as "abandoning the crowd ..." There is no gradual release valve from this pressurized situation. Jesus declares a sabbatical and takes off pronto. Even the disciples have to hustle to catch up with him. By the time the disciples are aboard, Jesus has already implemented his sabbatical by fixing up a cozy nest for himself in the boat's stern and settling down for a much-needed nap.

> For fast-acting relief, try slowing down.[3]
>
> —Lily Tomlin

It is hard for people to see rest as holiness, not laziness. Can you think of any activity more universally banned and panned than napping? Stand around any break room, teachers' lounge, or executive watering hole and what do you hear? Plenty of people decrying (or is it boasting?) how early they rose, how late they stayed up, how many days it has been since they have "really slept." When's the last you heard anyone brag about the great nap they caught yesterday afternoon? How about sleeping until noon on Saturday? When's the last time you heard someone exclaim that they couldn't wait to go home, put on their jammies, and crawl into bed?

Emerging lifestyles equate sleeping in with sloughing off. A siesta is an automatic admission that one is weak, overworked, or overwhelmed. Napping is an approved activity only for people in Pampers or Depends. When you're asleep, you can't answer e-mail, you can't respond to faxes, and you can't scan a split screen projecting stock quotes, news headlines, and office memos all at the same time. Those who sleep are seen as mired in intellectual sloth or eyes-closed nostalgia.

But are they? That same text describing Jesus' evening sabbatical morphs into one of the Bible's most dramatic miracle stories (Mark 4:35–41). A sudden squall descends on the little boat carrying Jesus and his disciples. Nonplussed by the storm, Jesus sleeps soundly in the boat's stern until, in panic and sheer despair, the disciples shake their captain awake with the howl "Teacher, don't you care if we drown?" (Mark 4:38).

Far from confirming the idea that succumbing to sleep is an invitation to trouble—a guarantee that while we rest events will render us impotent or incompetent—Jesus' undisturbed sleep proves just the opposite. In Genesis the all-powerful Creator celebrates the completion of the creative impulse by resting (Gen. 2:2). Resting is clearly a divine prerogative, not a sign of weakness or frailty. Only an unbelievably, unrelievably authoritative entity dares to lie down and sleep soundly. No other power is capable of disturbing the sublime confidence of a sleeping God.[4] Indeed God's gift of the Sabbath to created men and women clearly indicates the elevated status of human beings. Like God, men and women are called to hallow and treasure a time of rest.

Let's admit it. We're not too busy, too important, too needed, or too gifted to take a nap. We're too scared. We cannot close our eyes because we cannot bear to relinquish the little bit of control we have convinced ourselves we hold. We are terrified that in an unguarded moment we will lose all the reins of power we have so tightly grasped.

So despite feeling overworked, overwrought, stretched thin, and strung out, on any given night in USAmerica, seventy million hard-core insomniacs stumble up and down their hallways, staring at their television sets, pounding on their pillows. Add to that all those who spend just one or two nights a week working, worrying, and watching throughout dark sleepless hours, and it is easy to see why so many of us are in imminent danger of "hitting the wall."

Instead of trying one of the cultural remedies for our exhaustion—sleeping pills, herbal pillows, sleep music, white-noise machines, earplugs, eyeshades, adjustable beds, water beds, air beds, magnetic beds, isolation tanks—why don't we just declare that it's time for shore leave? Why don't we take the "liberty" of declaring a sabbatical?

There comes a time for leaders to jump ship and declare "liberty"—be it a week, a day, an hour, or a minute.

Fifteen minutes had gone by, and there I was—still standing outside a Dallas hotel, waiting for the person who was to pick me up. I knew I had to quickly make one of two choices: enter the moment, start worrying, and plan my next moves depending on how late or if she showed up; or suspend the moment and spend whatever time stretched out in front of me in another

time zone. I took the latter course, jumped ship, declared a sabbatical, and found liberty.

On that shore leave I walked the parking lot, praying as I walked, breathing the cool evening air, praising and thanking God for every person I had met that day, and rejoicing in every physical pleasure of the day I could itemize. When my ride finally arrived over an hour later, I had to be forced out of my sabbatical. I didn't want to leave.

We have a tradition in the Sweet household. Whenever there's an especially beautiful sunset, the entire family declares a sabbatical, drops everything we are doing, and gathers at the window to admire a truly Great Artist at work.

In the course of the last month, I have declared many sabbaticals. Some of the shorter ones:

- I declared a sabbatical … to loiter through the stacks of a Barnes & Noble while sipping a latté and picking up books and magazines at random.
- I declared a sabbatical … to call my wife in the middle of the afternoon to talk with her for twenty minutes about nothing.
- I declared a sabbatical … to share the powers and pleasures of good food with good company even though a deadline for this manuscript had passed.
- I declared a sabbatical … to place flowers and scented candles in every room of the house and to read a different book in every fragrance.
- I declared a sabbatical … to walk with protozoan purpose the two miles to my wife's and my favorite restaurant.
- I declared a sabbatical … to a sauna first, and then some knockabout fun with the kids.
- I declared a sabbatical … to the only safe haven I could find in the house: the bathroom.
- I declared some sabbaticals … to immerse myself in other people's stories and situations until time slowed down.

Embrace Embering

It's time spiritual navigators recover the ancient Christian tradition of Ember Days, which technically remained "on the books" of the Catholic Church until the sacramental shuffle of Vatican II. Ember Days were calibrated for both fasting and feasting. Prayer, petition, and penance were interlaced in a solemn but convivial occasion.

The roots of these Ember Days were probably as replacement celebrations for pre-Christian agrarian festivals, for there were originally four Ember Days, each corresponding to a different season. The name "ember" is not a reference to the dying coals of a fire but is a corruption of either the Latin *quattor tempora* (four seasons) or the Old English *ymbren* (periodic or recurring). Ember Days gave Christians a specific day to take time to reset and replenish the soul in response to the dawning new season of the year.[5]

An "Ember Day" took more than a day—initially three days at the beginning of the summer, three days at the end of the summer, and three days during the week before the winter solstice. The fourth Ember Day, celebrated during Lent, was added sometime during the fifth century.

Why should leaders retrieve this obscure embering tradition? These quarterly three-day celebrations were assigned so that the faithful might purposively enter into each new season of the year with reflection, jubilation, and restfulness. Picture the unlikely possibility of our culture giving everyone a day off to adjust to the switch to daylight-saving time, and you get the essence of an Ember Day celebration.

> How thin can I spread myself before I'm no longer "there"?[6]
>
> —Grateful Dead songwriter/digital age pioneer John Perry Barlow

Ember Days, like a weekly Sabbath or any unscheduled spontaneous sabbatical, allow the soul time and space to catch up to the body, and the body to catch up to itself before taking a deep breath and plunging headlong into the new duties, activities, and responsibilities of each new season. There are three basic paces that Ember Days put the soul through.

First: The sure and steady movement of the earth on its axis, which ushers in yet another new season, should bring our spirit to a focused mindfulness of God's unchanging divinity and unchallengeable power. Truly, if God be for us, who can be against us?

Second: When leaders take an Ember Day of rest and reflection, we are reminded of our call to be obedient children of God. Resting is not a sign of sloth, but a God-ordained command. As the Genesis story recounts so vividly, a period of active creativity and transformation is to be followed by a time of rest. God graciously hooked humans up to this invisible energy grid as a symbol of divine love. Sabbath days, Ember Days, sabbaticals of any duration are expressions of our obedience to a covenanted relationship with God.

Third: An Ember Day or a sabbatical invites leadership to abandon fear and to close eyes in confidence. Each approaching new season, new journey, or new project holds unknowable promises and perils. The claims tomorrow will make upon leaders are as deep a mystery as any distant star. God's gift of rest invites leaders to place our trust in God's providence and purposes, not our own.

From Shore to Shore

God's mission in the twenty-first century is a high-seas adventure. It could easily keep spiritual navigators at full sail most of the time. To maintain such a pace and still relish the feel of the wind at our backs and the spray in our faces, leaders need to take mental, spiritual, and emotional shore leaves. Where there is no "liberty," the leader perishes.

Once on dry land, however, there is always a temptation to overstay our leave, to turn a shore leave into an Unauthorized Absence (UA). The need for downtime, for a sabbatical or an Ember Day, is not an excuse to abandon ship altogether.

The thirteenth-century Spanish-Jewish philosopher/scientist Shev-Tov

Falaquera tells of five different kinds of passengers who disembark when they reach harbor.

1) The first group doesn't leave ship at all. They fear that if they went ashore, a sudden wind might come up and carry the ship away, leaving them behind.

2) The second group goes ashore but spends only enough time there to refresh themselves. They then return to the ship, find their quarters, and settle down.

3) A third group spends as much time ashore as they can. They wait until the wind whips up, when the sailors will want to raise anchor and leave. But this group waits to hear the trumpet. When the trumpet blows they rush back on board and must be content to live with whatever places are left on ship for them to inhabit.

4) A fourth group stays even after the trumpet sounds, until the sailors have stepped the mast. But even then they reason that the ship will not leave until she has raised her flag. When the flag is raised, they reason, "They will not leave until the sailors have eaten." When they see the ship leaving, they run to the shore, fling themselves into the water, and risk life and limb to reach ship and clamber aboard. They find very little room left on board and must live with the worst accommodations.

5) A fifth group falls in love with the port of call and decides not to return to the high seas. But after a while, according to this thirteenth-century philosopher/navigator, the "wild beasts appear and attack them. Now they weep and mourn, regretting that they did not go back to the ship, but it does not help them in the least, and soon all of them are lost."[7]

Leaders live from shore to shore, not on shore. We must not overstay our leave or confuse a sabbatical with permanent retirement. The goal of every ship that sets sail is to safely reach some new harbor. Every beginning is also an ending. And every ending is also a beginning. But a ship is made for the water. Without the waves crashing against her bow or the wind filling her sails, a ship is not fulfilling her true purpose. A ship in port is merely a still life of its shape, not an incarnation of its purpose.

Alpha-Wave Activities

When leaders declare a sabbatical and come ashore, the goal is not simply to "unplug" so much as it is to change frequencies. Submerged in everyday schedules, the human brain typically produces beta waves. These waves operate at thirteen to twenty-five cycles per second. Beta waves are produced by a brain that is involved in keeping the body talking, walking, or working at a particular task.

Though beta waves are good workhorses, they don't offer much assistance to the other crucial activities for which our brains are designed. The brain absorbs information best when it is in a state of "relaxed alertness." An alpha wave activity is any practice that clears the mind of everyday static and input clutter, opening the subconscious and airing out the mental crowding. Alpha waves are emitted when the conscious mind operates at only eight to twelve cycles per second. It is these longer, lackadaisical alpha waves that are present when we daydream, when we let our imagination roam on a long leash, when we crack open the window to our subconscious.

> In order to grow in grace, we must spend a great deal of time in quiet solitude. Contact with others in society is not what causes the soul to grow most vigorously. In fact, one quiet hour of prayer will often yield greater results than many days spent in the company of others. It is in the desert that the dew falls freshest and the air is most pure.[8]
>
> —Andrew Bonar

A true sabbath, whether stretched out over a twenty-four-hour day or squeezed into a twenty-four-minute stroll, is composed of alpha waves. It is not a sabbatical when you spend Saturday mowing the yard, cleaning the garage, catching up on a week's worth of laundry, paying bills, and returning phone calls. Those are beta wave chores.

On the other hand, standing in your garden, weeds and all, and breathing in the various scents of its flowers, grasses, earthiness, and fruits, concentrating on nothing but those smells and experiencing what each new scent makes you feel—that is an alpha wave escape, an afternoon delight, a healing sabbath.

Sabbaticals unleash and release the energy that is latent in your life. One physicist has calculated that if you could totally convert the amount of energy locked in one gram (0.04 ounce) of matter, it would be able to ...

- Lift fifteen million people to the top of Mount Everest.
- Boil four liters (a gallon plus) of water for each of fifty-five million people.
- Supply a modern city of fifteen thousand people with electricity for a year.[9]

The miracle of Sabbath-keeping is the turning of water into wine, matter into energy, seasickness into health. The miracle of the sabbatical is the creation of space where life is transformed into art.

Our tendency is to carefully carve out "leisure time" in our frantic schedules and then fastidiously fill every hour of that time with some specific "fun" activity. Leisure time is no longer leisurely but packed to overflowing with activities to keep us from being alone with ourselves, alone with a partner, alone with God. How many times have you needed a vacation to recover from your vacation?

One of the best things parents can do for children is simply let them play.[10] Without structuring all their time, let the children fill in their long blank afternoons with whatever ... tents made from blankets draped over chairs, conversations with stuffed animals or imaginary playmates, play-acting all the roles in a story that exists only as it unfolds from their own minds. It is in these hours of unstructured, free play that children, and all human beings, begin to grow their souls.

Architects now are designing "dead spaces" in public buildings—unspecified social spaces, uncultivated corners, and idle cubbyholes. "Dead spaces" can bring a building to life. Leaders require dormant, untilled sacred spaces in our personal lives as well. Quiet space is creative space, just as a field left fallow is a nurturing place, enriching itself for future productivity. Where it looks like nothing is going on can be where precisely the most is going on. There is no fullness without emptiness.

Telling Time

My wife, Elizabeth, brews a "good pot of tea," which should immediately tell you something. What makes a pot of tea "good" is "time." Good things take time. If you don't take time, good things aren't likely to happen. The best things in life are free, but they cost time. "Free time" isn't free.

If people can't take pleasure in it, they increasingly won't do it. Why? Because time is their most valuable commodity, and their time budget is their most pressed constituency. What "free time" people today have, they want to spend developing relationships and expressing themselves.

There is in today's culture a sense of "lost time," even of a "lost life"—hence the ubiquitous retort, "Get a life." Learning to "tell time" involves more than reading the hands on a clock. It involves developing a sense of timing that tells leaders when life needs breathing room for things to play out and work out. Leaders need to make room in life for life to emerge and manifest itself.

Life is fragile. It needs continual care and re-creation. Without the empty spaces of ember days, one cannot properly tell time, be creative, or take on the challenges of a collapsing world. Fallow times and sabbath moments add beauty to the soul, goodness to the heart, wisdom to the mind, and truth to the world.

> Plato says that men resemble children
> who want something and its opposite:
> They want rest and movement at the same time.
> It is unclear whether that is to act like a child.

Perhaps it is rather acting like a wise man to want rest and movement at the same time.[11]

—Jean Wahl

Life aboard ship requires constant alertness and watchful vigilance. But there is a peace and tranquility found riding the waves that is unmatched by any landlocked activity. What else could account for the fleets of aptly named "Sunday sailors"? Just as those who ride the waves every day find their liberty in shore leave, so those whose souls are parched on dry land run for the water whenever time allows. Even those who don't sail flock to the edge of the sea hoping to hear what David Sutton, in one of my all-time favorite poems "Water Music," calls:

"The music of not going anywhere
That quiet water makes against the land."[12]

Along with days of high winds, heavy waves, and hard labor, sabbatical moments and embering hours are available to everyone aboard ship. The crews of old sailing vessels sang together "sea chanties"—rhythmic, often ribald story-songs. The singsong, upbeat rhythms of these chants gave a buoyant beat to strenuous labor. A grinding beta-wave task—hoisting a sail, hauling a line, swabbing a deck—took on an alpha-wave quality.

For Christians sailing on the high seas, with no liberty port on the horizon, there is always a sabbath experience available. Jesus took special care to teach a sabbath technique to his disciples when he tutored them in the basics of prayer. Instead of a formal, time-slotted prayer to a Creator-God of the Universe, Jesus admonished his disciples to come to God at any time saying, "Abba/Father."

Prayer requires no special space or equipment. Prayer can be accomplished while hands are busy at other tasks. Prayer can transform a beta chore into an alpha experience. A prayer sabbatical is possible even while—perhaps especially while—moving full tilt across the sea. These are not "life ring" prayers ("Lord, help us survive!") uttered in moments of panic or desperation. Sabbatical prayers experienced aboard ship celebrate the unique conditions that being under sail create. Breathe a prayer to be caught up by the wind. Time a prayer to the rhythm of the waves slapping against the hull. Launch your prayers and your praises from what's going on around you.

They Also Serve

My mother, who wasn't totally convinced the TV wasn't "the Devil's blinking box," had a secret favorite program. It was called *Queen for a Day*.

If you could be "President for a Day," what would you do?

David Rice Atchison's answer to that question is one of my favorite presidential stories in USAmerican history. Zachary Taylor was the next president, but since inauguration day fell on the Sabbath, Taylor didn't want to be sworn in until Monday. President James K. Polk officially concluded his duties on Saturday, which left Sunday, March 4, 1849, as a day without a president. To fill the vacancy, the next in line, President Pro Tem of the Senate David Atchison, became President for a Day.

How did Senator Atchison spend his day as president? Asleep. Exhausted from concluding the affairs of Congress on President Polk's last day, Atchison arrived home late on Saturday night and went to bed.

He slept. And slept. And slept right through his once-in-a-lifetime, one-day-in-office as president of the United States.

What better thing could he have done? It was his privilege to preserve and pass on the institution of the presidency, and he could rest content knowing that the best thing he could do was not to mess with anything but be a faithful conduit of the office.

They also serve, who only lie and sleep.[13]

AQUACHURCH #7

NATIONAL COMMUNITY CHURCH, EBENEZERS COFFEEHOUSE

Washington, D.C.
www.ebenezerscoffeehouse.com

Ebenezers Coffeehouse is a first class, fully operational coffeehouse that seeks to serve the community on Capitol Hill. It is owned and operated by National Community Church and all profits go toward community outreach projects. National Community Church embodies the notion that a "sanctuary" is not a safe place from risk, but a safe place to take risks. Here at the heart of our nation's capital, as close to the seat of power as you can get, is a church that offers true Sabbath. Here is a pit to refurbish and refresh the soul. Ebenezer, as the origins of the name recount, serves as a memory marker for life's journey. Ebenezer Coffeehouse provides …

- A "pit" to stop and refurbish and refresh one's soul amidst the chaos of Washington, D.C.;
- a comfortable and relaxing place of worship and reflection as every Saturday night National Community Church offers two services on site;
- live music and other scheduled events such as dance lessons, poetry readings, and Open Mic nights;
- a venue for people within the community to book an event or performance;
- coffee with a cause—all coffee served at Ebenezers is "fair trade."

CAPTAIN'S LOGBOOK

PERSONAL LOG

Use these ideas to stimulate your thinking about how the principles of this chapter could affect your ministry. Consider sharing these ideas with other church leaders.

1 You can almost tell when people are beginning to go overboard. They get cranky; they run out of creative juices; they feel frustrated, uptight, weary. Let's get quickly and honestly to the point. Ask yourself the following questions:

- How close am I to The Wall?
- How weary is my soul?
- Can people "play" with me? What is the favorite "joke" my people tell about me?
- How ready am I for a serious discussion about a basic fact of life: "Humans aren't machines" (p. 190)?

Yes, we religious types know about "sabbath-keeping," but we still struggle with the practicality of it. Begin your soul-searching process by reading Matthew 11:28–30. Then analyze the following statement, especially as it relates to your personal life: The speed with which we live our daily (external) lives can and will directly affect the depth at which we live our devoted (internal) lives. On a scale of one to ten, where one is peacefully rested and ten is "don't prick me with a pin or I'll explode," where would you rate yourself?

2 Jesus sometimes escaped from the crowd by "going over to the other side."

- What do you do to regroup, to draw breath, to decompress, to rest and regain strength?
- Which of these haven't you done for a long time?
- Can you keep up the pace you are living now for the next twenty years?

3 Look up the hymn "Let All Mortal Flesh Keep Silence." Read the words silently. Then read them aloud or sing the song—and mean it.

4 With the boundaries between work and home more and more blurred (with cell phones, BlackBerrys, and e-mail), we need to be more deliberate about scheduling sabbaticals. Consider:

- Are you as massively disciplined about managing your private life as you are disciplined about your work life? Why or why not?
- If not, what can you do to be more disciplined about your personal and family life?
- What are the telltale signs that indicate your soul stands in need of restoration, that you need a sabbatical?

5 Read Exodus 20:8, and think about how the word *respect* applies to this commandment. Ask yourself:

- Do I respect myself enough to stop what I am doing to expose myself to what God is doing?
- Do I respect God enough to stop doing what I am doing to find out what God is doing?
- When was the last time I put myself in a situation where being was more important than doing?
- How did that experience birth a newfound respect for God and for myself?

6 Do you schedule a regular day off every week and observe it? If not, why not? Who and what are keeping you from taking your sabbath? If you are taking a regular sabbath, are you able to include your family members in any of it? Set a time right now to teach, schedule, and encourage your family to insert "instant sabbaticals" into their schedules (p. 194). Be sure to get your family's input about what the regular and "instant" sabbaticals should entail.

7 Consider the following practical suggestions for developing your sabbath taking:

- Read *Tuesdays with Morrie* by Mitch Albom, and keep a journal of your thoughts. Pay close attention to "The Sixth Tuesday," where the author talks about the need for "detachment."[14]
- Do a time log of your schedule for two weeks, and come up with several ways

to infuse your life with "being" (based on experience) as opposed to just "doing" (based on accomplishment). Your spouse may be very helpful in this process.

- Work on simplifying your life. Read *Simplify Your Life* (1994) by Elaine St. James and *Your Money or Your Life* (1999) by Joe Dominguez and Vicki Robin.
- Listen to some old music (How about James Taylor's "Up on the Roof"?), and let your mind and heart create some fresh experiences from some old memories.
- Create a Sabbath box. For more information on this see Wayne Muller's Sabbath: Restoring t*he Sacred Rhythm of Rest.*[15]

Ship's Log

Use these activities with your church leadership to help them understand and own the principles of this chapter and how they relate to your church's ministry.

1 Ask your leadership team: What does it mean to keep the Sabbath? After some discussion, work through each step of the four part "sabbath-keeping" process identified by Marva J. Dawn in her book *Keeping the Sabbath Wholly.*[16]

- *Ceasing* refers to a slowing down or stopping of our normal activities to honor our covenant with God. The first step to ceasing will include a repentance ("being sorry") for our work and the worry it causes us.
- *Resting* is defined as "the renewing of our whole being in grace-based faith." When was the last time you "rested" in this divine sense?
- *Embracing* is the move beyond the repentance of ceasing and the faith of resting into the application of Christian living. When was the last time you "embraced" life with tenacity and intentionality for spiritual things?
- *Feasting* is the simple but crucial call for celebration. When was the last time you had fun and gave God the credit for it?

2 Read the following passages, and make of list of reasons for keeping a sabbath: Psalm 127:2; Ecclesiastes 10:15; Psalm 23:3; Ecclesiastes 9:9; Hebrews 10:25; and Mark 8:36. With your leaders, match the reasons up with reality: Schedule sabbath time for your leaders and your church based on these reasons.

3 Discuss the following questions together:

- Why do so many people vacation at the shore?
- Why do you think so many people go to the shore and never enter the water?
- What's keeping us from getting wet?

If possible, move to a room where there are sofas, or at least plush carpet. Provide pillows. Have your leaders take off their shoes and get rid of any neckties. Then have them lie down and relax. Have them think about how nice it would be to be lying on the beach in the warm summer sun, with the waves lapping nearby. Allow five minutes of silent rest. Then ask:

- Who enjoyed this relaxing experience? Why?
- Who felt uncomfortable relaxing this way? Why?
- How is this like the way we feel uneasy about taking a sabbath?
- What can we learn from this experience to help us be more purposeful in taking and providing sabbaths?

4 In keeping with the Ember Days tradition, develop some special embering celebrations in your church. With your leaders, determine when those days should take place and what they should consist of. Remember what the purpose is, and don't crowd those days with activity.

5 Think about what's happening in terms of spirituality in our culture. Discuss:

- Do you think people in the twenty-first century are placing a higher value on the spiritual? Why or why not?
- How many marketing strategies can you identify that feature "good for the soul" messages? (Here's one to get you going, a motto for soup: "M'm! M'm! Good for the Body, Good for the Soul.")
- What is good about this emphasis? What's not so good about it?

6 Offer Eugene Peterson's definition of the sabbath as "uncluttered time and space to distance ourselves from the frenzy of our own activities so we can see what God has been doing and is doing."[17] Form groups of four to discuss the following questions:

- How is it that "Technology enslaves at the same time it liberates" (p. 192)?
- How can we begin uncluttering our lives?

7 Have your leaders discuss the following statement in groups of about four: "It is hard for people to see rest as holiness, not laziness" (p. 195).

- How true is this statement?
- Where did we learn this belief (that rest is laziness), and how can we unlearn it?
- How playful is our church? How playful do we encourage our people to be?
- Would we change anything about our church's schedule of events if we really believed that rest can bring holiness as well as wholiness?
- If "sabbaticals unleash and release the energy that is latent in your life" (p. 202), how can we help the church staff and leadership keep their sabbaths sacred and energizing?

Give each group a list of all the activities and meetings of your church. Be sure to list all committee and team meetings—everything that takes place in the name of your church. Then have groups consider which activities should be consolidated or eliminated to provide more opportunity for "sabbath." Seriously consider doing what your groups come up with.

MISSIONAL ART #8

SIGNALING WITH FLAGS AND SEMAPHORES: COMMUNICATION

If the world has not approached its end, it has reached a major watershed in history, equal in history to the turn from the Middle Ages to the Renaissance. It will demand from us a spiritual blaze.... No one on earth has any other way left but upward.[1]

—Alexandr Solzhenitsyn

Ask anyone who is looking for a candidate for almost any position. The top three most desirable traits in any applicant are: communication skills, interpersonal skills, and creativity. What destroys more leaders than anything else? What ends pastorates faster than an affair with the organist? Poor communication skills, poor relational skills, and lack of creativity.

In the modern world, we mastered the "Three R's": Reading, 'Riting, 'Rithmetic. In a Google world, leaders need mastery of the Three C's: Communication, Collaboration, and Creativity—missional arts #8, 9, and 10.

With Flying Colors

Semaphore communication is the signaling by flags or lights from ship to ship or ship to shore. Semaphores were used before the invention of the telegraph to transmit messages from one place to another or to convey visual distress signals. Small flags were held in each hand and were moved to different angles to communicate letters of the alphabet or numbers. The first of the Three C's is the C of communication: the ability to use signs, signals, language, and logs to convey messages.

To begin looking at this missional art, you must ask yourself, is your leadership culture-compatible? Is your church culture-compatible? I'm not talking about culture-driven or culture-determined, but culture-compatible. When we talk the truth or read the ethical riot act to this culture, can it hear what we're saying even if it hates us for saying it? To touch the heart, one has to know the heart.

Consider the following philosophy of communications: "If you would speak with me, you must first learn my language." The philosopher Voltaire spoke these words to those who would converse with him about the mysteries of life. He would deign to talk with you, but only if you smartened up to his level. Voltaire refused to dumb down.

Coming from a philosopher, these words sound arrogant and elitist. But the church speaks these same words to the culture every Sunday—and every other day of the week, for that matter. The church's Christianese language is not even a current one, but an outmoded print slanguage and jungle of jargon that is out of touch with how most people today live and move and have their being. The church must not lose its language. But it must not insist its language be learned before talking to the culture.

What if God had refused to dumb down? "The Word became flesh and made his dwelling among us" (John 1:14a). This is the essence of the Incarnation—God came down to us. God's good ship "Grace" did not disdain shallow waters. God didn't stand against us, but walked alongside us. The heart of the Incarnation is God's willingness to communicate through *kenosis* (emptying) toward the goal of *plerosis* (filling).

God's dumbing down was for our wising up.

It's not people who are right who change the world. It's people who can communicate their definition of right to others who change the world. To change the world for "right," leaders need to learn a new language, a language people can understand. The theory and practice of ministry are being transformed by new communications technology. This technology creates a whole new language, a whole new space, a whole new environment for leadership, worship, and education. You think the invention of farming was momentous? You think the invention of the printing press was momentous? The invention of the microprocessor makes the printing press look like a child's tea party. Every day brings another breakthrough wrought by microprocessing power.

For any leader to fail to pay attention to these revolutions is to fail to lead.

The whole debate about the nature of technology (electronics) is really a debate about the nature of an institution—the church. Imagine doing ministry in the modern world and boasting, "I don't read." Imagine doing ministry in the twenty-first-century world and boasting, "I don't do computers" or "I've never Googled." When is the last time you read a church publication challenging the church to embrace media literacy, or what I call "graphicacy"? Graphicacy involves more than slapping print up on a screen. The transition from Gutenberg to Google is the transition from linear to nonlinear modes of thought. To lead in the Gutenberg world, the watchword was "Get Linear." To lead in this Google world, the watchword is "Get Looped."

From the perspective of Googlers, communication happens in the church, but nothing is communicated. There's a lot of clucking, but not many eggs are being laid. Why are religious leaders having such problems "connecting"—making the transition from literacy to graphicacy, from linear to looped, from writing sermons to creating experiences?

Because we are prisoners of the pulpit. The sermon is still a viable and dynamic communication form, as the success of Comedy Central and the stand-up comedian testifies. But the sermon has not always been held hostage by the pulpit. Some of the greatest spiritual awakenings in Christian history happened when preachers escaped from pulpit prisons and started preaching from the aisles, the fields, the streets, the airwaves.

Wet Culture

New words are being invented every day to describe this new world: fourth discontinuity, bionic convergence, Cyborgian, transgenic, and on and on. But one phrase we will all have to get used to is "wet life." With so much "artificial life" out there, the term "wet life" is used to identify living things that are natural organisms.

For the church to be an expression of wet life, a living organism for the Spirit of God, it must master the cultures of the Web and the Wing. Two of the most striking and complex expressions in all of creation are the web of the spider and the wing of the bird. The Web and the Wing are wet culture's most compelling symbols of complexity.[2]

Wet life is complex life. It is not simple to define complexity. Seth Lloyd of MIT compiled a list of more than forty-five definitions of *complexity*.[3] This should not be surprising, since complexity means information that is so random and irregular that it cannot be compressed into description or definition.

The irony of all this is that complexity fosters stability, while simple systems are highly volatile. We are navigating a nonlinear world that is unknowable, unpredictable, uncertain. In nonlinearity, the system is more than the sum of its parts. In short, the future of the church is in making things more complex, not more simple; more complicated, not less. Simple communities are highly unstable; complex communities are stable. In fact, that's one of the problems with the elements of nature: We've simplified them to the point that they're now unstable.

Ditto the schools. We made school systems bigger, more organized and routinized, simpler, and more centralized (consolidated schools). In so doing we erased neighborhood schools and local participation. Sometimes better is smaller and more complex.

Ditto the church. We must go from "better is bigger" to seeing spiritual progress in much more complex and subtle ways. Sometimes "better" may be more "different" than "bigger." This does not mean an angry attack on megachurch promotion. But it does mean respecting the church as a complex adaptive system that can respond to challenges without having to wait for or depend on chain-of-command orders wafting down.

Where we went wrong in the past was to distrust the gifts of complexity, the blessings of complications. Our ancestors feared complicating the American identity through hyphenated heterogeneity. Historian David M. Kennedy has documented how wars have served as "homogenizing agents" that would through military service "yank the hyphen," as one contemporary put it, out of Italian-American, Jewish-American, Polish-American, and so forth. President Woodrow Wilson said that "any man who carries a hyphen about with him carries a dagger that he is ready to plunge into the vitals of the Republic." In the age of Gutenberg "one nation indivisible" meant one nation with hyphens removed. Variations of voice and register were the enemy of order and discipline.[4] In the age of Google "one nation indivisible" is an image that finds strength through the interconnectedness of a complex multicolored web.

> The Internet is going to break down boundaries and may promote a world culture, or at least a sharing of activities and values. But the network will also make it easy for people who are deeply involved in their own ethnic communities at home and abroad to reach out to other people who share their preoccupations no matter where they are. This may strengthen cultural diversity and counter the tendency toward a single, homogenized world culture. It's hard to predict what the net effect will be—a strengthening or a weakening of local cultural values.[5]
>
> —Bill Gates

The Internet was established on principles of trust, mutuality, reciprocity, and complexity—if you pass on my message, I'll pass on yours. Its origins lie in the 1970s, when the Pentagon established a decentralized, out-of-control computer-communications scheme that a nuclear assault could not knock out.[6] Nobody owns it. Nobody controls it. Nobody runs it. Nobody can turn it off. The simplicity of complexity. The order of chaos. The discipline of almost total anarchy. The bondage of freedom.

The church is a complex adaptive system. Leadership for uncharted waters is not afraid to complexify the journey or complicate the preparations. True leadership is the building of adaptive systems of incredible complexity without a master plan but with bottom-up, self-regulating control. This control starts with chaos and moves to order, starts with energy and moves to form, starts with spirit and moves to structure.[7]

Web Civilization

The NASA space program has transformed human existence by spinning off three things: Teflon frying pans, microchips, and the Internet. Microchips have only been around for twenty-five years, but they are the bricks and mortar of a new web civilization. This webbed culture has abandoned the center-to-periphery linear dynamics (that dominated railroads, interstate highways, and air traffic) of the machine for the complex field dynamics of an electronic webbed network, a woven tapestry with multiple centers.

We are crossing Rubicons all the time in this Web Civilization.

- Harvard University was given the first patent on a genetically engineered animal (the "oncomouse") in 1988.[8]
- Every day more text messages are sent than there are people on planet Earth.
- There is soon coming a time when people are never *not* connected to the Internet.
- More people are now associated with nondenominational churches than denominational ones.

And on and on.

Technologies have reshaped our understanding of the world in the past, as each new communication technology has brought with it new metaphors

that then shaped our personal (cognitive, psychological) orientation and social (political, economic, moral, religious) structures. For example, Industrial Civilization brought us big business, big government, program design churches, and smokestack spirituality. Web Civilization is bringing us decentralized, entrepreneurial, electronic structures and marketplaces, a small-town revival, and cyberspace spirituality.

Digitization is more consequential than industrialization—and it is just beginning. Martin Cooper invented the mobile phone in 1973: He made the first call on a handheld mobile phone on April 3, 1973. Now Western Europe has more phones than people. As of 2008, half of the world's population has a cell phone—the most dramatic and rapid dissemination of a technology in history. In the future, battlefields will be more in cyberspace than in physical space. All wars are now media wars more than they are military wars. The one with the best media campaign wins, not the best military campaign. Terrorist groups like Al Qaeda understand this, and carefully pick their targets to get the biggest media bang for the buck. They know that the shooting down of a helicopter, usually used only for transport or medical evacuations, produces one of the most graphically galvanizing sets of images that one can put on a screen.

The seventy-million-strong Net Gens—the second generation of environmentally concerned, artistically inclined, technologically savvy postmoderns—already have computerese (whether Microsoft "Windows" or Apple) as their first or second language. Public schools are now teaching third-graders to design their own Web pages; video-editing software is available for four-year-olds. The promise of interacting with Winnie the Pooh inspired our daughter Soren to master the mouse before she was three. Every parent of a three-year-old today has Webkinz or Club Penguin stories.

The basic distinctions of the future are between the in-the-know "cybersavvy" and the out-of-it "cyberklutzes," which some are calling "the gods/clods" scenario:[9] a highly educated and skilled cadre of professional elite, the high priests of technology who get things done, and the low-paying, gas-pumping, hamburger-service unskilled.

A low-tech anything is now a virtual impossibility—whether it be low-tech medicine, low-tech banking, low-tech agriculture, low-tech education, low-tech libraries, even low-tech churches. Digitization projects abound—for records, manuscripts, books, and magazines.[10] Lest you think this doesn't involve you and your ministry: In May 2008, a word search on books.google.com for "twenty-first-century Christianity" produced 1,910 hits for digitized books; "twenty-first-century church" had 1,650 hits; "emerging church" had 597 hits. And this is only the beginning.[11]

The challenge of this emerging civilization is that it can go either way: an Information Aristocracy or Digital Democracy. There are no absolutely positive benefits of technology. Technology has both negative and positive consequences, as oil spills and climate change attest.

> Why doesn't every public school student have a laptop? The Texas Board of Education estimates that giving laptops to its four million students would cost less than half the $1.8 billion the state has budgeted for textbooks over the next six years.

The electronification of the church, which began with the lightbulb and is still ongoing, is but the latest in a series of ecclesiastical negotiations between communications and culture.[12] For example, the alphabet aided the dissemination of Judeo-Christian ideas; the one-way medium of radio helped midwife totalitarian propaganda and regimes. It's up to religious leadership to make sure the future heads toward a Digital Democracy and that Web technology is tempered with faith and social values.

Exponential Revolution

The Internet has revolutionized our economic and social lives even more than our political structures. The World Wide Web, the primary Web metaphor and model of the future, is evolving faster than anyone can imagine. The metamorphosis of the papyrus roll into codex manuscript took place over a couple of centuries. The switch from codex to printed book took several decades. The transition from a linear culture of the page to a webbed culture of the screen scroll is taking place almost overnight.

Internet traffic is exploding. Roughly 20 percent of the world's population are now using the Internet (that's almost 1.5 billion people). What is more, the United States is behind a substantial portion of the planet

- The United States is a net importer of high-technology products.
- Japan is #1 in the world with broadband access.
- China today has more Internet connections and its free zones have higher bandwidth than does the United States.
- South Korea has forty times more communications bandwidth per capita than the United States.
- America's GPS can detect stationary or moving objects within ten meters (three meters for enhanced military version of GPS). The European Union and the European Space Agency, with backing from China, Ukraine, Israel, and India, successfully launched Galileo, which is much more accurate: It can detect objects within one meter.
- Digital technology has penetrated even the poorest places on the planet. My nephew Nikolas Sweet joined the Peace Corps and was sent to Thies, Senegal. He was given a cell phone, and amazingly never has to worry about being dropped. In one of his e-mails from 2007 he began, "Yesterday I saw a man in a rice hat chatting it up on his Sony Ericcson while driving a mule drawn cart filled with rubbish."

> The fiber-optic/coaxial cable that provides rapid access to the Internet gives us the world on a string.[13]
>
> —Gerald M. Levin, chair and CEO, Time Warner, Inc.

These are stunning jumps, unparalleled in history. As if more evidence were needed that the Web has become a mass medium, consider these figures. It took thirty-eight years for radio to gain fifty million domestic listeners.

It took thirteen years for television and cable to gain fifty million domestic viewers. It took four years for the World Wide Web to gain fifty million domestic users.

Home, Home on the Web

It's time to decide. It's time to break ranks and name names. Are you a twenty-first-century Reformer, or are you a defender of the existing power structures and delivery systems? Are you or are you not a part of this Revolution?

Our ancestors at great personal cost claimed the book as the heart of modern learning and communications. Will we claim the Web as central to learning and communications? The Protestant Reformers made the book the new delivery system for learning and faith development. Will we do the same with the Web?

For leaders, not having a Web ministry is more than being without a calling card, not using a Web site as a communication and community-building tool is to have fumbled the future. Most people won't even try out a new restaurant unless it has a Web site that is accessible, informative, and enticing. The Net boasts the potential for the biggest communications boost in the history of the church.

- The Net commences a whole communications system and a whole new delivery system for ministry.
- The Net makes it possible for the church to engage in one-on-one dialogue with each of its members, to learn about their dreams and daily minimum requirements of spiritual needs.
- The Net enables leaders to customize communication and to personalize teaching, healing, and preaching like never before in history.
- The Net helps remove barriers to communication and celebration—including time and distance. Already a wedding has taken place simultaneously at four different U.S. cities through Web-based electronic videoconferencing.[14]

- The Net helps leaders choose the best time and place to communicate.

As the potentials listed above make clear, the people's voice is getting louder, thanks to Internet technology. If your church can't re-democratize itself and customize its ministry through the Web, it's not a church of the future. If it can't become Web-friendly, with a data network to offer its members, it's a church for yesterday's people.

We must resist the temptation to take the thought patterns of a print culture and impose them in cyberspace. I call that categorical imperialism[15]—to imperialize the categories of one communication form by imposing them on another communication style. This is what happened when churches first tried to use "broadcast" television by throwing up on a screen their worship services. Ministry on the Web must be evaluated on its own terms and judged by the standards of Net culture. What works in other media most probably won't work on the Web.

A great example of categorical imperialism is Utah State University Professor M. David Merrill. Merrill was an early pioneer of computer-based training. But he has now renounced it because, as he puts it, experiential learning, action research, activity-based curricula "pulls us away from learning systematic bodies of knowledge." On the Internet, he argues, "there isn't enough guidance and structure there for someone to learn a systematic body of knowledge." More and more electronic education is moving us from "systematic instructional design."[16]

But that's precisely the point. In decentralized learning, heavily linear, ordered bodies of "Three R's" knowledge are suspect. The whole quest for a "systematic instructional design" was an Enlightenment project that no longer services the systemic, not systematic, linkages and lineages of the Web. Web Civilization is transforming education away from what students learn to what students want to learn. The desire to learn comes from within. Education first helps students yearn to learn and then secondarily teaches them to learn to learn. An education that makes students yearn to learn is at the heart of twenty-first-century leadership.

An education is not the filling of a pail, it is the lighting of a fire.[17]

—W. B. Yeats

Every communications system does some things well and some things badly. The promise of a Web Civilization is paralleled by the perils of a Web Civilization. Just look at the rise of terrorism in this wired universe. People are turning away from the ballot box and jury box and toward the cartridge box, aluminum tubes (airplanes) and weapons of mass destruction like anthrax (a lethal dose is about the size of a speck of dust, and five pounds could wipe out Washington, D.C.). A chemical weapon capable of wiping out an entire city can now be produced by any bright high school chemistry student.

The dangers of a high-tech world which turns computers into humans is fast turning into a "no-regrets" bio-electronic world that turns people into computers. With the increased use of push technology, the use of intelligent agents (also known as avatars or "information butlers" or "cyber valets") will increase. So why not put flesh on these digital creatures? We will see in many of our lifetimes the coming together of recombinant genetics, artificial intelligence, and Net connections in ways no one has even imagined.

So why not have software chips implanted in wetware flesh? Who would even consider that, you say? Soon parents will be given the option of having a chip implanted in their newborn with its complete genetic record, birth data, and parents information—a chip that would always tell parents where their kids are. What parent could resist the temptation of such "security"?

If the church doesn't help identify what's life-giving and what's disease-producing in the emergence of this new self-generated, self-adapting, self-modifying, self-diagnosing, self-repairing Web Civilization, a lot of other people will gladly oblige. The church has done this before. It was the Sunday school that gave rise to and modeled the public school system, which ushered children from all socioeconomic levels into print culture.

Wing Culture

The most powerful communicators in the Gutenberg era winged it with words. They were master wordsmiths. On the anvil of suffering, pain, and doubt, they hammered out words to live by and die for.

The most powerful communicators in the Google era wing it through sea and sky with images. Metaphors are how leaders chart the course for others to follow. Twenty-first-century leaders are master iconographers whose storytelling skills and metaphor powers graph the routes and guide the ship. The art of telling stories is one of the paramount leadership tools.

The building blocks of the body of Christ are stories. Jesus combined images and story into an oral icon called a parable. Leaders must combine images and story and shared cultural reference points[18] into a multimedia icon called a parable.

> Jesus was perfectly capable of laying out "Five Principles to Dynamic Praying," and the fact that he didn't should make us reflect.[19]
>
> —John Ortberg

Leaders must learn to be expert "story-catchers" and hunter-gatherers of parables through metaphors and images. The biblical image bank is wide open. At the mention of a human need or hardship, communicators can make withdrawals. Mining the past for images, leaders can mix and match metaphors from innumerable sites, cross-referencing images and ideas that can make the heart pound. The ability to create "wormholes"—interconnections between widely separated disciplines—is absolutely essential to creative leadership. Pick up and shake twenty-first-century communicators and they mix metaphors, scatter images, cross borders, and reel out stories only to reassemble them in startling new combinations.

Leadership is a new kind of visual artistry. Whereas in the past we created

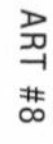

icons in stone, wood, and fabric, today's leaders now create visual icons in the air and among the audience through icon-parables.

> To change an organization you have to change its stories.[20]
>
> —Richard Stone, head of the StoryWork Institute, Orlando

What is icon-parable storytelling? An icon-parable is an image or metaphor that conveys a lifetime of experiences and stories. Icon-parables story people's lives. Icon-parable storytelling helps us make decisions or reverse decisions we've already made. Without icons, the Google generations are spiritually ill-fed.

Certain ideas, events, missions, and people, but most especially icons, serve as magnets that organize into coherent shape scattered filaments. Icon-parables line everything up, gather scattered wits together, make everything fall into place, and put everything into perspective.

There are various kinds of iconic stories. "Stories of identity"[21] help convey values, build morale, develop role models, reveal inner mechanisms of community. These icons serve as carriers of identity, values, and memory. They are the primary carriers of religious culture.

> Krispy Kremes are more than doughnuts—they're stories. People get a dreamy look in their eyes when they talk about them.[22]
>
> —Mike Cecil, minister of culture (sic) for Krispy Kreme Doughnut Corporation

Brand Identities[23]

In many ways, the process of "branding" your church is the twenty-first-century equivalent of "planning" processes (short-term, long-term, strategic) so beloved by moderns. Unlike mainline denominations, companies now offer what are being called "brand experiences" through "brand franchises" and "brand identities" so that you can feel a sense of community with others just through phrases like "Just Do It" (Nike) or "Think Different" (Apple).

1. Nikeism

The genius of Nike's Phil Knight was to realize that his company was not in the business of making sneakers, but in creating stories of heroism and a style of rebellion that people could experience. Nike's celebrity endorsers spin rebel stories of heroism in which you and athletes can participate as equals in this athletistocracy. Nike now sells its yellow bracelets at $1 a pop to support the Lance Armstrong Foundation for cancer research. It wanted to raise $5 million; it quickly raised $20 million in online sales alone. Yet you will not spot one swoosh on those yellow bracelets. Nike's brand is so strong it can do good without bragging.

For another example (e.g., "No Fear," "Mission Statements") of how the world steals the church's best lines, partly because we don't know we have them, consider the very name "Nike!" which is Greek for "Victory." Some scholars think that "Nike!" was a baptismal cheer, yelled by the community when a soul crossed the finish line into eternity.

2. Disneyism

Ditto Walt Disney World, Disneyland, Disney stores, Disneyshopping.com, Disney movies, Disney Channel. They all exist to evangelize the Disney brand experience through interactive activities with cartoon characters. Disneyism makes us a part of a community, a story, an ongoing dialogue, and a learning community through "fun-filled learning" on the Web and "edutainment" DVDs. In 2008 Disney launched "The Year of a Million Dreams" in which the focus is less on visiting the attractions of the Magic Kingdom than experiencing the magic of the kingdom. To make real the make-believe, Disney now encourages interactions with the happy Disney characters and smiling employees through pin-trading, and princess makeovers in the castle (where Cinderella sleeps, and now you can too).

3. Cocacolization

What do Coke and Pepsi make? Not soda pop. They manufacture culture. They create logos from which people can share experiences, logos that nourish communal identities and a distinctive sense of belonging.

The power of a brand connection is revealed in the blind taste tests of Coca-Cola and Pepsi. When people don't know which brand they are sipping, their flavor preferences are evenly divided between Coke and Pepsi. But when told which brand they are drinking, 4 out of 5 choose Coke. There is something bigger than flavor.

4. Nickelodeon

The Nick brand is dominant with kids, and kids are loyal. Why? Nickelodeon has penetrated the very hearts and souls of its customers, and it knows kids even better than kids know themselves.

Volvo, Saturn, and Harley-Davidson have cultivated cult followings of their cars and bikes. The Volvo Saved My Life Club turns real-life stories of car crashes into emotional attachments and reverential testimonials. The diehard Harley Owners Group (H.O.G) (650,000 members) celebrates anniversaries with festivals, rallies, concerts, factory tours, and motorcycle parades.[24]

Brands are all the more important in Web culture, for they show people what information can be trusted. For example, *The New York Times* and *Wall Street Journal* brands have power on the Net because they stand for journalistic integrity and factual authenticity.

What does your church embody? How will your church communicate its message to a twenty-first-century culture? These are questions AquaChurch leaders must ask and answer.

Communication's Four Tacks

In a very real sense, "brand" can be but another name for "soul."[25] And "soul" is something that is built from within, not invented from without. When experiences are built not around the church's needs but around the aims and ambitions and hungers of the people, "soul" is being conveyed. People feel "soul" and want to live "soulfully."

You can't control the winds, but you can trim the sails. In summary, there are four tacks into the wind for communicating a message, conducting a mission, establishing an identity, building a brand in Google culture, or best yet, growing souls in this twenty-first-century culture.[26]

1. Make the Net Work

Use the Web. To communicate with this new Net culture, leaders must experience and employ the Net. This is more than simply being Web-friendly. It is also more than a Web site.

It is a Web ministry.

How do you help people become attached to your Web site? Enable them to play, have fun. Eddie Bauer has "virtual dressing rooms" where you can mix and match clothes or scan in your home's floor plan and see how its furniture fits in. Lands' End lets you create a virtual model of your body shape to test out the clothes. Clairol invites you to scan in a photo of yourself and test out new hair colors. Amazon.com keeps track of your reading interests, seeking to anticipate your needs.[27]

2. "Give Away the Farm"

In a Web Civilization, you give away content. The Grateful Dead intuited this "information-wants-to-be-free" ideology of the Net with their succession of giveaways. TED and Pop!Tech do the same today, charging thousands of dollars to attend their conferences, but webcasting free of charge all the presentations of their conferences.

The only people who don't have to "give away the farm" are those who are giving big-time experiences. For this people will pay big bucks. The ultimate "big-time" is the experience of God. For this people will pay "big"—pay with their lives.

3. Tell Big Stories

Stories are the skeletal structure of the soul. Is there energy in your story? Is your body in your story? Is there passion in your story? Is your story more about God than about you? The last step in exploration and discovery is to close the loop. To close the loop is to tell the story, to share what you've learned.

You bring closure to your journey by telling its story. Robert Ballard, one of the great explorers of the modern world, puts it like this: "Columbus' journey, according to myth, began when he said to Queen Isabella, 'Give me your jewels, and I'll explore the world.' His journey wasn't finished until he returned with word of his discoveries."[28]

4. Fill Everything with Jest and Zest

"Are we having fun yet?" Jest and zest are the psychic glues that will hold things together in future culture. Laughter is already such a determining mode in today's culture that not only are the social and medical benefits of humor now taken for granted, but there are now even "corporate humor consultants." David Levin, who was trained as an information-technology consultant, was the "minister of comedy" at Ernst & Young. His role as a court jester was to get people to take themselves less seriously and to create humorous videos for company gatherings.[29]

Be playful, be funny, and have fun. If you're having fun, you're more creative, more energetic, friendlier, and optimistic. We can say something serious too seriously. But remember: For the Christian, the purpose of life is not jest but joy.[30] Oswald Chambers defined a joyful spirit as "the nature of God in my blood."[31] Joy is the lifeblood of the church. The joy of the Lord is a tidal wave of confidence and strength. And the key to joy is not keys to a Jaguar or pluckings in pursuit of the bluebird of happiness.

There's an old mountain saying: "It's not the piston or the box, but the steam." The church must harness and harvest passion and put to work the roaring, reverberating energies of zest. Zest is the source of the acute powers of concentration that enabled Isaac Newton to become so preoccupied with scientific and theological problems that he forgot to eat or sleep. Edwin Land, inventor of the instant camera and many theories of vision, worked at his desk for days on end, unaware of the passage of time.

Another old mountain adage says, "God uses desperate people." Pleasures abound for the soul when you go with your passion. Do you really believe in what you're doing? Or better yet, do you really believe that what you're doing is part of God's doing?

There is a bumper sticker that reads, "God is simply fun." To be sure, God is love. God is joy. God is peace. But when we live out of zest and jest, God is also "simply fun." The life of faith is comedy above all.

AQUACHURCH #8
LIQUID CHURCH

Morristown, New Jersey
www.liquidchurch.com

Communicating a timeless message is important, but so is the ability to "catch a story." Liquid is an AquaChurch that has a remarkable capacity to catch the story of what God is up to in the community and communicate it effectively through worship. Each week leaders at Liquid work to deliver a dynamic and message that illustrates who God is and what a life-giving relationship with Christ means. Through its relevant teaching, dynamic worship, and creative outreach, Liquid has experienced seven years of rapid growth and changed lives. They continue to work toward a vision of becoming a local church with a global influence by "streaming God's grace from New Jersey to every corner of the world." Liquid:

- Provides four live worship services every weekend featuring incredible music, relevant Bible teaching, and cutting edge multimedia;
- Offers a church for the "unchurched" and "overchurched," intent on changing the way you experience church.
- Worships through an online congregation in addition to the New Jersey site. Each service is streamed online so that anyone, anywhere can be a part of the community;

- Has a heart for not just those who worship at the weekend services, bur for serving their neighbors and world—especially the poor, marginalized, or hurting.
- Seeks creative ways to show God's love and be the hands and feet of Jesus on a street level. They have done Extreme Home Makeovers (Church Edition), Free Markets, God-sized tips, and gas giveaways.

CAPTAIN'S LOGBOOK

PERSONAL LOG

Use these ideas to stimulate your thinking about how the principles of this chapter could affect your ministry. Consider sharing these ideas with other church leaders.

1 Would you agree that "we are prisoners of the pulpit" (p. 215)? Ask yourself:

- How has our lack of media literacy or "graphicacy" encouraged this?
- What can I do to make the sermon a more dynamic communication form?
- What can I do to make the transition from simply writing sermons to creating experiences?

2 If you can buy or borrow it, listen to Amy Grant's 1997 *Behind the Eyes* CD, which some say is the best album she's ever produced. As you listen, think about the following questions:

- Does she ever mention God or Jesus directly in this album?
- Why would some call this album "the most profound theologically of her career"?[32]
- What insights can you gain from this CD that would make your ministry more effective?

3 Explore some of the spirituality sites on the Internet. BuddhaNet.net offers online courses and meditations to download. At www.aish.com/wallcam,

you can type messages that students in Jerusalem print out and place in the Western Wall. At ewtn.com, the Global Catholic Network will take you on a spirituality tour. The Virtual Mosque site www.islamicity.org/Mosque will conduct a tour of mosques around the world. A large library of resources can be accessed at the home page for the Presbyterian Church (USA) at pcusa.org.

Also check out some of the "zines." A "zine" is a magazine that appears only on the Internet, like www.zinebook.com or web-source.net/web/Ezines for listings of "zines." Consider what your church might be able to do on the Web for your church members.

4 Consider what you can learn from Richard Branson's "Virgin" brand. See the latest edition of his *Losing My Virginity: How I've Survived, Had Fun, and Made a Fortune Doing Business My Way* (2004). He's dyslexic, but one survey in Britain ranked him as the most intelligent man in the country—one up from Stephen Hawking. He's also hugely successful in choosing which companies to start and give the "Virgin" name. A company or product can't bear the "Virgin" label unless these five conditions are met:

- It must have high quality.
- It must be innovative.
- It must provide good value for the money.
- It must have a sense of fun.
- It must be challenging to existing alternatives, also known as the "Big Bad Wolf" theory. "We look for the big bad wolves who are dramatically overcharging and underdelivering," says Branson.

Virgin Atlantic offers first-class experiences at cut-rate prices. For Branson, the only hierarchy is this one: Employees first, customers second, and shareholders third.

5 Take a moment to consider how the following facts have affected the way you personally do the "work of ministry": Personal computers are now in more than 70 percent of homes (though the United States is way behind other countries like Iceland, Sweden, and South Korea). Around 1 million text messages are sent every 30 seconds.

- What is potentially good and bad about these trends for the way you do your day-to-day ministry?
- What is potentially good and bad about how these trends affect your church's weekly communication process?
- What opportunities may you miss if you don't take advantage of these modes of communication?

6 Do you believe that for leaders not to use "a Web site as a communications and community-building tool is to have fumbled the future" (p. 222)? If so, how have you begun to utilize the power of the Internet to study and prepare to communicate? If not, what do you plan to do to employ this communication tool in the future? Make a list of ways you would like to be able to use the Internet. Choose the two that seem most valuable, and commit to begin using them within a month. If you don't know how, seek help from within your church.

7 How well do you embody the admonition to "Make Everything Full of Jest and Zest"? Why do you think so many religious people have difficulty having "fun"? What does this lack of fun say about our ability to enjoy God? Name the last time you "adored" and/or "enjoyed" God.

Ship's Log

Use these activities with your church leadership to help them understand and own the principles of this chapter and how they relate to your church's ministry.

1 Study Philippians 2:1–13 to examine how "God's dumbing down was for our wising up" (p. 214). Spend time analyzing the "dumbing down" process involved with the incarnation (God becoming human through Jesus). Be sure to understand that it was the "emptying" of Christ that allowed for the "filling" of the believer. Discuss the following questions:

- Why is it so difficult to "dumb down" the Christian message?
- Why is it so necessary to "dumb down" the message?

Brainstorm practical ways your church can engage in authentic incarnational Christianity that balances doctrinal purity with communicational clarity.

For further study, you may want to read the first couple of chapters in Marva Dawn's book *Reaching Out Without Dumbing Down* (1995).

2 Whether we like it or not, the imagery of advertising is the language of the people. Discuss this question: To communicate the gospel to people outside the church, can we escape using that language?

Form groups of about three. Give each group newsprint or poster board and markers. Have each group create an ad for the ministry of your church. Encourage leaders to keep in mind the ideas in this chapter—include visual images and metaphors; maybe even design a Web page.

3 Have your leadership group examine the idea that "the church is a complex adaptive system" (p. 218). Think of the word *complex* from the standpoint of how the church is "community-based," and think of the word *adaptive* from the standpoint of how the church is "culturally attuned." Ask:

- What would need to happen in your church in order to have a bottom-up, self-regulating control that starts with chaos and moves to order, starts with energy and moves to form, starts with spirit and moves to structure?
- See Ephesians 4:1–16. How biblical is this kind of control?
- How possible is this kind of control?
- Seriously consider how you can help your church move to this more "bottom-up, self-regulating control" system.

4 In 1998, it was the official position of the Church of Scientology that every member should have a Web site. To this end, church members were given a CD-ROM with a template for creating one's own Web site and for linking to the church's home page as well as making the site identifiable to popular search engines.[33] Ask:

- What effect do you think this position has on church members?
- How effective do you think this method is for reaching people outside that church?
- What can we learn from this example?
- What might we want to do in response?

5 Check out the design of Shane Claiborne and Christ Haw's book *Jesus for President* (2008). Are there generational differences over whether you love the look and feel of this book, or whether you hate it? What do you think the future might look like in terms of books?

6 Read the response to new technology by a nineteenth-century ancestor. These words were spoken by one of the leaders of the American Tract Society:

> What new marvels of science and art may characterize the age, we know not; but we know that Christ is "Head over ALL THINGS to his church," and that every invention by which the world is made smaller and wiser, will facilitate the plans for making it better. The steamboat and the rail-car, and the telegraph, and cheap printing, and cheap postage, enable good men and good institutions to more than double their efficiency, and to concentrate the labors and the influence of a century into a brief generation. Shall these advantages be thrown away? Shall we content ourselves with the post-coach speed of the eighteenth century, in schemes for evangelization, while all worldly schemes are propelled with the locomotive speed of the nineteenth century? Shall we creep along the beaten path our fathers trod, and because they trod it, eschewing or neglecting all the increased facilities Providence has given us for publishing the great salvation, while steam, and electricity, and the

> printing-press are left to be the agents of ambition, avarice, and revolution? Or is not the voice of God ... sounding in the ears of his people: "I the Lord have given you power and wealth, mountains of iron and valleys of gold, a boundless territory and a free government.... I have added the ocean steamer, and the rail-way, and the steam printing-press, and the telegraph; employ all these for my glory and for the establishment of my kingdom! Use them all, till it shall be announced along the lightning wires that encircle the globe, 'Their line is gone out through all the earth, and their words to the end of the world.'"[34]

Discuss:

- When is the last time you heard a leading Christian saying something like that?
- How does this ancestor's response to the challenges of that day compare to our own whinings and bleatings?
- What is keeping us from sounding like this?

7 Have your leaders wrestle with the following questions:

- What kind of Web ministry could our church develop to communicate with our congregation? To minister to our community?
- How can we monitor both the promise and perils of this strange new world of Web Civilization?
- Should the church be providing information on how to filter and screen out inappropriate material from this nondiscriminating center of information?

Together, take a look at the Web to see some possibilities beyond providing simple information about your church:

- What if you could put on the Internet an announcement about a birth in your family, a photo of a baby with family members, a guest book, or other features. Could your church provide this "ministry" to its members within a biblical framework? Did you know that social networking sites like Facebook, MySpace, Flikr, Twitter already accomplish this?

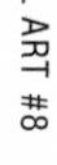

- What about a Web site where you can find recommendations on which books your kids shouldn't miss—recommendations from all sorts of people, such as pastors, friends, and teachers?
- What about your church's Web site linking to www.screenit.com, which reviews movies for parents?

MISSIONAL ART #9

VALUING THE CREW: COLLABORATION AND TEAMWORK

Come, follow me …
and I will make you fishers of men.
—Jesus (Matt. 4:19)

In nineteenth-century British history, two figures loomed large on the landscape: William Gladstone and Benjamin Disraeli. It was said that when you dined with Gladstone, you thought that you were with the most interesting, brilliant, and dazzling conversationalist. And it was said that when you dined with Disraeli—an equally charismatic figure—you felt that you were the most interesting, brilliant, and dazzling conversationalist.[1]

Which are you most like—Gladstone or Disraeli?

Sir Ernest Shackleton was most like Disraeli. During his lifetime, what he was most noted for was not his heroic 1909 polar expedition that reached farther south than anyone before him. Nor was it his *Endurance* expedition (1914–1917), which brought a twenty-two-foot open boat from Elephant Island to South Georgia Island. Some have even called this daring feat of seamanship "one of the greatest epics of survival in the annals of exploration" and "one of the greatest boat journeys ever accomplished."[2]

What Shackleton was most noted for was his team-building ability to draw legendary levels of leadership out of his crew.[3] In spite of nearly impossible weather conditions and some of the worst living arrangements of any crew in history, in spite of daily difficulties in obtaining observational sightings for the making of their positions, in spite of mutiny and dissent, Shackleton had a single-minded determination to do what was best for his crew. What made the Shackleton team work was his insistence that getting a project done was more important than who does the project, who controls the project, or who gets credit for the project. In the words of his biographer, "The mystique that Shackleton acquired as a leader may partly be attributed to the fact that he elicited from his men strength and endurance they had never imagined they possessed; he ennobled them."[4]

Shackleton equipped his team with a mantra they heard over and over: "Optimism is true moral courage."[5] As the captain of the ship, Shackleton refused to discriminate between the weak and the strong, the sick and the well. They would all survive or none survive.

They all survived.

> May the Lord help you to do your duty & guide you through all dangers by land and sea. May you see the Works of the Lord & all His wonders in the Deep.[6]
>
> —Inscription in ship Bible presented by Queen Alexandra to the crew of the *Endurance*, May 31, 1914

Participation and Connectivity

Gutenberg leadership highlighted the noun "equipment." Google leadership stresses the verb "equip." The first time the word for "equip" is used in the Gospels is when Jesus finds a father and his two sons in a ship, "preparing" their nets (Matt. 4:21; Mark 1:19). The Greek word for "prepare" is *kartatizo*, which means to repair the rends, to make whole again. But it also means to make someone what they ought to be—to "equip," to "prepare," to "strengthen" someone for a mission. "Equip" doesn't mean to fix the nets yourself, but to enlist and empower others to do what God is calling them to do.

In ecclesiastic ecosystems, people at the lowest levels must be given every decision-making power and entrepreneurial boost to rise to the top; creativity in all staff, including those at the lowest level, must be given free reign; teams must be encouraged to be self-organizing; power and authority must be shared by everyone.

When you drain complexity and chaos out of any living system (as The Order of St. Roberts, master plans, "orders from headquarters" can do), you snuff out that system, for you damage the organism's natural immunological ability to adapt to new conditions and future-fit itself for unprecedented challenges.

Leadership is less about employing people than empowering people. Leadership is less about controlling people than releasing them. This does not mean that other people will not put their lives in your hands. But the whole purpose of an air traffic "controller" is not to keep planes on the land, but to get them off the ground and into the sky. What do "controllers" do? They clear pilots for takeoff.

Missional art #9 is the art of collaboration. The future belongs not so much to movers and shakers but to leaders who can work in teams. In fact, the movers and shakers of the emerging-church culture are teams, which must become the dominant model for ministry and mission. There are no more clergy and laity. There are only ministers. Missional art #9 is the art of making every member as good a minister as you are endeavoring to be.

On stage a Victorian actor died a very elaborate and melodramatic death. Suddenly, from the audience came the cry, "Die again!" So he did.

So do we. Again and again we die when we fail to understand that …

- to be a great preacher, you first must be a great listener;
- to be a great worship leader, you first must be a great congregation;
- to be a great leader, you first must be a great team player.

All Israel are responsible for one another.

—Ancient Jewish proverb

It Takes Two … or More

Marvin Gaye was right all along. In fact, Jesus said it first: "For where two or three come together in my name, there am I with them" (Matt. 18:20). Google culture may encourage a connectional, collaborative style, but it was here long before we arrived on the scene.

It was here with Noah. Someone has conceived an alternative to *All I Really Need to Know I Learned in Kindergarten*. It's titled "All I Ever Needed to Know I Learned from Noah."

1. Be prepared. It wasn't raining when Noah built the ark.
2. Stay fit. When you're six hundred years old, someone might ask you to do something REALLY BIG.
3. Don't listen to critics. Do what has to be done.
4. Build on high ground.
5. For safety's sake, travel in pairs.
6. Two heads are better than one.
7. Speed isn't always an advantage. The cheetahs were on board, but so were the snails.
8. If you can't fight or flee, float.
9. Take care of your animals as if they are the last ones on earth.
10. Don't forget that we're all in the same boat.
11. When the doo-doo gets deep, don't complain. SHOVEL.
12. Stay below deck during the storm.
13. Remember: The ark was built by amateurs; the Titanic was built by professionals.
14. If you have to start over, have a friend by your side.
15. Woodpeckers on the INSIDE are often a bigger threat than the storm outside.
16. Don't miss the boat.
17. No matter how bleak it looks, there's always a rainbow on the other side.[7]

Look again at numbers 5, 6, 10, and 14. Who said, "No one is an island"?

Don't we feel alone as we float down the great river of time? After all, we must put on our own clothes, maintain our own books, keep burning our own lights, sail our own ship. No matter. We are all single lanes in search of two-lane and four-lane highways that bridge to other islands.

To live afloat requires a crew of compatibility and respect. Assembling the right crew is the heart of any expedition. Some solo expeditions one cannot evade, such as birth and death, but solo navigations are the most dangerous journeys anyone can take.

The missional art of collaboration involves both selecting a crew and equipping that crew for the rowing of a galley ship. Electronic media especially mandates leadership skilled at team functioning. Where mass print culture was an isolating experience, electronic culture is by its very essence a collaborative, communifying function. The modern era undervalued the missional arts related to connectedness. In fact, collaborative skills are more valuable to leadership than technical skills. No church can do multisensory worship or multimedia education without the deployment of teams.

The days of the single scholar working alone at a cubicle or desk are as fading as the days of the linear-narrative monograph. Scholarship is now a social enterprise. My oldest son, a PhD in the fields of biology, ecology, and toxicology, publishes articles whose masthead lists of authors make the cluttered titles of law firms look positively roomy. If truth be told, scholarship was always more of a collaborative enterprise than the modern world let on. Just ask any graduate student.

> Far from being the product of one brilliant mind, the Declaration of Independence was a collaborative document showcasing the uncommon wisdom of common people throughout the thirteen colonies. Thomas Jefferson was chosen to be the draftsman because, as John Adams put it, "You can write ten times better than I can."[8]

"Won't You Be My Neighbor?"

Twenty-first-century culture is a sink-or-swim society. It creates sink-or-swim scenarios. But the biblical witness is another: We sink or swim together. The actions of one affect all.

This connectedness reaches to the subatomic level of our universe. We now know that once two electrons have connected or touched in some way, they can never be the same again. In fact, no matter how far apart the electrons go, what happens to one happens to the other. When one changes, the other changes. The connection between them goes beyond "cause-and-effect" because this kind of "cause" and "effect" are not tied together in time and space. There is no time lapse between what happens to one electron and what happens to the other. The changes are instantaneous, simultaneous, immediate.

We do not inhabit a causal universe but a connectional universe in which everything is a part of everything else. Why should we be surprised? Wasn't Jesus trying to tell us this when he brought the far distant and the up close together in his warning, "Whatever you did for one of the least of these brothers and sisters of mine, you did for me" (Matt. 25:40 TNIV)? No matter how far apart we may be, in some sense we are all one. The classic image of chaos theory is "The Butterfly Effect." What chaos theory really means is that God made the world such that the mere waving of a butterfly's wings in Beijing could birth a tidal wave in Washington.

In a connectional world, not only does every action have consequence, but every action has consequence on everything else. Collaboration extends outward and inward at the same time. Geneticist Richard Lewontin even argues that the chemical composition of the atmosphere is as much a product of what earthlings are doing as a precondition of their life.[9]

In the African concept of *ubuntu*, if one person is not treated properly, no one is treated properly.[10] The connectedness of a community is such that the devaluation and dehumanization of one is the devaluation and dehumanization of all. A Jewish parable by Rabbi Shim'on ben Yohai tells of some people sitting in a boat: One of them took a drill and began to drill beneath himself. His companions said to him, "What are you sitting and doing?" He replied, "What business is it of yours? Am I not drilling beneath myself?" They said to him, "But the water will rise and flood the ship upon all of us."[11]

When the storms of life are raging, stand by me.[12]

—Charles Albert Tindley

We are all in the same boat, linked in ways we cannot yet even conceive. Our financial markets are so enmeshed that a failure anywhere reverberates everywhere. Our environments are so interconnected that what one region does about its water has universal impact. There is even an online computer simulation game, "SimCity," that is based on reality: not if, but how does industrial growth affect deforestation; not if, but how do taxes impact the polls; not if, but how do consumption patterns affect the growth of private security forces, which now outnumber the police four to one worldwide and ten to one in South Africa and Russia.[13]

"Mayday! Mayday!"

There will be storms in life. Guaranteed. And storms don't come one at a time. Guaranteed. "The singular disadvantage of the sea," novelist Stephen Crane wrote in *The Open Boat*, "lies in the fact that after successfully surmounting one wave you discover that there is another behind it just as important and just as nervously anxious to do something effective in the way of swamping boats."[14]

Mariners whose ships are going down issue a "Mayday." The word comes from the French *M'aidez*, which means, "Give me aid." Who will answer your "Mayday! Mayday!"? The waves are crashing all around you. Your boat has capsized. You are sinking fast. "My God, my God, why have you forsaken me?"

"Mayday! Mayday!"

Rescue missions are team efforts.

Teamwork-Obsessed

The Christian tradition is teamwork-obsessed. The doctrine of creation trumpets a God who shares creative power with us, who insists we be co-conspirators in our own story, collaborators in our emergence. The doctrine of redemption is the universe's story of pulsating and materializing relationships. The very doctrine of the Trinity is based on a relational God living in community both within and without.

The early church imaged the three persons of God in a variety of ways, including a circle. The seventh-century Greek theologian John of Damascus described the relationship of the three persons of the Trinity as *perichoresis*, which means literally "circle dance." In Greek, *choreuo* meant a round dance used in banquets and festivals that usually involved singing—hence "chorus."[15] The perichoretic image of the Trinity portrays the three persons of God in a circle movement, the "choreography" of a "dancing God." Later, the modern world preferred to image the Trinity as a triangle, where the Father is "on top" and a hierarchical image of the godhead clangs piercingly. If the modern world created a flat-earth church, the early church was both in the round and flat. Biblical spirituality is both a line dance and a circle dance.

A collaborative model is at the heart of Christian faith. Jesus himself was teamwork-obsessed.[16] He spent his ministry not founding local communities or growing a mega-following for himself, but building a handful of itinerant disciples in first-century Palestine into a great team that could create a culture of perichoretic love. He called out his disciples in many cases in teams. He sent out his disciples always in teams. He made healing a collaborative affair and insisted that those who were about to be healed cooperate in their own healing.

For Jesus the possibilities of the promise take place in community: "When they accept you," Jesus told his disciples, "they accept me." What is more, "If you embrace the least of these," Jesus said, "you embrace me." Individual Christians are spiritual fractals of the body of Christ. Baptism is a communal ritual, a water branding and initiation rite into the household of faith. After all, the Lord's Prayer is addressed to "Our Father."

> A cord of three strands is not quickly broken.
>
> —Ecclesiastes 4:12c

A strange salvation is at work here that frightens those who can only say "I." Work alone and you get nowhere, Jesus taught. Work together with me and you get everywhere. Indeed, "all things are possible."

To build a great church, build great teams.

Collaborative Personality

Leadership in the modern world was the power of charisma and command. Only a few people had it. These were gifts. Leadership in the Google world is collaboration and interaction. Everybody has it. These are learnings.

Have you ever noticed that people who have played team sports have a different spirit about them than those who haven't? Teams are groomed "We-first" to "think team" ("We're number one") rather than the "Me-first" of the "star syndrome" ("I'm number one"). When Rick Majerus was head coach of the University of Utah basketball team, he attributed the team's presence at the 1998 Final Four with these words: "We break every huddle with the cry of 'Team.' We play it, we yell it, we believe it."

The improvements that come to leadership from the cry of "Team" are not like the car "improvements" that came with catalytic converters. In the catalytic converter model, all one had to do was attach a new filtrating device to the old, dirty engine and the pollutants were removed. It is not enough to attach collaborative gadgets to leadership styles and leave everything else unchanged.

Rather, collaboration is a systems thinking that modifies how life is lived and how change is generated. Collaborative leadership is built around images, logos, metaphors, ceremonials, stories. Nobody can really be in overall charge anymore when one understands the interrelationship of seemingly independent variables. The ultimate interconnectedness of all of life is based on the biblical principle of collaboration: "In Christ all things cohere." That mysterious glue of grace links all that is and all who are with all that was, and all who were with all that shall be.

For example, it is not enough simply to rename "committees" as something else, even something as good as "ministry action teams," if they keep functioning as committees. Similarly, it is not enough to shift from staff-based to team-based if there is still a "big-boss-with-the-hot-sauce" manager mentality where "big-cheeses" issue directives that underlings accomplish. In a team-player mentality, leaders direct the issues and identities of associates who team up to perform missions and accomplish projects without ever being asked. In a team-player mentality, no leader ever goes to a continuing education event or conference without taking others.

> The Authorized King James Version of the Bible … must be the only work of literary genius written by a committee.
>
> —P. D. James

The missional art of collaboration transforms everything—from how leaders behave to what leaders believe and become. In the modern world leadership was getting ahead of others. In the Google world, leadership is getting along with others and getting others to go along with you.

The essence of collaboration is this: You can't be an individual without collaborating with others. You can't stand alone. As IBM learned first and Apple came around to seeing, we must become "compatible" with each other. When people draw energy from one another, they do everything better. Where there is no collaboration, there is no reverberation.

> The monk is he who is separate from all and united with all.[17]
>
> —Evagrius of Pontus

Huge groves of red cedars dot the western coast of the United States. From a distance they appear tall and sturdy and strong. But underground, their roots are shallow. When one falls, others often follow. The only thing that holds up these majestic trees is that they lean on each other. Their branches literally reach out and touch one another. Their roots intertwine and support one another. Not one of them can stand alone.

True leaders never say "I," either in speech or spirit. A collaborative personality has shifted from what theologians call autonomy to autopoiesis,[18] from an independent, rational self to an embedded, relational self. Collaborative leaders help others to look at each other not as separate entities, but as a series of parallel processing organisms where everything is connected to everything else.

- In autonomy, everyone is a "law unto himself/herself." In autopoiesis, every life system is a part of something larger than oneself, "with each part existing both for and by means of the whole," writes complexity biologist Stuart Kauffman, "while the whole existed for and by means of the parts."[19]
- In autonomy, an organism articulates and manifests the directives of some command central. In autopoiesis, an organism is self-renewing and has the power to generate itself while at the same time it is "highly autonomous, each one having its separate identity, which it continuously maintains."[20]
- In autonomy, an organism has boundaries that keep it separate from the world around. In autopoiesis, boundaries are connecting membranes that open the organism to the complex world outside.

In the future, everything must become connective. Can the church be the sacred place that makes possible life's maximum opportunities for interaction and collaboration and synergy? Can the church be the place where office and rank mean less and less, and where teamwork rules?[21]

Log On and Link Up

The mantra of the future is a collaborative one: "Log On and Link Up." Leaders Get Linked. Leaders Get Connected.

The Web is about community and connectedness. It is the twenty-first-century watering hole. Moderns use the Internet as an information medium. For postmoderns the Internet is a social medium. They use it as a water cooler and bar stool.

Why computer viruses? Because early inventors never imagined how this technology would be used as a social medium. They saw it more like a typewriter, a solitary machine used in isolation from others. They simply couldn't foresee the social uses of computers, including sharing software. They couldn't predict the reality every parent now faces: Kids can establish global social relationships totally beyond parental control.

One of the greatest hoaxes perpetrated on the contemporary mind is that electronic culture creates passive people. In fact, many of North America's most prestigious seminaries are on record banning outright or panning online learning because we allegedly live in a world where "people mistake the virtual experience for the real." According to this mentality, "Kids are just as likely to sit in front of their computers and 'play' baseball as go outside and pitch and bat."

Exactly the opposite is true. When residents of the Google world surf the Net, they want to surf Big Sur more. Electronic culture creates interactive, not passive people. The more chat groups, virtual tours, and Web sites are available for conversation, the more cafes open up where you can set the table with conversation and coffee or simply be by yourself in a crowd.

I started an online doctor of ministry team at Drew Theological School. These twelve doctoral students with Web-friendly ministries from around the world would do part of their coursework online and part on campus. The degree was designed to bring together the up close and far distance. When the time for their first "intensive" arrived, I was worried. How would they function alongside the other doctoral groups that we were starting and were already in place?

What happened surprised everyone, especially me. Before any of the online students arrived on campus, they had connected online and had already invested hours in getting to know each other. They coordinated travel arrangements that maximized their resources, including renting a van at the Newark Airport to cut down on limo expenses. They planned a trip together into the city, decided what ministries to visit there, and made reservations at Manhattan restaurants. When their feet touched down on the Drew campus, there was no doctoral group that even came close to the camaraderie, esprit, and organization of this one. They had bonded like no group I had ever mentored. The Web had deepened relationships, not diminished them.

> Wild nights! Wild nights!
> Were I with thee,
> Wild nights should be
> Our luxury!
>
> Futile the winds
> To a heart in port—
> Done with the compass,
> Done with the chart.[22]
>
> —Emily Dickinson

The Relationship-Driven Church

At his confirmation hearings as deputy secretary of state in 1981, Judge William P. Clark, a Californian friend of President Reagan, could not name the prime minister of Zimbabwe. This provoked much mirth and ridicule among "foreign policy professionals." But Clark had one priceless asset for his position: superb access to and trust of the commander in chief. The Judge Clark dictum is this: To make change, make connections.

More than two millenniums ago Aristotle said there are five things no one can ever have too much of: health, knowledge, love, confidence, and

friends. But in a Facebook, MySpace culture, there is now more power in relationships than we have seen in half a millennium. In the Gutenberg world, people sought meaningful relationships. In the Google world, meaning *is* relationships. The content *is* the connection.

What flower power was to the sixties and punk was to the seventies, club culture was to the nineties and naughts. Why is twenty-first-century culture a dance culture? What was it about "raves" and "dancing with the stars" that almost became a spiritual awakening to so many?

I asked a Dallas raver about this, and he answered immediately: "At a rave you get a feeling of community."

I countered, "You mean instant intimacy?"

"That's it," he replied excitedly, not sensing my pejorative tone. "I become part of a rave community," he admitted.

"I can see how dancing would help break down a sense of individualism and foster a sense of unity and community. But does the community continue? Do the relationships last?" I pressed.

"They're now my best friends," he said proudly.

Can the church build new kinds of relationships with members and nonmembers, collaborative relationships over combative relationships? The biggest factors determining whether new members will dig in or drop out are answers to these four questions:

- "Can I make friends in this church?"
- "Is there a place where I will fit in?"
- "Does this church need me?"
- "Can I be me here?" (Especially for a younger "rave" generation, freedom of expression without judgment is key.)

A "no" answer to these questions means the member leaves after about six months. A "yes" answer keeps them for six months, after which the questions become different:

- "Are my new friends as good as my old friends?"
- "Does this group address specific needs in my life?"
- "Is my contribution valued?"

The average church loses 6–12 percent of its membership per year. The official reasons? One to 2 percent, death; 3–4 percent, transfer; 2–6 percent, inactivity/reversion.[23] The unofficial reasons? The church's rigid, frigid aura as well as other factors that get in the way of the church advancing people-relationships and God-relationships.

Teammates who are skilled at managing relationships and releasing the power of relationships will be some of the most valuable leaders of the future. Emerging leaders practice random acts of attention and recognition.

A Good Crew

What is an authentic community? What is an authentic self? What makes an authentic team? The following are critical elements:

1. Mission

Every team needs a mission. This mission may or may not come with a handy "plan" or highlighted "trip-tic" attached. It's not true that leaders cannot lead unless they know where they're going. Sometimes God sends us on missions we don't understand and don't want. Forget the need for definite outcomes. Getting the right outcome is less important than doing the right thing and obeying orders.

Essential to every mission is a focused sense of calling. A team is being deployed "for such a time as this." The leadership skill necessary for "mission" is not visioning "God's plan" but voicing "God's call" and bringing onboard everyone who will be obedient to that call. Such "voicing" skill requires a unique social intelligence—one that can sense the spirit of a group, take its pulse, know how each person fits together (not "fits in"), personalize communication so that each hearer feels special, and most critical, help teams to think in terms of mission. The psychodynamics of teamwork is not asking what's best for me, but what's best for the mission. Leaders in the modern world helped underlings to "think institutional." Leaders in the twenty-first-century world help teammates "think missional."

Ministry teams are less "gift-based" than "mission-based." Gift inventories and tests are modern attempts at mapping and at flipping nominating committees into head-hunting businesses. People today resent tests or inventories telling them what to do. Besides, tests will tell you what your natural bent is, what you're naturally best at. Inventories will tell you for what ministries you have a natural "gift-mix."

But no gifts inventory tells you what's in your heart, or what's in God's heart for you, or what you can do supernaturally. Sometimes the community needs you to do what is lacking rather than do what you want to do or what you're psychologically programmed to do. There is an old camp-meeting saying that needs resurrection: "God doesn't call the equipped; God equips the called."

Besides, in mission-based teams, people are always surprising you with their "gifts" and "abilities." Strong leadership can extract participation while keeping the mission up front.[24]

2. Otherness

In the cosmic and quantum worlds, there are always multiple sides or parts to all wholes. If there is a quantum experiment that shows that particles can't hold positions contradictory and simultaneous, I don't know about it.

What makes a great team is "otherness." For a long time psychologists have talked about "significant others" with the accent on the "significant" and not the "others." In modern "significant others," the "significant" familial, professional, social, or romantic "others" were too alike to be "other."

AquaChurch teams are as marked by "otherness" as the Jesus TeamNet. Jesus brought together political opposites on his team: Simon the zealot and Matthew the tax collector. Jesus brought together a mix of generalists and specialists with the advantage to the generalists, who can keep in mind the big picture. Jesus mixed up age groups and generational gestalts, with advantage to the younger who make us less blind to the possibilities of what we can discover.[25] Jesus nurtured young talent, let them go, and let them rip. Mission teams must begin to read—like Jesus did—the printouts of cultural difference, dissonance, and diversity.

For the sake of the mission, missional teams will seek out "PALS" (Partners, Affiliations, Liaisons, Strategic alliances). Sometimes teams will even pursue PALS that are as "unholy" as they are "strategic." Some strategic but "unholy" alliances already out there?

- The Sierra Club and the National Rifle Association collaborated to stop the expansion of the Houston airport into the Katy Prairie.
- Cattle ranchers and conservationists have locked arms to promote land trusts to protect land from development.
- Farmers and big-city mayors are partnering to promote responsible land-use policies.

> The key to being a successful skipper is to see the ship from the eyes of the crew.[26]
>
> —Pacific Fleet Commander D. Michael Abrashoff

3. Trust

What the language of "virtues" was to Gutenbergers, the language of "viruses" is to Googlers. It is as important to develop positive spiritual viruses as it is positive social viruses. One of those "viruses" that brings together the social and spiritual is "trust."

Trust is a team's most precious commodity. I call it the connective tissue of the body of Christ. Reggie McNeal calls trust "the currency of teams."[27] In fact, the need for bringing back old-fashioned social viruses like trust and loyalty is more acute than ever in electronic culture. The social trust virus, which is based on "you're like me, therefore I trust you," is hard enough. In 2007, only 24 percent of the USAmerican people said they trusted their government.[28] The spiritual trust virus, which builds relationships of trust with people who are different from you, is harder yet.

A trust based on diversity, not likeness—if not a blind trust—is at least a farsighted trust. Trust has been defined as "building a bridge as you walk on it."[29] Plank by plank we build that bridge of trust, laying down a plank of

respect here, a plank of responsibility there, a slat of motivation there, a panel of protection here, celebrating small successes to build team confidence, and rigging systems (masts, booms, ropes, and sails) that scaffold the lives of "others" with charity, dignity, loyalty, and security.

4. Succession

The word *success* has a double ring. We know the popular meaning of "success" as leading the pack, getting ahead, being first. But the word *success* also means following behind, falling in from the rear, and staying in step. When you "succeed" someone, for example, you follow that person, you walk behind that person, you step into someone else's shoes.

A "successful" team is one that knows how to deal with "succession" issues, the most critical of which is loyalty. Leadership is not just the ability to work in teams; it is also the ability to inspire "successors" and mark others for successive sailings—people who will keep the mission going and raise it to new levels.

Twenty-first-century "people skills" raise to prominence the ability to pick a crew and be a crew. All organisms experience growing pains, which means that sometimes teams must be disassembled, reduced, expanded, or reconstituted. The team you start a mission with is not going to be the team you end that mission with. Exercises help discover who doesn't belong on the team, as well as who needs to "succeed" on that team.

5. Collaborative Competence Framework

The missional art of collaboration depends on one's willingness to become a collaborative person and develop collaborative competence frameworks. This does not mean one gives up the identity of the "self." But it does mean that the "self" takes its meaning, shape, and direction from one's community and tribe.

Ralph Ellison defines jazz as an act of community that is punctuated with individual creativity, ingenuity, and genius:

> True jazz is an art of individual assertion within and against the group. Each true jazz moment ... springs from a contest in which

> each artist challenges all the rest; each solo flight, or improvisation, represents (like the successive canvases of a painter) a definition of his identity: as individual, as member of the collectivity, and as a link in the chain of tradition. Thus, because jazz finds its very life in an endless improvisation upon traditional materials, the jazz man must lose his identity even as he finds it.[30]

A collaborative competence framework that brings the individual and the communal together operates out of four grids:

- *Collaborative Accountability:* Popular culture is a prime resource for ministry, but popular culture can be hijacked very quickly by reactionary forces: Metaphors, unlike "points," are easy to pick up, warm and fuzzy, and easily susceptible to private interpretation; Gutenberg peoples easily mistake "having an open mind" with letting their brains pop out; in a world of complexity and ambiguity, discernment needs the confirmation of the community. In short, a collaborative style requires a communal check and accountability. The community is a key learning instrument in collaborative leadership.
- *Collaborative Learning:* Collaborative leadership operating out of collaborative competence frameworks is open to stacking new learning habits on top of old ones—like triple-loop learning. In the words of business guru Robert Hargrove, "triple-loop learning involves altering the particular perspective, underlying beliefs, and assumptions (or old rules) that shape who we are as a human being … Double-loop learning (similar to triple-loop) involves altering the rules or underlying patterns of thinking that determine the way we think, interact, and solve problems. Single-loop learning involves trying to do the same thing better or gaining some transactional tips and techniques."[31]
- *Collaborative Style:* Authentic leaders circulate an attitude of creative cooperation and solidarity through constantly evolving

projects, missions, and deadlines. It's not true that you're only as good as your next project. But your leadership is only as good as your next mission. The heart of a collaborative style is multiple frames of reference that can juxtapose different types of people and projects. Witness "The Three Tenors."

- *Collaborative Space:* Leaders need spiritual design as much as "smart design" in their use of space. A "sick building syndrome" can afflict the soul and mind as well as the body. Healthy space is team space, shared space, not a hierarchy of space with royalty inhabiting offices fit for the gods while everyone else lives in convict cubicles. Already in the business world the walls are coming down in office space. More and more senior managers now sit in open offices with no doors. The dimly lit cubicle with one's own private space is becoming more rare. Pittsburgh's Alcoa has banished all private offices, even for its CEO. So has Cisco Systems, where an office isn't space in a building, but any space any employee is. The future is "teaming rooms," "commons," "playrooms." People need their own personal spaces, their cliff dwellings, but personal space is basically electronic space (laptops and portable phones) conjoined with team space—hangouts like water coolers, living rooms, and snack bars dominated by casual learning, dress, and connectedness.

> Anyone who is popular is bound to be disliked.[32]
>
> —Yogi Berra

On Romanticizing Collaboration

Ferdinand Magellan led the first circumnavigation of the globe, crossing the equator in 1519. The *Victoria* and eighteen crew members returned to Spain in 1522 in the first vessel to circumnavigate the globe.

But Magellan set off with five ships, not one. The dash in the years 1519–1522 tells a tale of many obstacles and ordeals. One of the ships wrecked in rough seas. The crew at one point survived on sawdust, leather strips from the sails, and rats. But by far the greatest challenge Magellan faced, a challenge that almost sank his mission and many others before and after, was mutiny—by three of his Spanish captains (Juan de Cartegena of the *San Antonio*, Gaspar de Quesada of the *Concepcion*, and Luis de Mendoza of the *Victoria*).

Comedian Carol Leifer has a warning to people going on a cruise: "If you thought you didn't like people on land ..."

It is not true that the more people rub shoulders and bend ears, the more they come together, or come to agree. USAmerican people spent the better part of two years hashing over Bill Clinton and ended up more divided than ever.

> Jesus Christ only had to make twelve appointments—
> and one of them was a bummer.[33]
> —Media mogul Ted Turner

Collaboration is as much about making enemies into friends—not fiends bound for that fire-and-brimstone burning lake—as it is about helping bosom buddies work together. The love of family and friends is not a distinguishing mark of Jesus' disciples. The love of enemies is.

Jesus learned from his ancestors that either we are all children of one God or none of us are. "Have we not all one Father? Did not one God create us? Why do we profane the covenant of our fathers by breaking faith with one another?" (Mal. 2:10). But Jesus went from there to make the love of enemies a centerpiece of spiritual practice. Christians love their enemies. For enemies make Christians better Christians.

Why do Christians think it necessary to diminish others to enhance Jesus' reputation? Disciples of Jesus are called to understand, not judge, real-life people. Authentic evangelism is not raining on the Buddhism parade, or on the Islam parade, or on anyone's parade. Authentic evangelism is telling the stories of Jesus to everyone who will listen. And others' willingness to listen to us depends on our willingness to listen to them. The days of "Show and Tell" evangelism are over. The era of "Shut Up and Listen … Then Lift Up Christ" have begun.

The missional art of collaboration involves listening to contradictory points of view, even those that unsettle us the most. Leaders listen to the stories of their enemies; they hear the stories of those who disagree with them; they do not mock crude religious belief. Part of the mystery of how the church manages to fudge nearly all its opportunities to share and embrace the greatest story every told is found right here. If you want this culture to hear your story, you must listen to a lot of stories you find offensive and troublesome.

> A thousand friends are too few; one enemy is too many.
>
> —Turkish proverb

The Lighthouse

Lighthouses shine. That's it. They don't blow horns. They shine. And in that shining, the lighthouse provides mariners a navigating beacon that serves multiple functions. It guides the ship in times of fog and distress, warning mariners where the rocks are hidden and how to find the shore. Its light can also symbolize the "lights of home" to those returning from voyages or to all with a sense of lost belonging. Finally, its beacon signifies a goal, a vision, an impossible possibility toward which a person strives and one day hopes to reach.

To miss the light of a lighthouse is to find misfortune, to overlook home. Leaders can spot and decode the flickers beamed out to sea by lighthouses.

A church outside Geneva, Switzerland, maintains a centuries-old tradition. Everyone who comes to church brings a light from home. This happens not just on Christmas Eve for a candlelight service; it happens at every service.

The three-hundred-year-old sanctuary starts out dark, and then slowly becomes light as the worshippers bring their unique lights and hang them on hooks that jut from the church's walls.

When the congregation meets a parishioner who was absent from worship, they say, "We missed your light."

When we say we're created in the "image of God," the word *image* is less noun than verb. We are created more to image God than to be images of God. Are we reflecting God's glory in our lives? Or is the world missing our light?

AQUACHURCH #9
GRANGER COMMUNITY CHURCH

Granger, Indiana
www.gccwired.com

Collaboration and teamwork are definitely descriptive words of Granger Community Church. Granger has incorporated teamwork throughout its organization to provide:

- a casual atmosphere
- friendly people to provide guidance and direction
- today's music, powerful dramas, high-impact media presentations
- messages relevant to daily life
- an amazing children's space
- a Starbucks-esque café where you can relax, recharge, and relate in your comfort zone, with a coffee in your hand
- the assurance that everyone matters to God—and to GCC

CAPTAIN'S LOGBOOK

PERSONAL LOG

Use these ideas to stimulate your thinking about how the principles of this chapter could affect your ministry. Consider sharing these ideas with other church leaders.

1 How do you feel about your team-building abilities? Do you agree with the following statement: "No church can do multisensory worship or multimedia education without the deployment of teams" (p. 243)? On a scale of one to ten, how do you rate yourself in terms of collaboration? How do you rate your current ministry team in terms of its ability for collaboration? How supported and encouraged do you feel as a leader in your church? What do you do to support and encourage your closest team members?

2 Memorize 2 Corinthians 3:6, the priesthood of all believers verse.

- What does this verse say to you about the need for collaboration?
- Has your lack of collaborative leadership been killing your church through the letter of the law?
- How does the Spirit give life through teams in your church?
- How could the Spirit give more life to your church?

3 Think about this one sentence by Thomas Wright: "To know is to be in relation with the known, which means that the 'knower' must be open to the possibility of the 'known' being other than had been expected or even desired, and must be prepared to respond accordingly, not merely to observe from a distance."[34]

- How does this thought relate to your fears about empowering others in your church?
- In view of this statement, how does faith fit into empowering others?
- What's most difficult for you in thinking about a more collaborative form of ministry leadership?

4 Do personal study to help in developing your collaboration skills. Two important resources might be the following: E. Stanley Ott's *Transform Your Ministry with Ministry Teams* and George Cladis's *Leading the Team-Based Church*. Set tangible, realistic, written goals, and remember, collaboration is learned behavior. "Leadership in the modern world was the power of charisma and command. Only a few people had it. These were gifts. Leadership in the Google world is collaboration and interaction. Everybody has it. These are learnings" (p. 247).

5 Consider the words of Pacific Fleet Commander D. Michael Abrashoff: "The key to being a successful skipper is to see the ship from the eyes of the crew" (p. 255).

- If this is true, what can you do to develop more empathy for your people?
- This chapter says that being a team player would enhance your leadership; that being a congregation participant will prepare you to be a worship leader; and that being a listener will improve your ability to be a speaker. Do you believe all of that? If so, do a written analysis of ways you can practice following, participating, and listening.

6 Study the four grids for a "collaborative competence framework" (pp. 257–58), and pick one or two as part of a self-development plan. For instance, what would it mean personally and specifically for you to establish "a collaborative style [which] requires a communal check and accountability" (p. 257)? Also, what would it be like if you seriously considered reshaping some of your office space according to the concerns found within the discussion on "team space"?

7 The Fellowship of Christian Athletes in Kansas City, Missouri, sponsors weekly accountability groups at which these ten questions are answered weekly by each of the members:

1) Have you spent daily time in Scriptures and in prayer?
2) Have you had any flirtatious or lustful attitudes, tempting thoughts, or exposed yourself to any explicit materials that would not glorify God?

3) Have you been completely above reproach in your financial dealings?

4) Have you spent quality time with family and friends?

5) Have you done your 100 percent best in your job, school, etc.?

6) Have you told any half-truths or outright lies, putting yourself in a better light to those around you?

7) Have you shared the gospel with an unbeliever this week?

8) Have you taken care of your body through daily physical exercise, proper eating, and healthy sleeping habits?

9) Have you allowed any person or circumstances to rob you of your joy?

10) Have you lied to us on any of your answers today?

Consider:

- Do you have anyone holding you accountable in this way?
- What might be the result of you and your church leaders having this kind of accountability among yourselves?

Ship's Log

Use these activities with your church leadership to help them understand and own the principles of this chapter and how they relate to your church's ministry.

1 Examine the following questions with your church leaders:

- How many people in our church are mentally and spiritually prepared to shift to a navigational journey?
- For those who are unprepared, what combination of things can we do to help them make this move?
- What new opportunities for mission and ministry would ensue if we moved to an AquaChurch model?
- What are the top three features that drive your own personal leadership and that make contributions to the church? Are they areas of giftedness or willingness?
- How would an AquaChurch mentality change the way our church organizes its own life and ministry?
- How would it change the way you find new solutions to old issues?

2 George Cladis writes how authors Kevin and Jackie Freiberg, in their book *Nuts! Southwest Airlines' Crazy Recipe for Business and Personal Success*, attribute much of Southwest Airlines' success to their treatment of customers like "sacred creations of God." The authors write that Southwest employees "view customers as, to use Martin Buber's term, sacred thous who should be treated with dignity."[35]

When the customer is a sacred thou, you scour the gate area for the lost teddy bear; you park his car when he's running late for a flight; you get out your credit card and pay for her ticket when she's lost her purse; and, yes, you even take him off the streets and give him a job.[36]

Discuss with your leaders:

- Does it surprise you to read this kind of language in relation to a secular business enterprise? Why or why not?
- How does this statement compare to the way our church treats its guests? its members?

Develop a list of ways your church would need to change to treat people who attend this way. Choose two to begin on this week.

3 Businesses are now drafting "declarations of impossibility," which they then deploy teams to turn into possibilities. Form groups of three or four to draft some "declarations of impossibility" for your church. Remember, if you can do it without divine help, what is the "impossibility"?

After about ten minutes, have groups report, and list their declarations on a chalkboard or newsprint. Then, as a group, choose three to begin praying about and working toward their accomplishment.

4 If possible, take your leaders outside, and light a bonfire or a campfire. Be sure to include the items in the quote below. As you sit around the fire, discuss the following thesis with your leaders:

"Successful change is like a bonfire. It starts with a match, which may have to be repeatedly struck (the change maverick). The flame then moves to the newspaper (the creative minority); the paper may have to

be rekindled several times. If the newspaper burns, it ignites the kindling (the critical mass), which eventually sets fire to the logs (the committed majority), which then burn using their own resources for fuel and enabling everyone (the competent masses) to use and benefit from the resulting light and heat."[37]

- How does this metaphor compare to the way new things happen in our church?
- What issues do we want to start on fire?

Choose one issue at a time, and work through the following questions as they relate to each issue:

- How will our church benefit from the heat and light of this fire?
- How can we be the matches? How could we also be charcoal lighter fluid?
- What are going to be the toughest logs to get burning?
- Who should be the paper and the kindling?

5 In a book by Os Guinness titled *The Call*, he makes the statement that "there is not a single instance in the New Testament of God's special call to anyone into a paid occupation or into the role of a religious profession."[38] Conduct a brief study of Ephesians 4:11–13, and ask:

- Why do Christians have a difficult time understanding that the Bible makes no distinction between the clergy and laity, only between gifts and opportunities?
- List at least three reasons why doing away with this distinction will be important to doing ministry in the next millennium.

6 Engage your team once again into a discussion about your church's use of the Internet. Discuss:

- If it is true that Gutenberg people use the Internet as an "information medium" and Google people use it as a "social medium," then how will that affect the way our church organizes its Web page (p. 250)?
- Is it possible to integrate these two approaches in an interactive Web page that allows for both informational and social contact?
- Check out the Web site for World Gardens (www.worldgardens.com). The virtual cemetery will post (for a small fee) a Web page for a deceased loved one that can

include his or her photograph, a biographical sketch, a bulletin from the memorial service, and e-mail for condolences. Why can't our church provide the same service to its members for free?

- What other important communication services could our church provide for our people?

7 Encourage your team to study the "fact over feeling," "obedience over giftedness" concept related in this chapter. Study the story of Gideon in Judges 6—7 as it relates to this principle.

Ask:

- Did Gideon see himself as gifted in the area God wanted him to serve? Explain.
- What made it possible for God to use Gideon?
- How does this story parallel the stories of the call of Moses (Ex. 3:1—4:17) and Isaiah (Isa. 6:1–8)?
- How do these stories relate to the concept of "obedience over giftedness" expressed in this chapter?
- How would our congregation respond to the admonition "to do what is lacking rather than do what you want to do or what you're psychologically programmed to do" (p. 254).
- What are the benefits as well as the detriments of this approach for helping people understand their sense of calling?

MISSIONAL ART #10

USING THE GYROSCOPE: CREATIVITY

Imagination is more important than knowledge.
Knowledge is limited. Imagination circles the world.[1]

—Albert Einstein

One of my favorite stories out of David Buttrick's vast homiletic repertoire is of a poor, black woman in the bayous of Louisiana. With very little money and even less education, she raised over a dozen children who had suffered parental neglect, abuse, or rejection. After the kids had grown into healthy, productive adults, a newspaper "discovered" her deed and "featured" her in one of those stories the papers love to run at Christmas.

When asked why she had taken in all these kids, particularly when it was so hard, she looked the reporter in the eye, and a great smile spread across her face: "Because I saw a new world a-comin'."[2]

A new world is "a-comin'." Whether it will be the one envisioned by that saint of the bayous, or whether it will be more like that portrayed in *Blade Runner* and *I Am Legend* movies, depends on the type of leadership the church contributes to this emerging new world.

In this new world, changes occur overnight. Boris Yeltsin converted to Orthodox Christianity so quickly it took him months to learn how to cross himself properly. I fully expect to wake up to an entirely different world than the one I went to bed in. More changes now occur in one decade than occurred

in entire centuries in the past. In this new world, the key to leadership is not replication, but innovation; not implementation, but imagination; not "follow procedures," but "imagine and create."

A gyroscope is defined as a "rapidly spinning wheel set in a framework that permits it to tilt freely in any direction" so that the momentum causes it to retain its attitude however severe the framework is tilted. The human body has an internal gyroscope: the heart. This eight-ounce supernova and its electromagnetic field bring into balance the brain's left and right hemispheres, and are in a real sense the source of creativity itself.[3]

The uses of a gyroscope on ship are as multiple as the uses of the heart in the body: from internal guidance systems to antiroll equipment to automatic pilots to stress reduction of the structures. A gyroscope allows mariners to meet changing conditions with an unchanging orbit, a regularity of design, a gravity. Without a gyroscope and its true and unchanging axis, mariners are in a motion without direction, a motion without emotion or purpose.

A spirituality without imagination is a spirituality without inner guidance and without sea legs. Without the gyroscope of creativity, which enables us to rotate about any axis however challenging or threatening, we cannot maintain our balance in life. Without the gyroscope of creativity, we cannot keep on an even keel. The gyroscope of creativity keeps us ticking through life's storms and stresses. Our creativity gyroscope stabilizes us in turbulent times, reduces the rolling of our ship, and defines direction. Without creativity you die, even if you live.

> It would be an unsound fancy and self-contradictory to expect that things which have never yet been done can be done except by means which have never yet been tried.[4]
>
> —Francis Bacon

A World of Artist Servants

Creativity is the gyroscope for twenty-first-century mariners, and it is understandable why some would make this the missional art of the new world. The overlap of the emotions and the intellect is called the imagination, a gyroscope that spins toward transcendent realities in our lives.

It used to be that a ship on an expedition would have one "ship's artist" aboard who would be responsible for creative input and artistic interpretation of the voyage. These were positions that artists would actually apply for. Now every person is an artist.

Every person is a creative genius at something. Every artist is less a special kind of person than every person is a special kind of artist. Being creative is what makes us "in God's image." We are all creatologists. Every one of us must be an innovator, an inventor, a creative genius. These creatology titles are no longer reserved for a select few, but for every single one of us—whether we like it or not. The future does indeed belong to right-brained people.

Plato's dream of a nation of philosopher kings was countered by Jesus' dream of a world of artist servants.

> Try to remember God is a Great Artist. Artists like other artists. Expect the universe to support your dream. It will.[5]
>
> —Julia Cameron

Why is this missional art now more important than ever?

1. Fast and Loose World

A gyroscope is more essential than ever before in this fast and loose world where the only thing certain is uncertainty. Count on one thing: what works today won't work tomorrow. The most successful churches in the world today weren't even a glint in some preacher's eye twenty years ago. Some of the greatest fortunes being made today are from products and ideas that weren't even conceivable ten years ago.

Creativity is an absolute necessity in navigating a profoundly changing and chaotic world. What is the world's fastest growing industry? Biotechnology. More USAmericans now build computers than cars. More make semiconductors than construction machinery. More work in data processing than petroleum refining. One of the world's wealthiest individuals is not an industrialist, but a knowledge worker.

There is no way to "manage" such a world. Hypercontrolled churches, like all hypercontrolled institutions, are teetering and toppling all over the landscape. The need to prepare for ongoing adaptive change makes innovation and creativity the key missional arts in navigating the profoundly changing and chaordic[6] world of the twenty-first century. Creativity is the only intelligence without a shelf life.

One study of corporate success strategies concludes that McDonald's founder Ray Kroc's secret was not in perfecting the world's best hamburgers, the world's best corporate strategies, financial management, or motivated employees. Rather, Kroc's genius lay in fashioning a corporate culture that fostered creativity and focused everyone's creative skills on a single mission.[7]

> Create like a God. Command like a King. Work like a Slave.[8]
>
> —Sculptor Constantin Brancusi

2. Home-Cooked, Not Store-Bought

Where the industrial economy required efficiency, the information economy requires creativity. Today's workplace expects made-to-order innovation and built-to-market creative problem-solving. In fact, the Nomura Institute in Japan has identified creativity as the next stage in economic evolution following agriculture, industry, and information.

Why? The triumph of the individual and the triumph of the individual style. Google culture is a badge culture, but the badge is found in the personal freedom to be original, not in positional goods. People crave community, but at the same time they want the freedom to be an individual: iPhone, iPods,

iTunes, IM. The individual is now in charge. Nobody wants to be "same" or "average" or "normal," but "different" and "one of a kind," "handwritten" and "homegrown." People seek personal expression above everything, hence natural over artificial, boutiques over behemoths. Fashion statements are now less about status than they are individual identity. The emerging generations are not devoted to their jobs or the institutions that employ them. They are devoted to challenges in which they can express themselves and unleash their creativity.

If your church thinks "mass," whether "congregationally" or "on average," it will list in these tumultuous waters. There is vigilant resistance to litmus tests or anything else that grinds us into some required shape. Disciples now relish having a song that sounds very different than that sung by any other. In Jesus' question to his disciples "What are you doing more than others?" (Matt. 5:47), there is an alteration of the cultural question from "How can I be different?" to "How can I be different in a way that makes a difference for God?" Or better yet, "How can I be different in a way that makes this world a different place and that connects it with God?" Or best of all, "How can I be a disciple of Christ, which in itself makes me different?"

> Damn your principles; stick to your party.[9]
>
> —Founder of modern conservatism Benjamin Disraeli

No postmodern disciple feels, or acts, as any normative standard "oughts" them to feel or act. All definitions are adversaries. The test for the church is this: Can the church be creative and free enough to let people be who they are, or more precisely, help people become who God wants them to be? Can the church let the vigor and uniqueness of its members' personalities shine through? Will the church view its high-souled members through the lens of weirdness or wickedness?

An unexplored mystery of the Incarnation is Jesus as an artist who expresses himself creatively and sacrificially at the same time. Biblical scholar Elizabeth Barnes shows how Jesus lived life "vigorously, richly, committedly, unreservedly, stumbling and rising, in other words, sacrificially. Only so does one travel the road modeled by Jesus the Christ."[10] Jesus both expressed himself fully and denied himself utterly. Self-expression and self-sacrifice belong together, not apart. "By living the full genius of who he is sacrificially," Barnes concludes, "Jesus expresses and glorifies God."[11]

3. Renaissance Civilization

Throughout history, "renaissance period" was but another name for the mind "jumping the rails" in search of new insights into living and dying, working and worshipping. For example, massive creativity was unleashed in the aftermath of the Reformation as the Bible became "the people's book."

Similar creativity is being unleashed now by the Internet and its opening of various "disciplines" to the air of cross-fertilization and cross-communication. Members of cyberchurch communities are asking new questions like What have decades of hymn-singing, creed-reciting, church-building, altar-calling really gotten us? Are there cyberspace, SecondLife ways of being the "body of Christ"?

People get "unstuck" in their spiritual lives when they move from "reproductive" thinking to "productive" thinking. In reproductive thinking, we solve problems by reproducing how we solved them in the past. In productive thinking, we look at the problem differently, rethink the ways of seeing it, and invent new ways of thinking and acting. Productive thinking is the trademark of artists.

In productive thinking, a "celebrant" becomes an artist and worship becomes an art form. Robert Shaw, the greatest choral conductor of the previous century (the era known as the twentieth century actually dates from 1914 to 1989), once suggested at his Nashville, Tennessee, workshop that just as the church saved the arts in the medieval world, it may be the arts that save the church in the new world dawning. Whether Shaw had in mind the high, folk, or pop arts is less relevant than that worship is being transformed and "saved" by the celebration arts.

4. Altered Religious Sensibilities

"It's just your imagination!"

With these words we were chided as children into dismissing our imaginative powers. With these words we learned not to take our imagination seriously. Religion was heavily rational. Print culture was heavily cerebral and principle-oriented. Protestantism especially became a rational movement that intellectualized life and theology.

The Enlightenment forced upon Christianity a new epistemology: the rationalization and abstraction of belief, which exorcised the mystic from each of us. Imagination was a casualty of modernity's drive for efficiency, logic, and control. In fact, the most prominent atheist in the world today, Oxford biologist and Britain's "top intellectual" Richard Dawkins, uses the lack of imagination against Christians in particular, and religion in general. "Religions are *not* imaginative, not poetic, not soulful. On the contrary, they are parochial, small-minded, niggardly with the human imagination, precisely where science is generous."[12] Where the emotional and imaginal found expression in the modern period was in music and literature, not religion.

The true religious vision is less intellectual than imaginal. "Both the affective and the imaginative, strongly stimulated by audiovisual images, are becoming the central part of human and religious functioning."[13] Google-world Christians have clipped the wings of reason and are riding the winds of a prodigal imagination and supernaturalism. Imagination has become one of the church's most valuable commodities. Successful ministry in the future requires imagination.

Need more proof that the base of spiritual life is imaginational more than rational? Take the angels phenomenon. *Time* magazine did a feature on the "grass-roots revolution of the spirit" titled "Angels Among Us" in which it asserted that 69 percent believe in the existence of angels and 46 percent believe they have their own guardian angels. Harvard Divinity School even periodically offers a course on angels.[14]

Why is this happening? From the University of South Africa, David Bosch observed just before he died that the "reason" championed by the

Enlightenment "has been found to be an inadequate cornerstone on which to build one's life."[15] Even if we are not at *The End of Physics*, as one scholar argues, David Lindley admits that physics is not "able to explain everything in the universe" and that physics is reaching "the end of all the things it has the power to explain."[16] Andrew Harvey decries the way the "concentration camp of reason" has suppressed our powers of intuition, wisdom, and unity.[17] Even atheists are now claiming to have a spirituality.

An unimagining faith is as undesirable as an unreasoning faith. Without imagination, all hearts are closed, all desires unknown.

The point is not to abandon rationality, but to expand rationality to embrace imagination and experience. Lutheran seminary professor Donald H. Juel argues just such a position for reading the Bible. He places the "indispensability of imagination" at the heart of biblical interpretation, which opens up biblical "scholarship" to everyone just as the Bible itself was first opened up to everyone with the Protestant Reformation.

> For several decades, biblical studies has been dominated by source-critical approaches that give the appearance of being scientific and careful. I continue to be impressed, however, by their limited usefulness and their inability to persuade. And upon further reflection, it strikes me as a definite advantage that in a field where method becomes so sophisticated and esoteric as to lie beyond the ability of any but the professional, it is still possible to lay bare the truth of a text with tools that are quite within reach of any who can read. The results of such work may turn out to be more interesting, more significant, and more convincing.[18]

5. Double-Ring Phenomenon

What is the essence of creativity? What releases the powers of the imagination? Mixed metaphors.

According to one study of fifty-eight geniuses, including Einstein, Picasso, and Mozart, "all [their] breakthroughs occurred when 'two or more opposites were conceived simultaneously, existing side by side—as equally valid, operative and true.' The research report continues: 'In an apparent defiance of logic or physical possibility, the creative person consciously [embraced] antithetical elements and developed these into integrated entities and creations.'"[19]

The post-critical method is built on a premise laid out by Niels Bohr, the father of quantum mechanics. On an atomic level, he argues, "two mutually exclusive ideas can both be right." I shall never forget reading two scientific announcements during the same week. Scientists in Britain announced that they had invented a fabric that could take the smell of body odor out of clothes. No more smelly socks. Another group of researchers in France announced that they had created a new highly sexual perfume made from the scent of body odor found in socks. With the double-ring sounding everywhere—just listen to the down-and-outs and the up-and-ins simultaneously—the potential for creativity has never been higher.

Creativity expert Bryan Mattimore's research reveals that the essence of genius and the heart of imagination itself is the taking of diverse characteristics already present in nature and combining them in new and fresh ways.

Leonardo da Vinci's cardinal rule of creativity? Combine opposites, mix and match difference. When da Vinci was serving as an apprentice, his father, Ser Piero, presented him with a shield and a challenge: Paint something on the shield. Son Leonardo decided to paint for his father something that would, as he put it, "terrify the enemy." He collected in his room the makings of his model: "lizards, newts, crickets, serpents, butterflies, grasshoppers, bats, and other strange animals." Out of the mix of these creatures he fashioned a monster, horrible and horrifying, which released a poisonous brimstone breath and ignited the air into flame.

When his father came to pick up the shield, he "received a great shock" and almost fell over backward with fright. To Ser Piero, his son's creation appeared "nothing short of a miracle."[20]

The acceptance of paradox
as a feature of our life
is the first step toward living with it
and managing it.[21]
—Charles Handy

Barriers to Creativity

The church faces serious barriers to creativity that must be pulled down.

Barrier 1: Distrust

The church has become a culture of distrust, a culture where people don't trust one another, especially not the "Whipperuppers."

"Whipperuppers" is a phrase used by novelist Elizabeth Smart to describe those igniters in life that would jump-start creativity and inspire the imagination.[22] Whipperuppers are "different." They don't do normal. A little odd, a little off, whipperuppers look, dress, act, talk somewhat strangely. They display a certain back-of-the-class restlessness that can be rather excessive, even oppressive.

Since all creative acts are by definition off-center (eccentric), "a departure from the established norm,"[23] a test of creativity is this: How well does your church tolerate and treat the whipperuppers? According to one study, there are at least fifteen characteristics that apply to eccentrics, in descending order of importance. How does your church fare at integrating and empowering the oddity and quiddity of those who are (1) nonconforming; (2) inventive; (3) curious; (4) idealistic—want to make the world a better place; (5) happily riding more than one hobbyhorse; (6) aware from childhood that they are different; (7) intelligent; (8) opinionated and outspoken; (9) noncompetitive; (10) unusual in eating habits and living arrangements; (11) unconcerned about the opinions of others; (12) mischievous sense of humor; (13) single; (14) often the eldest or only child; (15) bad spellers?[24]

Without whipperuppers there can't be creativity. "Companion" is a nautical name for a permanent ladder on a boat. "Companionway squatter" is someone who insists on sitting on the steps and getting in everyone's way. The church is more sensitive to and understanding of companionway squatters than whipperuppers. Alas, the church even tolerates fools more gladly than it does whipperuppers.

Barrier 2: Unfriendly System

The church lacks mechanisms for good information sharing, especially in bloated bureaucracies where to ask lots of "why" questions or not to take things for granted is an act of apostasy.

The ultimate corporate hierarchy, according to the world's reigning strategy guru, Gary Hamel, is not a hierarchy of experience or entitlements or titles. It is a "hierarchy of imagination." And that means, in his words, "giving a disproportionate share of voice to the people who up until now have been disenfranchised from the strategy-making process."[25]

If there is to be a reimagination of the church, it will be because of the energetic feedback loops and double feedback loops of an open system that nurtures creativity-friendly environments. The church needs to employ its immense imaginal resources in the service of spiritual enrichment and betterment.

Barrier 3: Imitative Environment

The church must rebuild an impoverished and sometimes nonexistent innovation infrastructure. Novelist Saul Bellow once complained that, "In the USA today the facts appear to have it all over the imagination."[26] This is even more true in the church, where the watchword has not been innovation, but replication. A lot of religious leaders are very sure of their ground, partly because they always tread squarely in the footsteps of those who have gone before.

Instead of rewarding those who display re-creative audacity, we tend to punish the "creative" types. Those who create their own paths are used as examples to show others the dangers of "breaking rank."

In 1500 Erasmus was denounced as a dangerous innovator because he suggested children be allowed to say something at meals "when an emergency arises."[27]

Ministry by imitation, replication, and reproduction gets applauded. Ministry by imagination, innovation, and production gets made a guillotining matter. It's time the church ceased prowling around for institutional and programmatic fixes and used its imagination instead. Creativity is the church's ultimate subversive weapon.

If we're looking at Jesus, our motto should be "Go Thou and Do … Likewise." If it's anyone else, our motto should be "Go Thou and Do … Otherwise." Go to Saddleback Valley Community Church, Lake Forest, California (www.saddleback.com). Study Rick Warren and Company. But when you return home, refrain from a lemming-like rush toward replication, and move toward innovation instead. Attend a Catalyst Conference (www.catalystconference.com), Q Gathering (www.fermiproject.com/q), or one of Ginghamsburg Church's "Change the World Conferences (ginghamsburg.org/changetheworld),"[28] but don't go home and replicate what the speakers are doing. Instead, let that visit and its baring of "best practices" inspire you to new births, new heights, and new adventures. In the past, we put together "to do" lists. Perhaps it's now time to come up with "to create" lists.

Barrier 4: Image-Averse Communities

Google culture displays a promiscuous, if not incontinent, love of metaphors. Both in spite of and because of the fact that it is a media-rich culture with a lightning rush of images and metaphors, many of our religious communities find visual delights highly suspect and murky. In fact, some see icons as little more than "visual drugs" for an image-crazed culture.

Imagination gives us access to worlds of vision and thought otherwise denied us. But such a statement begs the larger question: What is imagination?

Philosopher Mary Warnock defines imagination as the power to produce images in the absence of the objects themselves imagined.[29] Imagination is nothing more than the ability to make images.

Religion is a work of "imaginative rationality"[30] where what images you have matter a great deal. In fact, blind people like Victorian Scottish minister George Matheson ("O Love That Will Not Let Me Go" and "Make Me a Captive, Lord") may be able to "imagine" better than the rest of us. The truth is that we need more insights that are the product not just of critical observation but of "imaginative rationality." An artist absorbs material through images and then reproduces it in living form. Art is nothing more, nor less, than the production of images: in painting, in film, in poetry, in sound.

The modern era equated images with debaucheries of the mind. Loopiness was the same as looniness. Metaphor was seen as a primitive and faulty method of communicating truth. Aesthetic modes of reasoning were suspect. The modern world represented truth through propositions. It slotted thought into fixed categories. It seriously believed that God thinks in propositions, in principles, in laws, and that theology was the "thinking of God's thoughts after him." The notion that God could think in models, in stories, in narratives caused modernity to hold its nose.

Yet Cambridge physicist Stephen Hawking himself confesses that when he lost his ability to speak because of Lou Gehrig's Disease, his thinking became less linear, consecutive, and sequential and more loopy, spatial, and concurrent. He began to "see" more "spatially" in his "mind's eye," and once he made this shift he imagined multidimensional models of the universe he never grasped before. Benoit Mandelbrot, who coined the term "fractals" in the 1970s and developed the whole area of fractal geometry, argues that the scientific abhorrence of images stopped with the discovery of the double helix shape of DNA. The only way you can conceive of DNA is to think of this shape, which means that "the secret of life is something you can look at."[31]

Images are not the last word. They require interpretation and adjustment. But until at last the image or metaphor strikes like lightning, people's "imaginations" will not be moved.

Critical Creativity

How embarrassing that the institution that worships the Creator is so often bankrupt of creativity. Where ought the world's most creative spaces be if not in the church? Yet where is one less likely to find daring creativity and wildfire imagination? Are the worlds of economics, entertainment, and the arts the only places where creativity can "pay off" and the creative spirit be celebrated? Why did universities offer degrees in creativity training before seminaries?[32] Why must the church always flock to the St. Peters (the departed sage Peter Drucker, Peter Senge, Laurence Peters, Tom Peters) of Wall Street and Wal-Mart?

The church has an imagination deficit. Such a drift and atrophy of spiritual imagination exists that we are now in a crisis—simultaneously—of spiritual creativity and reproduction.[33] It's hard to imagine two worse crises.

The word *creative* was initially used exclusively in reference to the divine creation of the world. "Creation ... and creature have the same root stem. This context remained normative until at least the [sixteenth century]," when the transformation of thought we now describe as Renaissance humanism[34] expanded the word to include and indicate present or future making—that is to say, the making of, by, and for humans.

"Creativity" as a missional art of spiritual navigation is critical creativity: It aims not at novelty, but at innovation that specifically continues the divine work of creation. Not everything "new" is creative. To be truly creative, the leader cruises in channels where the mysterious undercurrents of divine creation continue their churning.

Understood this way, we really do no creating. All is discovery. What leaders do in "creating" is "discover" what God is already up to. As philosopher Walter Benjamin put it, "creative work is the prayer of the soul."

Publishers/creatologists Thom and Joani Schultz put it this way: "Creativity is not the goal. Creative activities can (and should) be used, but each should add to students' understanding and application of biblical truths. If your curriculum is creative but seems to focus merely on facts, it's time to reread the Parable of the Sower."[35]

Creativity is not directed to our own glory but to the glory of God.

Yada, Yada, Yada

"Now this is eternal life," reads John 17:3, "that they may know you, the only true God, and Jesus Christ, whom you have sent." What is the first reason for our existence, learns every good Roman Catholic, Lutheran, and Reformed child? The first reason for my existence is "to know God."

So what does it mean "to know" in the biblical sense of knowing?

The Hebrew word for "to know" is *yada. Yada* is one of those Hebrew words many people have heard of, and not just because of *Seinfeld*. The Hebrew term for sexual relations is *yada*—"to know," demonstrating the intimacy of knowledge in the Hebrew mind. "And Adam knew Eve his wife; and she conceived" (Gen. 4:1 KJV).

When you know something in the biblical sense, you conceive.[36]

Adam knew Eve, and they conceived … and something was born. When you know someone or something, when you really know them in the biblical sense of knowing, you conceive … you give birth … you create … you bring forth art. In other words, knowing is ultimately an aesthetic of creativity.

When God knew God, God conceived … and the universe was born. When one hydrogen atom knew another hydrogen atom, they conceived … and a Big Bang was born. But the Big Bang does not just happen once. The Big Bang happens at every birth, as one cell from the father gets to know one cell from the mother, and an explosion of gametes is born that gushes forth a galaxy of nuclear, cytoplasmic, and membranous material known as a human being.

When God knew the universe, the universe conceived … and Christ was born. When Christ knew the universe, Christ conceived … and the church was born. When you know Christ, "I know that my Redeemer lives" (Job 19:25), you conceive … and a new life in the Spirit is born. When you know your knowing, when you know that you know, you conceive … and culture is born.

When people know other people, they conceive … and friendships, and marriages, and children are born. When an artist knows a thought, a thing is born—a thing of beauty known as a poem, a play, a party, a musical piece, a dance—and sometimes the birth process is a difficult one.

Even when you know yourself, you conceive … and what is born is not self-knowledge, or narcissistic introspection, or the self's knowledge of its own peculiar needs and interests,[37] but wisdom about fulfillment of your creative, re-creative, and procreative purpose for living. Again, knowledge is not a technological concept. Knowing is the central aesthetic activity of creation.

We are conceivers, all! Here is the *imago dei* in us: knowing God we conceive, knowing God we ourselves are birthers of the image of God. All existence is a participation in the existence of the Creator. The more knowledge we bear, the more knowing we do, the more we bear our Creator's image, the more we do our Creator's will.

Or let me tease you a bit by translating this into the dictionary of economics. One of the problems in our economic system today is that we have listened to Adam Smith, who got so much right except this one mistake: He based an economic system on human self-interest as the driving, motivating force behind human endeavor. That is why the "free" market is advantageous for the rich, the clever, the gifted, the inventive, the educated. But it is disadvantageous to the poor and uneducated, the less favored and more helpless. The "free" market frees the rich but exploits the poor.

What if we were to base an economic system on conceiving—not on self-interest—as the driving, motivating force underlying human action? What if conception rather than consumption were to govern the marketplace? What if capitalism were to be so conceived that the free play that is now allowed to selfishness in economic pursuits were allowed to conceiving? What if the U.S. tax code were as biased toward conception as it is now toward consumption?

We would become a society of conceivers rather than consumers. In other words, we would behave artistically. We would become artists. We would all

think of ourselves as artists. Everything would be practiced as art—even politics, even ministry.

The Great Creator is still creating. Creation is the only true never-ending story. In fact, the Bible teaches that the earth, once created, itself becomes creator: "Let the earth bring forth." Every moment is an act of creation.

How does creativity take place? Through conception. Through "knowledge" that turns to acknowledgment. For true knowledge leads to acknowledgment. When knowledge knows knowledge, wisdom is conceived.

To continue to compose the Unfinished Song of Creation, we need to see ourselves as conceivers of creation. When you know anything biblically, you conceive ... and something is born. That "something" is a participation in God's own creativity.

> Deep assignments run through all our lives;
> there are no coincidences.[38]
> —J. G. Ballard

The art world is the whole world. The true test of your mastery of missional art #10 is this: What are you conceiving right now that is transforming your world? What artwork is being born in you and through you right now that is available for others? In the words that Steven Jobs, Apple's founder, scrawled on an easel in January 1983 when Apple was behind the eight ball: REAL ARTISTS SHIP.[39]

AQUACHURCH #10
BRIDGEWAY COMMUNITY CHURCH

Columbia, Maryland

www.bridgewayonline.org

The term *mosaic* best describes the group at Bridgeway Community Church, a multicultural congregation in Columbia, Maryland. As an AquaChurch, Bridgeway embodies creativity by showing how the many colors come together to form God's beautiful mosaic of creation. They have dedicated themselves to removing unnecessary barriers to trusting Christ and building bridges of care and compassion in the communication of God's love. Bridgeway fosters creativity through this multiplicity by:

- celebrating the diversity of colors, classes, and cultures that invites all to come and worship together;
- making the chief command they obey "love God and love people" and their mission "to build into one another as we build bridges to our community";
- having in their vision the goal of being a multicultural army of devoted followers of Christ;
- utilizing the acronymn BRIDGES to describe their values: Building into one another; Reconciliation; Instruction; Dynamic worship; Growth; Evangelism; Service/Stewardship.

CAPTAIN'S LOGBOOK
PERSONAL LOG

Use these ideas to stimulate your thinking about how the principles of this chapter could affect your ministry. Consider sharing these ideas with other church leaders.

1 Reflect for a moment on your early years. Try to remember who first encouraged you to dream, to think beyond the possible. Was it a parent, relative, teacher, friend, or perhaps a person whose lack of dreams caused you to hunger for more? Do you still dream as much as you used to dream? If not, why not? What happened that made you trade in your view of tomorrow for a warmed-over version of yesterday?

2 Write "God" on a sheet of paper. Now put the pen in the other hand, and write "God." How does it feel to try something new? Jot down your feelings, still writing with your "wrong" hand. Ask yourself:

- How are those feelings like the way people feel when they're asked to change old habits and try new things?
- Where in my life am I now "changing hands"?
- Where is my church "changing hands"?
- What can I do to help people overcome their discomfort?

3 If imagination is "the overlap of the emotions and the intellect" (p. 271), how well are you doing with the balance of those components in your personal and professional life? Take a sheet of paper, and create two columns. In one column list the people in your life who add to your ability to be creative. In the other column, list those who subtract from your ability to be creative.

Think:

- How often are you with these two kinds of people?
- How could you start spending more time with those who add to your creativity than those who subtract?

4 If religion is a work of "imaginative rationality" in which the images we have matter in life-changing ways, how are you doing with your imaginative rationality (p. 281)? As you prepare to teach, are the insights simply a product of critical observation or imaginative rationality? Spend a few minutes picturing yourself more as an artist who "absorbs material through images and then reproduces it in living form" rather than simply a truth-teller who depends on rationality and reasoning. Draw something that represents who you would like to see yourself become.

5 Pull out your last two messages, and analyze them.

- Were they simply products of critical observation or of imaginative rationality?
- Did you move beyond the obvious to the new or different?
- Did you use your "sanctified imagination" to go beyond what the text said to what it said to you?
- Did you use your creative writing skills to tell a story in a warm and winsome way?
- What can you do in your preparation process to help you add more creativity?

6 The University of Chicago's Mihaly Csikszentmihalyi gives the following suggestions for enhancing personal creativity. Think about how you might use these ideas to add creativity to your life and your ministry.

- Try to be surprised by something every day.
- Try to surprise at least one person every day.
- Write down each day what surprised you and how you surprised others.
- When something strikes a spark of interest, follow it.
- Recognize that if you do anything well it becomes enjoyable.
- To keep enjoying something, increase its complexity.
- Make time for reflection and relaxation.
- Find out what you like and what you hate about life.
- Start doing more of what you love and less of what you hate.
- Find a way to express what moves you.
- Look at problems from as many viewpoints as possible.
- Produce as many ideas as possible.
- Have as many different ideas as possible.
- Try to produce unlikely ideas.[40]

Ship's Log

Use these activities with your church leadership to help them understand and own the principles of this chapter and how they relate to your church's ministry.

1 Summarize for your leaders the famous "Grand Inquisitor" episode of *The Brothers Karamazov*.[41] Discuss:

- Do you agree with Dostoevski that if Jesus were to return to earth today, he would be much too radical, strange, and eccentric for the church he founded? Explain.
- How should this story affect the way we look at our ministry today?

2 Discuss these "Ten Tips Toward Creativity in the Workplace" by Robert J. Sternberg, IBM professor of psychology and education at Yale University, and Todd I. Lubart, visiting professor at Ecole Superieure de Commerce de Paris:

- Reward creativity in those who display it.
- Take sensible risks.
- Overcome obstacles; don't let them overcome you.
- Think for the long term.
- Keep growing.
- Beware of the dangers of knowing both too little and too much.
- Tolerate ambiguity.
- Reconceptualize unsolvable or intractable problems.
- Find what you love to do.
- Know when to shape environments and when to leave them.[42]

Ask:

- Which of these do we do a good job at? Explain.
- Which of these do we not do so well at? Explain.
- Which of these do we want to work on to encourage creativity within our church's ministry?

3 Consider together: Is your church's problem not so much a lack of money as a lack of imagination? "It costs a lot of money to build bad products," Norman Augustine, CEO, Martin Marietta Corp., once said.

Those who are trying to move us from a benefit-based welfare system to an asset-based model have done some refiguring of what kind of assets people could build up if they had gotten the money directly as an asset rather than as a benefit:

a) Walter Williams, of George Mason University, pointed out that the money spent in the United States on poverty programs since the 1960s could have bought the entire assets of the five hundred largest companies in America "plus virtually all the U.S. farm land. And what did it do? The problems still remain and they are even worse."[43]

b) Economist Thomas Sowell has figured out that if the entire social welfare budget of the government were simply given to the poor instead of being administered by government, that average "poor" family would have some $70,000 per year.

- What lack-of-imagination examples do you see in our church?
- What creative examples do you see in our church?
- How can we avoid the ruts of lack-of-imagination thinking?

4 List fifteen creative ways you can de-average your church's ministry. Then form groups of about three, and let each group choose one of the creative ideas to develop. Be sure no idea is taken by more than one group. Have each group brainstorm how that idea might take shape if resources were not a problem. Encourage them to be wildly creative—no holds barred! Then have them come up with a creative way to present their developed idea to the rest of the group. They might use a skit, a mural, a song, or anything else that requires creative thinking.

You might want to make this a project that takes a couple of sessions. Once the ideas have been presented, evaluate each one with your whole group, and determine which ones to pursue further. Be sure you don't limit God's creativity in helping these ideas become reality.

5 Have your leadership team research the Creative Education Foundation in Buffalo, New York (www.creativeeducationfoundation.org), or the Center for Research in Applied Creativity in Ontario (www.basadur.com/company/center.htm). Have leaders report on the following questions:

- What can we learn about innovative thinking from their findings?
- What innovative thoughts for our church came to you while doing this research?

6 Ask your leadership team to identify the "new world a-comin'" people in your church (p. 269). Discuss:

- What is it about these people that makes them visionaries or what Elizabeth Smart calls "whipperuppers" (p. 278)?
- Are they respected and revered in our church or ignored and ridiculed? Explain.
- How can we support and encourage the creativity that comes from these people?

7 Have your leaders analyze the following statement: "Both the affective and the imaginative, strongly stimulated by audiovisual images, are becoming the central part of human and religious functioning" (p. 275).

- Do you believe this statement? Why or why not?
- What can we do to help our church better address the "less intellectual" and more "imaginal" aspect of this postmodern world?
- How can we be sure that our use of the imagination does not impinge or infringe on—or stray from—biblical truth?

MISSIONAL ART #11

LEARNING FROM THE SHIP'S LOG AND LIBRARY: INTELLECTUAL CAPITAL

'Tis of great use to the Sailor
to know the length of his Line,
though he cannot with it fathom
all the depths of the Ocean.
'Tis well he knows, that it is long enough
to reach the bottom at such Places as are necessary
to direct his Voyage,
and caution him against
running upon Shoals, that may ruine him.
Our Business here is not to know
all things, but those which concern
our Conduct. If we can find out those
Measures, whereby a rational
Creature, put in that State,
which Man is in, in this World, may,
and ought to govern
his Opinions and Actions
depending thereon,
we need not be troubled,
that some other things scape
our Knowledge.[1]

—John Locke

An old story portrays three people of the cloth fishing on a small lake—a Protestant minister, a Catholic priest, and a Jewish rabbi. The priest watches in astonishment as his companions, one after the other, climb out of the row-boat and walk across the water to the concession stand. Assuring himself that his faith is as great as theirs, he steps from the boat and promptly sinks. The minister turns to the rabbi and says, "Do you suppose we should have shown him where the rocks are?"[2]

Leaders need to know where the rocks are before venturing into the water. That's why "change" is a loaded word. Rocks can be either stepping stones or stumbling blocks. You can either walk on them or run aground on them. When it comes to information, more can mean less.

A Learning Culture

What makes the difference is a learning culture of knowledge management where data (undigested facts) can become information (facts organized by outside sources but not yet integrated into your thinking), which then can become knowledge (internalized information), which can be turned into wisdom (integrated knowledge).[3] In the corporate world, CKOs (or chief knowledge officers) specialize in turning information into knowledge if not wisdom.

A ship is itself a learning culture, and those ships that learn faster sail faster and farther than those that learn slowly. Every ship has onboard a log and library. The log chronicles the journey, its tests and tales of an untheorized nature. The library intensifies the ship's intelligence-gathering capabilities. If leaders are to navigate through ever more complex environments and seas of information, they will need to keep better logs and collect better libraries.

Why did Nehemiah suddenly mourn, weep, fast, and pray? Why did he decide to go to the king with a request that could have gotten him killed? Why did he buck everything and everybody, even stirring up the anger of his own people? Why did he take on the impossible, dare disgrace, and risk ridicule and persecution?

What absolutely changed his everything was the wisdomization of his ministry. Nehemiah was given data that turned to information about the survivors of the devastated city of Jerusalem. Nehemiah then internalized this information about the fallen gates, the falling-down walls, and the flouting of Yahweh into knowledge. Once Nehemiah's leadership was knowledgized, he was able to integrate the reality of the situation his people were facing so that his ministry was transformed from internalized knowledge ("Let us start rebuilding" [Neh. 2:18]) to integrated wisdom ("I am carrying on a great project and cannot go down. Why should the work stop while I leave it and go down to you?" [Neh. 6:3]). Nehemiah's wisdomized ministry refused to be distracted or detoured from the work of rebuilding the walls of Jerusalem.

Missional art #11 is intellectual capital and the cultivation of a learning culture. Twenty-first-century leaders are willy-nilly intellectual capitalists. In fact, knowledge is the capital commodity of twenty-first-century culture. The source of wealth today is not material, it is informational. The pursuit of wealth and influence today is the pursuit of information, and the application of information to the world in which we live. Information is power. Leadership is either well informed or ill equipped and nonexistent.

> I keep six honest serving men;
> (They taught me all I knew)
> Their names are What and Why and When
> And How and Where and Who.[4]
>
> —Rudyard Kipling

More than a thousand senior corporate managers from across America were asked this question: "Which would you rather have: a 25 percent larger line of credit at your commercial bank, or 25 percent more accurate information on what your customers are doing?"

Ninety-nine percent took information over money.

Or to put it in economic terms, "the money is in the blades, not the razor."[5] The cultural capital of knowledge has created new wealth and is at the heart of wealth creation. It has also created new classes that are dominating the scene. In a knowledge economy, it is the knowledge transactions, knowledge assets, knowledge management, and knowledge products that take center stage and create value.

It is imperative to understand the relationship between knowledge and power.[6] In fact, intellectual capital is the pivotal point at which politics and culture and science and economics converge to coalesce into that dirty word, "power."

But "power" need not be "dirty." Power in a Google world is best defined as access to resources, information and support, and the ability to rally cooperation.[7] The differences between power-driven knowledge and spirit-driven knowledge diminish the more power is decentralized, driven downward to the people and upward to God.

Like technology itself, information (even more so knowledge, and most so wisdom) are not somethings that accumulate willy-nilly. They are products that must be created. They are expensive. They are risky. They depend on the willingness of a learning culture to invest in research and development.

Jesus was begotten, not made. Disciples of Jesus are made, not begotten.

Wisdomization of Leadership

Leadership is soul work, but it is also wisdom work. Of all the knowledge occupations out there, leadership is the most knowledge-intensive vocation. Aside from what you carry in your heart, what you carry between your ears is your most valuable tool of the trade.

The value of knowledge capital is hard to overestimate. In fact, the very word *disciple* means "learner." In Greek, *mathetes* (which we translate as disciple) comes from *mathano*, which literally means "student" or "learner." Only those churches will survive and prosper that empower all their members with the intelligence and decision support that can exercise, organize, and mobilize brainpower into missional muscle.

But "thought leaders" will not navigate these waters properly—indeed we

will drift about with flotsam on this postmodern tidal wave—unless we first do some sustained biblical and theological thinking about information itself. Spiritual navigators are not called to be easy riders of the world's information seaways. But we have to be on them—and with more than information or knowledge when we're riding on them. One good thing: We don't always have to leave our homes to get on them. Ten-year-old kids with children's computers and laptops are discovering corporate America's secrets and dabbling in international espionage without ever leaving their bedrooms.

Google culture is information rich but wisdom poor. Spiritual leaders must know how to wisdomize their ministries and missions. The church must become one of culture's chief "wisdom refineries" for the conversion of gross data into high-grade wisdom. Leadership that is "rendered" without wisdom—the verb is sadly appropriate—can do more harm than good. If the essence of education is that it is "what's left after all else is forgotten," then wisdom—not knowledge—must be a leader's final word. Friends of knowledge may or may not be friends of the human race or of planet Earth.

Any trawling of human history in the twentieth century turns this up immediately. Never have humans been smarter, and never have humans been dumber or meaner. On the final page of Clive Ponting's obituary for the twentieth century, he writes,

> The scale of the destruction of human life in the twentieth century was unprecedented. Hundreds of millions starved to death because of the permanent maldistribution of the available food in the world. In addition, about 100 million died in the great famines of the century. This compares with the perhaps 10 million who died in natural disasters and the 25 million killed by motor vehicles. War killed another 150 million, government repression about 100 million. The total of 14 million who died in the century's genocides was, on this scale, comparatively small, but they were the victims of the greatest acts of deliberate murder.[8]

The church must become a learning culture that it may become a wisdomizing force in twenty-first-century culture. The biggest issue of the wisdomization of leadership, however, is helping others to see and hear, ask and think the right questions. The business of wisdom is determining the real from the bogus problems and the smart from the irrelevant questions. In the same way the battle of New Orleans was fought and won after the war was over, in the same way the French military strategized during World War II, many of our churches are solving problems that no longer exist or fighting battles after the war is long over. In the same way the Yugoslavs fought in the 1990s over issues key to the eleventh century, our churches are fixated on problems that belong to worlds that are no more, while the problems of the coming world are largely unknown and unaddressed. Elephantine theological forces are locked in battle over social and intellectual mice, and the church—unlike its founder—is proud of its innocence of the ways of the world.

And yet wisdom also is knowing that the more things change, the more some things stay the same. Wisdom warns us that we have seen it all before. Shakespeare's *Titus Andronicus* (1593) boasts one human sacrifice, nine murders, four executions, two rapes, four amputations, one act of treason, and one birth out of wedlock. The same sicknesses abound in cyberspace. But so too in print culture. In times of rapid transition, wisdom keeps us from overreacting.[9] Wisdomized leaders know when a wider isn't necessarily a wiser use of technology. Too much novelty can be disorienting to the soul and distracting to the church's mission.

Who shut up the sea behind doors,
when it burst forth from the womb,
when I [God] made the clouds its garment
and wrapped it in thick darkness,
when I fixed limits for it
and set its doors and bars in place,
when I said, "This far you may come and no farther;
here is where your proud waves halt"?
—Job 38:8–11

The Plimsoll Point

God gave spiritual navigators a plumb line. There are design limits to creativity. The line on the ship is called the Plimsoll line.

Sea vessel captains take pains to watch a hull marking called the Plimsoll line. More and more things can be added to the boat as long as the water level remains below the Plimsoll line. When that level is reached, the boat has taken on too much cargo and is in danger of sinking. No matter how much rearrangement takes place on board ship, the problem is the carrying capacity itself, which has been breached. Either one respects the Plimsoll line, or one is sunk. Literally.[10] To go over the Plimsoll Point is to go beyond the point of no return. In a storm, to save the ship that went beyond the Plimsoll line, sailors often cast cargo overboard. Hence Jonah.

God said to Adam and Eve: There's the Plimsoll Point. You can put lots of things on this spaceship Earth and do lots of things, such as "tend the garden," "be fruitful and multiply," "walk with me in the dew of the garden," and on and on. But amid a garden full of things you can put onboard ("You are free to eat from any tree in the garden" [Gen. 2:16]), there is one big Plimsoll Point. See that tree over there—the tree of the knowledge of good and evil? Leave that one alone. That's the Plimsoll Line.

Spiritual leaders will need to be wisdomized to get at least one jump ahead of the field—and sometimes two—to show to this culture its Plimsoll Points.

- It's OK—bring onboard genetic engineering to enhance agriculture and ignite a second Green Revolution.
- It's OK—load up biotechnology that can create bug-resistant potatoes, apples, pears, and other fruits.[11]
- It's OK—transgenic beets, even parrots that can withstand cold North American temperatures.[12]
- It's even OK—transgenic pets that combine the beauty of a kuvasz with the intelligence of a poodle.

- It's OK—take one organism's DNA and insert it into another like "beetatoes" (a beet and a potato) or "apriums" (that's apricots and plums).

But combine the genes of the human species with plants or animals? You've gone beyond the Plimsoll Point.

- It's safe. Tinker with DNA to eliminate almost two thousand single gene diseases, such as Huntington's Chorea.
- It's safe. Manipulate DNA to reduce the diseases with genetic predispositions, such as dozens of cancers.
- It's safe. Take seriously agrogenetics and the identification and implantation of disease-resistant genes, especially in plants.
- It's safe. Even perhaps take nuclei from nonviable embryos, and use them to produce life-saving tissues or organs.

But take nuclei from the cells of mature humans, and use them to produce children? You've gone beyond the Plimsoll Point.

Human cloning in the quest of immortality? Past the Plimsoll Point.

Harvesting of body parts for use in prosthetics? Past the Plimsoll Point.

The old eugenic dream of choosing our descendants? Past the Plimsoll Point.

Wisdomized leadership understands that cloning reverses God's design of creation, which is away from sameness and toward novelty, complexity, and "difference," what the sages call "the perfection of the universe."

- It's safe. Use all sorts of technology in this time of expanded human existence, and expand what it means to be created in God's image.

But the ultimate human-machine interface, wiring our brains to computers through DMMI (Direct Mind-Matter Interaction) technology? Downloading our brain into a computer, also known as extropianism? Past the Plimsoll Point.[13]

One vision of the future applauds the idea that by 2040 it will be possible for people to routinely scan their brains into a computer and create self-replicas. Even if the technology makes it possible, should we "MINDCOPY" (we already do DISKCOPY) the brain electronically, bit by bit, connection by connection, synapse by synapse, neuron by neuron such that reinstantiated humans can have nanotechnological bodies?[14]

You've reached the Plimsoll Point.[15]

> What a shame—yes, how stupid!—to
> decide before knowing the facts!
> —Proverbs 18:13 TLB

Cultivating a Learning Culture

If leadership is to be wisdomized, multiple kinds of learning cultures will need to be cultivated. A fully stocked library of resources for the creation of a learning culture onboard ship would include volumes on the following kinds of learning, every one of which could take volumes to expound:

All-Time/Just-in-Time Learning

The human brain is only 38 percent developed at birth. All other mammal brains are 98 percent developed at birth. To be a human being is to be a continuous learner.

A leader is always preparing for the next expedition and is always learning more about the sea. Learning is a never-ending process of continuous preparation—"perpetual learning" or "lifelong learning." There is no "graduation" in all-time learning, only ceaseless commencements.

There is no shelter from the fallout of knowledge. The first word processor didn't appear until 1970; the first silicon chip not until 1971; the first personal computer in 1975. A little more than thirty-five years later, 75 percent of U.S. households enjoy Internet access.

> Winston Chen, the chair of Solectron, says that "twenty percent of an engineer's knowledge becomes obsolete every year."[16]

Today's out-of-the-box breakthrough can become tomorrow's out-of-date antique faster than you can say "eight-track." The top of the class today will not be the top of the class six months from now without an all-time learning culture. The cream of the crop today can quickly become the skimmed milk of the earth tomorrow or the dregs at the bottom of the cup twelve months from now if we aren't being stirred by continuous learning.

> In times of change, learners inherit the earth, while the learned find themselves beautifully equipped to deal with a world that no longer exists.[17]
>
> —Eric Hoffer

Unless leaders keep on their information toes, unless leaders work diligently to stay current, they automatically become archaic, and the information base on which they make crucial decisions gets more and more flawed. Much of what leaders in the church are trying to do has so long passed its use-by date that it's a wonder anybody is left to lead. If nothing in your ministry has changed in the past year, you're not keeping up.

Some Christians have minds that haven't changed in fifty years. Not even rocks stay that still. Every day, it seems, the world changes without church leaders being aware of it or caring enough to take note.

Cyberspace merges life and information to the point where everything is moving "at the speed of mind," as they say in Silicon Valley. In this kind of world the competitive imperative of speed is greater than ever before. In a world of "Next-Day Delivery," even "Next-Second (instantaneous) Delivery," who will develop "Next-Day Ministry" or "Just-in-Time Ministry"? Where are the "Jack-be-nimble, Jack-be-quick" churches?

Total Learning Experience

Google residents have different cognitive styles and learning capacities from Gutenberg citizens. Some scholars contend people now learn one of three ways: visually (what they see), audibly (what they hear), or

kinesthetically (what they feel and touch). David Kolb counters with four discrete modes of learning: concrete experiences (CE), reflective observation (RO), abstract conceptualization (AC), and active experimentation (AE). Whether your learning modalities are based on visual, auditory, and kinesthenic learners, or (with Kolb) Divergers, Assimilators, Convergers, and Accommodators,[18] total learning experiences incorporate multiple information streams in the learning enterprise.

In fact, a lot of young people with the alleged disease of "attention deficit disorder" are really multiple learners (especially kinesthetics) in need of total learning experiences, not drugs. In the Gutenberg world, ADD was known as BAD … or "boys will be boys."[19]

Google generations learn not through lock-step, lecture-drill-test marches of Industrial Age classrooms and corridors but through multisensory webs of stimulation and inspiration.

> In school, you're told what to study. I discover my own interests and pursue them.[20]
>
> —Charles Loyd, one of 1.5 million homeschooled kids

SDL Learning

Complexity theory is focused on the ability of self-organizing systems to learn and be creative. Complexity scientist Stuart Kauffman has formed a new company called Bios that is attempting to translate complexity theory into the language and life of the workplace. We need someone to create a mission (Theos?) that will translate complexity theory into the language and life of the church. One of the best places to begin is the way in which complex systems move toward self-organization, self-adaptation, and self-learning.

SDL (Self-Directed Learning) skills set students free to assess their own needs, with direct access to resources to meet those needs, and with critical evaluative skills to assess how well they are doing.

SDL is basic to future leaders, whose more active and independent learning styles make them naturally self-directed learners. No one can teach Google kids how to learn. Postmoderns teach themselves. This is not to say that SDL skills aren't teachable.

SDL incorporates many learning styles, including traditional classroom-based and lecture-based learning, but also digital learning (sometimes called CBL, which is Computer-Based Learning), multimedia learning, multilingual learning, and much more. At its best, SDL brings together the Up Close and the Long Distance—two learning modes that have fought one another in the past.

> No one would think of lighting a fire today by rubbing two sticks together. Yet much of what passes for education is based in equally outdated concepts.[21]
>
> —Gordon Dryden and Jeannette Vos

Web-Based Learning to Learn

The Net changed everything, including how one learns. The creation of a learning info-structure is more crucial to ministry that the building of organizational infrastructures.

Google generations learn more from electronic resources than from print. There is no option but to fully computerize the educational wing of your church, to install at least one screen in every sanctuary or worship center, to make Internet access easy and abundant. Don't be an Internot Church (those afraid or reluctant to use the Internet).

The problem is that the Net can be the biggest waste of time and also the biggest time saver. Science fiction writer Arthur C. Clarke compares people's approach to the Internet to the person who tried to quench his thirst by opening his mouth underneath Niagara Falls. We need our thirst quenched and get drowned instead.[22] Can the church help by providing the plumbing necessary to bottle and serve the deluge of information?

We cling to the guideline of moderation, but what's a moderate amount of nearly infinite information?[23]

—*Journal of Social and Evolutionary Systems* editor Paul Levinson

Web-based learning is radically different from the first generation of catalog-of-courses-and-a-box-of-videotapes methodology of distance learning. Cyberlearning is a whole new way of accessing and processing information that doesn't so much replace earlier learning styles as bring them all together and bring to prominence some earlier ones. For example, books, videos, the Internet are great sources of information. But without interactions with people, they lose their edge. That's why conferences and conferential learning is more important now than ever.

What to do about cyberhate? Create home pages and Web sites and chat lines and bulletin boards that are dedicated to social justice, forgiveness, racial equality.

What to do about cyberporn? Build family sites online. Instead of family photo albums pasted into a book, scan family pictures into the computers, and put them on the Web site. Create a virtual church directory that is interactive and constantly evolving.

What to do about chat rooms? For inspiration see the "Y? Forum" (www.yforum.com), a Web site also known as The National Forum on People's Differences, where people can discuss sensitive topics.

What to do about cyberspirituality? Why not have your church put daily devotionals on its Web site? Or approach MySpace and Facebook missionally? What about SecondLife? Your church's ministers of videography can put your members online doing devotionals.

Tell me, and I will forget,
Show me, and I may not remember.
Involve me, and I will understand.
—American Indian proverb

Home Learning

The home, not the school, is the primary locus of learning. Parents, not teachers, are the primary educators of children. Churches, not theological schools, are the primary educators of ministers.

In the last thirty years, there has been a revolution in our understanding of how the brain actually operates. The names are different—"super learning," "accelerated learning," "integrative learning," "brain-based learning," "whole-brain learning"—but the phenomenon is the same: Base learning on how the brain actually functions, not on some socially theorized developmental schemata.

The first four years are absolutely as critical to spiritual and moral development as they are to social and intellectual development. A child's spirituality begins before it is born. Churches that help parents understand and address a child's "learning windows" from the womb onward will lead the way. If working parents can expect nursery-care centers to stimulate their child's intellectual development from day one through a variety of stimuli, why are our churches lagging behind in offering children sounds, images, and touches to stimulate their spiritual imaginations as well?

Double/Triple-Loop Learning

One of the key marks of an "adaptive" learning culture is "double-loop learning"—the self-adaption of a system to new information in such a way that innovation and creativity are intrinsic to the system itself. A learning culture learns from experience by evolving and growing in response to changing conditions.[24]

Christianity is not a single system of thought, but a living, lasting exploration of the divine. It has been through double-loop and triple-loop learning when Reformers in the past got ahead of the curve and helped the church not just anticipate or understand what's around the corner,[25] but decide what corners to take, cut, and close.

> I dream far ahead, but I do not plan far ahead.
>
> —Fred Gibbons, president, Software Publishing Group

Part of the church's difficulty with bringing into play double- and triple-loop learning is precisely that: One has to "play" to "bring into play." Organizational psychologist Karl Weick has used the term "galumphing" to describe a kind of purposive playfulness that helps organizations to innovate and adapt to new situations. "When people build new activities and recombine acts, they may learn more about what's being recombined."[26]

Here's an example of a "galumph." Make a video of a person who does not know Jesus. Then make a video of a person who thinks he knows Jesus but is turned off by him. Then make a video of a person who knows Jesus. Now compare the three. What have you learned? Haven't you "galumphed" yourself into a new awareness of Google-world evangelism?

There is one double-loop lesson that every generation seems to miss. The church thinks that when it says "this will never happen," it actually never happens. The truth is that if you have an idea that something might never happen, the chances are someone out there is already trying to make it happen.

If it doesn't sound ridiculous at first, don't trust it to be true ... at least true of the future. In the words of Peter Drucker, "We know two things about the future: It can not be known and it will be different from what exists now and from what we now expect."[27] Leaders must be open to a radical future and give people the time to adjust to outlandish ideas and the opportunity to try radical things.

Learned Ignorance

In a world where change is permanent, one has to be prepared to unlearn everything and begin all over again in the course of a lifetime. Leaders are constantly unlearning some things. Church culture is as much an unlearning culture as a learning culture.

Leaders must settle for nothing but the latest intelligence, the best information. But leaders must also realize that information is perishable. If learning is at base "making sense of things," then we may need to unlearn some things so that we can make sense of things like never before.

People know too many things that aren't true. People see too many things

that aren't there. Leaders can "discredit" their assumptions and successes and begin again. The spiritual art of "learned ignorance" (theologian Nicholas of Cusa) or "intelligent ignorance" (Dayton, Ohio, inventor Charles F. Kettering)[28] entails an agility of thought, even an ability to do about-faces in a rapidly changing world.

Don't expect consistency. Gutenbergers looked for conceptual coherence. Googlers require of themselves continuities, not consistency or coherence. If the truth be told, so too did Gutenbergers. John Wesley could sermonize for hours on the vice of gambling, yet he drew lots to decide whether to marry.

Karl Weick says that firefighters are most likely to get killed or injured in their tenth year on the job. Why? Because that's when they start taking their knowledge for granted. They begin to think they've seen everything there is to see in the field of fires, and they "become less open to new information that would allow them to update their models."[29]

> The modern era tried to beat mystery into submission. Its "M.O." was bright fluorescent lights to banish the shadows and shade and to illuminate every defiant iota of space with a white artificial light.

Our greatest threat may be the notion that what we don't know isn't worth anything. Our greatest challenge may be how to come to know what we don't know. If truth be told, the more we know, the more we know we don't know. In the future, bad news must travel as fast as good news, and what we don't know must be embraced as heartily as what we do know.

The bounds of the human mind are not the bounds of the divine. The difference between a chimpanzee's brain and a human brain is only a couple of percentage points. Tiny genetic differences beget gargantuan differences in brainpower.

How many percentage points separate us from God? No wonder newly humbled scientists are boasting about their not-knowing. The new science

has discovered limits and insists we respect nature's limits, whether relativity theory's speed of light or chaos theory's "uncertainty principle" or evolutionary theory's Homo sapiens origin.

The toll of wisdom is not a loss of wonder for the deep mysteries of nature and life. Quite the opposite.

Multicultural Learning

Know and understand your culture and your people. But create a culture that prizes learning about other cultures and traditions. In fact, the more welcoming and willing to learn from others a culture is, the more vital and vigorous that culture is itself.

To diminish others is to deaden oneself—even when the "others" are people who disagree with you or dislike you. Leaders know the negative impressions people have of them, so they can offer the opposite.

In the 1790s the population center of the United States was in Maryland. In the 1890s the population center had migrated all the way to somewhere in Missouri. From 1985 to 2005, the ten fastest growing states were in the Pacific Northwest, the Desert Southwest, and the South. The same kind of shifting toward the Pacific and the South is happening on a global basis. Two hundred years ago the center of the church was in Europe. Today the center of the church is in Africa (actually, Timbuktu).

If we could shrink the Earth's 5.7 billion population to a village of one hundred people, the resulting profile would look like this:

Sixty Asians, fourteen Africans, twelve Europeans, eight Latin Americans, five from the United States and Canada, and one from New Zealand or Australia.

Eighty-two would be nonwhite.

Sixty-seven would be non-Christian.

Thirty-two percent of the entire world's wealth would be in the hands of five people.

All five people would be citizens of the United States.

Sixty-seven would be unable to read.

Fifty would suffer from malnutrition. Thirty-three would be without access to a safe water supply.

Eighty would live in substandard housing. Thirty-nine would lack access to improved sanitation. Twenty-four would not have electricity.

Only one would have a college education.[30]

On this global planet, we can eat Kentucky Fried (USAmerican) for lunch; drink Cuban coffee from Kenya in Canada with sugar from the West Indies; wear Italian perfume (Bulgari) in Auckland, New Zealand; celebrate St. Patrick's Day in a Spanish Sushi bar … you get the picture. Increasingly the children of the world are partying together. Increasingly the children of the world are marrying together. And increasingly (remember, this is the generation that watched the Twin Towers collapse in which Anglos, Asians, Hispanics, and Blacks perished together) the children of the world are dying together.

Shared Learning

The more "knowledge" is shared, the more valuable it becomes.

The more "knowledge" is shared, the more knowledge is learned. Nothing pushes the learning curve so much as to have people who just learned share what they have learned with others.

The metaphor of the human brain as a sponge (I don't know who first came up with this visually obvious comparison) helps to explain the concept of "shared learning." Sometimes a sponge is in a soak mode, where it draws into itself all sorts of information and competencies. But there comes a time when, if we are to add anything more, we need to move to a squeeze mode—we squeeze it out and pass on the wisdom to others. The more we keep to ourselves the sponge's contents, no matter how unconventional the sponge's information-gathering habits, the less fresh material we have to fill ourselves. Sharing learning ensures vigorous learning.

Why is it doctors crave the latest information about the human body? So they can squeeze that information out in healing. Why is it physicians learn the latest techniques and technologies of medicine, or at least learn the experts to whom to refer their patients? So they can squeeze that information out in healing.

Why don't religious leaders have similar cravings about the soul that physicians do about the body? Why don't religious leaders have as much of a teachable spirit as our colleagues in medicine?

> There is no frigate like a book
> To take us lands away.[31]
> —Emily Dickinson

Book Learning

Even though print is now a digital enterprise, the notion that people read fewer books in a digital culture is fiction. An old maxim my mother taught me—"Leaders are Readers"—is more true now than ever. Adults are purchasing more books every year. More books are being published every year.

In the United States alone, more than 155,000 books are published each year. That's over 400 books per day—beyond anyone's speed-reading ability! We know what that Inquisition censor meant when he wrote, after being instructed to update the *Roman Index of Prohibited Books* (1559), "what we need is a halt to printing, so that the Church can catch up with this deluge of publication."[32]

We can never fully "catch up," but we can stay close. How? By reading a lot more than we do. Set aside fifteen minutes a day to read a book. That becomes almost two dozen books a year. That increases your lifetime reading by one thousand books, or five times what you read in college.

> There is nothing
> that doesn't bear looking into.[33]
> —Last lines of poet Nadya Aisenberg's "At Akumal"

Endtroducing

Most of us read from left to right, from beginning to end, from introduction to conclusion. We may be back-door readers of a few magazines, but by and large we move from front to back.

In Hebrew one reads from right to left. This is the way the Ten Commandments are traditionally read—what seems to us from end to beginning. Learning to read Hebrew is a creativity exercise: Simply the experience of reading both ways—front-to-back, left-to-right/back-to-front, right-to-left—expands the parameters of how your brain processes information and helps one think creatively.

The spiritual art of endtroducing is the ability to challenge what is for you convention, to step outside your customary frameworks, and to enlist "looking-glass logic" to invert what you see. An endtroduced reading of a biblical passage would go from the culture to the author and finally to the world of the text. The Hebrews used the ancient spiritual art of endtroducing when they consulted unconventional sources for direction and advice. For example, ancient mariners used birds to determine whether land was in a navigable distance and in what direction.[34]

The willingness to learn from strange and sundry sources is more important than ever in a world where all boundary lines are blurring. It's not just that boundaries are not the subject of fierce dispute anymore. Boundaries simply don't exist anymore.

- In the world of business, the lines between business and pleasure, home and office are blurring so much that they almost can't be distinguished.
- In the world of journalism, the lines between mainstream (*The New York Times*) and tabloid (*National Enquirer*) are hopelessly blurred.
- In the world of the church, the lines between clergy and laity, established churches and church plants need to be blurred if they already aren't. (Any pastors who aren't in the midst of planting new churches are at odds with their own time.)

- In the world of network television, weathermen are interviewing celebrities, and legal consultants are announcing news.
- In the world of the arts, the borders have collapsed between high culture and popular culture.
- In the world of psychology, adults are discovering the child within, and children are becoming adults faster than ever. One CBS/*New York Times* poll found that half of teenagers enjoy the same type of music as their parents.
- In the world of biology, prion diseases (Creutzfeldt-Jakob disease, bovine spongiform encephalopathy) are crossing species barriers without anyone knowing how, why, where, and when.
- The worlds of science and theology have so blurred that Sheldon Glashow of Harvard compares superstring physicists to "medieval theologians."

The three core technologies making and shaping the twenty-first-century world are in themselves blurred boundaries. Bioengineering is symbolized most powerfully by the human gene mapping competition between The Institute for Genomic Research in Rockville, Maryland, and the government-sponsored $3 billion Human Genome Project in Atlanta, Georgia.[35] There are already dozens of DNA-based drugs on the USAmerican market, with hundreds in clinical trials and thousands in the planning stages.[36]

Biomimetics, the science of mimicking biological structures for use in material designs, brings together researchers in molecular biology, material science, biochemistry, and mechanical engineering. Nature's products are stronger than our own. How is spider silk stronger than steel and tougher than Kevlar (parachutes)? How are rhino horns self-healing? How can rats eat through metal? How can beetles survive nuclear fallout? Abalone shell is 98 percent chalk, yet it has a breaking strength that is twice that of any high-tech ceramic composite. To unspool their secret—a complexity of structure—a complex of sciences is required.

The second core technology of the twenty-first century is mind machines, both those created through top-down artificial intelligence—especially expert systems—and those created through bottom-up neurocomputing and neural networks.[37] The difference? Neural networks can handle fuzziness, expert systems can't.[38]

The third core technology is miniaturization. Matter is made up of molecules, and molecules are made up of atoms. Scientists are now working on what they call "quantum computers" where information is stored on atoms themselves. If each atom could store one bit of information, a single grain of salt could contain as much information as the RAM in all the computers in the world.[39] Look at the changed world you and I are living in. It used to be we debated the number of angels that could dance on the head of a pin. Now it is the number of bits and bites.

Since 1988, scientists have been building micromachines the width of two human hairs.[40] Microtools, micromotors, micromovers, microsensors are but the first generation leading to the ultimate "small machine," a motor or tool built out of the most plentiful raw material in the universe itself, atoms. To make things out of atoms, one atom at a time, requires a collaboration among biology, chemistry, physics, engineering, digital technology, and economics that returns science to the way nature has operated since the beginning. "The distant future is where computers, genetics, and micromachinery are one and the same."[41]

It is not enough anymore to read and study the academic superpowers and the scholarly superscholars in one's discipline or field. Roaming, roomy reading is a twenty-first-century imperative. In fact, sometimes one needs untethered reading habits—reading that is spontaneous in origin, promiscuous in range, unpredictable in destination, like a river meandering even as it flows forward. Google-world leaders read anything and study everything, from restaurant menus to airline magazines to magazines randomly picked off the Barnes & Noble racks. Some of my best ideas are whipped out of a souffle of clippings, columns, novels, and newspapers.

For nine years my wife and I wrote the preaching resource *Homiletics*; fifty-two sermons a year for nine years equals 468 published sermons. Each one of these sermons I assembled like anyone builds a fire. From a wide expanse of territory you pick up a wide variety of kindling, and collect it in various places (files, notebook, compact discs, pockets), including the fireplace itself. The bigger pieces of logs that provide the major heat and light for the fire come from just a couple of trees: the Bible and the tools that release its energy, theological treatises, church history texts, and pastoral experience.

No matter how full the fireplace becomes with tinder and logs, it does not catch fire unless something outside itself sets it ablaze. It may take just one little stray spark, or a whole matchbook of frustrated strikings, or the pumping of a bellows, but what finally turns a fireplace into a blazing pyre is the presence of an igniting thought, fact, perspective, or question that is external to the carefully crafted pyramid itself.

What sets any creative effort ablaze after you have built the fire? Isn't it often a snatch of something that doesn't seem to fit anywhere and comes from a strange source? Isn't it the intermingling of new and unexpected combinations of ideas, songs, movies, phrases, encounters? Isn't it an external spark that consumes the wood stored in the fireplace?

Transformation comes most often from endtroducing.

AQUACHURCH #11
REDEEMER PRESBYTERIAN CHURCH

New York City, New York
www.redeemer.com

In the heart of New York City, Redeemer Presbyterian Church offers an intellectual and relevant message of the gospel by a very educated leadership staff. Since its beginning, Redeemer has been an AquaChurch that keeps up with the ever-increasing knowledge of its culture. The church accomplishes this by:

- Providing an intellectually stimulating presentation of the gospel;

- Seeking to develop a ministry to college students and recent graduates as the heart and future of our society;
- Offering classes to equip the congregation with a gospel-centered worldview and skills to grow in fellowship with God, community with one another, and service to the city;
- Encouraging pastors and lay leaders to take the next step in their leadership knowledge through conferences, training seminars, resources, and retreats;
- Creating a School of Gospel foundation within the church that coordinates all the educational classes and seminars offered.

CAPTAIN'S LOGBOOK

PERSONAL LOG

Use these ideas to stimulate your thinking about how the principles of this chapter could affect your ministry. Consider sharing these ideas with other church leaders.

1 This chapter gets personal. It deals directly with the issue of a leader being a lifelong learner. (Remember, the human brain is only 38 percent developed at birth [p. 301]!) So, how are you doing?

- How has God wired you?
- Are you more intellectually inclined, where study and learning come easily? Or are you more of a people person for whom the library is more like a dungeon than a learning laboratory?

Either way, think about establishing a "learning culture" around your daily ministry.

- What one book could you read to enhance your learning?
- What one schedule change could you make to ensure a better learning culture?
- What one conference could you go to that might encourage growth in this area of your ministry?

2 Ask yourself: How can someone who is a disciple of Jesus—the same Jesus who had an implacable itch to engage with the world—have the problem of not knowing what to do with oneself or not having enough to do? What would you say to such a person?

3 Think about the world of the future: "Nanotechnology" is based on a "nanometer" which is a thousand times smaller than a micrometer, one-billionth of a meter. A typical atom is 0.2 nanometers. The period at the end of this sentence is about 700,000 nanometers.

- What kinds of changes does this technology signal for your future?
- How might it affect the people you minister to and with?
- How might it affect the ministry of your church?

4 As an exercise in endtroducing, go to your local Barnes & Noble bookstore, and pick up at random and read magazines or newsletters that have nothing to do with anything you'd normally read. Spend at least an hour, preferably an entire afternoon.

5 Spend a week studying the life of Nehemiah. Carefully examine how he utilized the four components of the knowledge management system (data, information, knowledge, wisdom) to create the learning culture necessary for rebuilding the walls of Jerusalem. Consider developing a leadership training series or planning retreat around what you discover.

6 Think about this statement: "The biggest issue of the wisdomization of leadership … is helping others to see and hear, ask and think the right questions" (p. 298).

- What are the top five issues your church is facing today?
- What are the processes in place that help your church address these issues? How are these processes functioning?
- What are some of the questions your leaders need to formulate to get clarity about doing ministry in this Google world?

- What things need to be changed and what things need to remain the same? How do we honestly know the difference?
- How would your church/your life change if you switched questions?

7 Reflect on the study about firefighters that concluded they were most likely to get killed or injured in their tenth year on the job (p. 308).

- What does this say about the necessity of a personal and corporate learning culture?
- Who do you know whose ministry has been negatively affected because they've stopped learning? Why did that happen?
- Who do you know who has "not taken their knowledge for granted" and has kept alive the quest for learning? What effect has that had?

If possible, take each of these people to lunch and tactfully try to learn why each turned out as he or she did.

Ship's Log

Use these activities with your church leadership to help them understand and own the principles of this chapter and how they relate to your church's ministry.

1 Ask leaders to name some of the wealthiest Americans in the past. Then ask:

- How did each of these make their money?
- Who's the wealthiest man/woman today?
- What are the differences in the sources of their wealth?
- In what ways is knowledge power?

2 Form groups of three or four. Have leaders follow along in *AquaChurch 2.0* as you read aloud the following quote: "The laws of physics and of economics are very different at the micro level, and understanding both is necessary to appreciate the dynamics of the bio-economy that is taking shape. When scientists and engineers work with micromachines, weird things happen. Friction, for example, is a bigger problem because dust specks act like boulders and moving microtools through air molecules is slow going. Although it is not yet clear what the design limits are, how small things can get, it is clear that small equals tough. At the molecular level a spider's web is as strong as steel. For microengineers, the major occupational hazard seems to be either inhaling the equipment or sneezing it into oblivion."[42]

Have groups examine this quote and discover parallels between the challenges microengineers face and the challenges your church faces. Ask:

- How is what's described here similar to what we struggle with in the church?
- What are the unknowns we face?
- What are the knowns we need to deal with?
- How can this exercise help us be better prepared to deal with the future?

3 Form pairs, and give each pair paper and pencils. Have them spend at least fifteen minutes answering this question: What changes would occur to your church if you designed your educational ministry to teach congruently with the ways people actually learn?

Have leaders report on the changes they would foresee, and discuss with your whole group which ones you should begin implementing.

4 Analyze the knowledge management system necessary for the development of a well-functioning learning culture "where data … can become information … which then can become knowledge … which can be turned into wisdom" (p. 294).

- What do you think of the components of this knowledge management system?
- When has a process similar to this been used in our church to solve a problem or to create a new ministry? Describe it.
- How would you rate the "learning culture" within our church? Using the previously stated components, try to identify how each of the four steps are carried out within our church setting.

5 Examine the following definition of power: "Power in a Google world is best defined as access to resources, information, and support, and the ability to rally cooperation" (p. 296).

- Which part of this definition (gathering or rallying) is the most difficult in our church?

- If the "differences between power-driven knowledge and spirit-driven knowledge diminish the more power is decentralized, driven downward to the people and upward to God" (p. 296), how can we begin to decentralize the power in our church?

List ways you can begin this decentralization, and then determine which ones to begin right away.

6 Encourage your team to think seriously and practically about some issues raised in this chapter:

- Is it time for a minister of research and development?
- What is the ministry parallel to "Next-Day Delivery" service that is escalating in our world (p. 302)?
- Could we create a mission (Theos?) that would translate complexity theory into the language and life of the church (pp. 303–4)?
- How can churches, not theological schools, become the primary locus of learning for our future leaders (p. 305)?

7 Read the amazing statistics concerning the earth's population profile (pp. 309–10). Form groups of four to examine the statistics in more detail. Tell groups to pretend that these one hundred people are your potential congregation (or multiply each number by ten to make a congregation of one thousand). Have groups answer the following questions for that world church:

- How would our ministry have to change to address the people's needs?
- What would we have to learn to reach these people?
- How do these statistics reflect directions our world is going?
- What can we learn from this exercise to enliven the ministry of our church?

Have groups report on their discoveries, and then determine what steps you should take toward creation of a learning culture in your church.

MISSIONAL ART #11 1/3

FEELING THE WET FINGER: INTUITION

The Spirit will take from what is mine and make it known to you.

—John 16:15b

Before sailors knew the science behind magnetic north, they navigated by putting their finger to the winds. Charts showed these winds stemming from what was called a "compass rose." Artists often portrayed on cathedral and castle ceilings puffy-cheeked cherubs blowing the twelve winds of the compass rose. In times past, sailsmanship was in large measure learning the science of the winds.

Missional art #11 1/3 is intuition, putting one's finger to the winds to help in dead-reckoning (estimating one's position), to hasten dead-aft sailing (sailing with the wind straight behind you), or to locate the eye of the wind—the exact direction from which the wind blows. Missional art #11 1/3 is the aptitude for distinguishing puffs and tempests, and the artistry of maneuvering and reversing through gusts and gales.

Why is this missional art #11 1/3 and not #12? Because 12 would be too neat of a package—the emerging world is not that simple. Because this one follows and builds from all the others. Because intuition is dangerous without the other eleven missional arts.

There are some who point the wet finger heavenward after learning the first two missional arts. They think that once they have found the North Star and can use the compass, all they need to sail is the wet finger. But leaders aren't ready for the wet finger rite of passage until they have mastered the previous eleven skills. For without the other eleven missional arts, your boat may be seaworthy, but you aren't.

The wet finger carries the secret of the missional arts: It's in the air.

Red Sky in Morning

> When you breathe, you inspire. When you
> do not breathe, you expire.[1]
> —Exam answer of an eighth grader

That eighth grader's answer probably didn't earn him an A, but it is as true a statement as any we can make about the human condition.

There is more to living than breathing in and out. There is more to being alive than managing and meeting physical needs.

The more valiant the search by the "hard" sciences for the basics of and basis for life, the more "soft" variables surface that refuse to comply. Some factor doesn't fit into the latest equation; some nagging remainder skews the curve. A qualitative force beats at the heart of this pulsating universe that goes beyond the rational and defies all endeavors to explain, predict, quantify, or fully fathom.

One of life's "soft" mysteries is "intuition." Insights grasped without explanation, conclusions reached without evidence, truths revealed without truths' riggings—these we chalk up to a "sixth" sense we call intuition. Intuition is the wild card of navigation, an opportunistic leadership skill that can turn any ship into a splendid sailing vessel or into a ship of fools.

> Red sky in morning
> Sailors take warning;
> Red sky at night
> Sailor's delight.
> —Jesus

In the old days of sailing, a vessel had to wait for a flood tide before it could sail into port. The Latin term for this status was *ob portu*; that is, a ship positioned in the water facing a port, waiting for the moment when it could sail safely into harbor. This is where we get our English word *opportunity*.

Intuition is the ability to seize the moments and "read" the signs—the signs of the times, the signs of the sky and sea, as well as the "scape" signs, such as mediascape, storyscape, spacescape, agescape.

Leaders "steer." Leaders set the course. Leaders choose which lanes to sail in. "Steering" is a strategy that requires leaders to read the waters, read local currents, read locations of distant stars, recognize jetsam and flotsam, respect the roiling waters and wailing winds, jury-rig anything to make a rescue or make it safely to land. It requires remembering the give and take of the waters to know when to drive and when to drift, when to launch in bad weather and when to weather the storm, when to change tack and when to stay the course.

Back in the 1970s, General Electric had to choose to unload one among three of its more creative investment ventures: nuclear power, computers, or jet engines. Extensive market research was conducted, exhaustive data were compiled, and a corporate decision was made. GE unloaded computers.

Trust your intuition. Not your desires. Not your data. Not your designs. Trust your intuition.

The missional art of intuition is not simply the ability to jump in over one's head in places where very few can swim. The missional art of intuition is an everyday thrival skill in which over-one's-head decision-making, out-of-left-field observations, and winds-of-change opportunities become wild-card judgments that actually chart the journey itself. Authentic leadership is a combination of the rational and the intuitive, the visible and the invisible.

Respiration (the correct answer in the science test mentioned at the beginning of this chapter) can be measured. The intake of oxygen and outflow of carbon dioxide and other gases can be assigned specific ratios. The health of the body can be gauged according to the relationship between these numbers. But instinctive forecasts, hunch actions, and uncanny guesses are as much a sign of a healthy, fully operational human being as any other of the body's vital signs. The only difference is that the phenomena of intuition refuse to slide onto some measurable scale.

> Raise your sail one foot and you get ten feet of wind.
>
> —Chinese proverb

You respire when you move forward by breathing in and out. You inspire when you move forward by intuiting your way ahead. In many ways, the missional art of intuition is the culmination and completion of all the other missional arts.[2] It is the embodiment of the principle that the whole is greater than the sum of its parts.

Rule Breakers, Rule Makers

For a Google world, where facts aren't the focus anymore, a well-honed intuitive sense is as important as intelligence and as critical as a continually fresh flow of information. Ironically as our lifestyles and life requirements have become more dependent on technology, the worth of a well-read, well-fed intuitive sense has become more precious. The more technologically progressive, the more interconnected humans and machines, the more intuitively adept leaders must become.

The microchip and cloud computing has reduced response time to nanoseconds, far outpacing human reaction-response times. The faster the pace of change, the less rationally predictable the future becomes and the more intuitive our responses need to be. As our worker-bee PCs take on more of our daily workload, only an intuitive mind and spirit can sense the way information is flowing and the wind is blowing. It takes sharp intuition to navigate the rapids of rule-breaking change.

You don't think the rules have changed? Even the rules of grammar have changed. According to two new Oxford Press dictionaries, it's now permissible to consciously split infinitives. A preposition is something we can end

a sentence on. And we can even feel free to begin a sentence with "and." Or even "but." But only if we don't overdo it....[3]

> This is what the Lord says—
> he who made a way through the sea,
> a path through the mighty waters ...
> —Isaiah 43:16

Jesus was the ultimate Rule Breaker and Rule Maker. As the rules changed for the early Christians, the apostles steered the church with the "wet finger" of intuition. In their "outside-the-box" leadership, they played hunches, minted some new myths, and proved that it is possible—through the power of the Holy Spirit—to see what we can't comprehend. Recorded in the fifteenth chapter of Acts, a historic meeting was held in Jerusalem among Peter, Paul, James, and other apostles. The decision reached was not an easy or popular one: to set to the side Jewish law and preach to the Gentiles.

A letter went out announcing this new direction and justifying the decision. It read: "It seemed good to the Holy Spirit and to us ..." (Acts 15:28).

Incredible! The apostles picked up the winds of the Spirit and piloted the church in a whole new direction. How? Among those present at this meeting was the Holy Spirit, whose presence and purposes were intuitively received by the apostles. They resisted the winds of public opinion—even majority rule—and surfed the fresh waves of the Spirit.

By the way, majority rule is so often not intuition that in every place in the Scriptures where majority ruled, the result was a disaster. In Acts 27, Paul told the ship's crew not to set sail. But the crew voted and decided to launch anyway.

The result? The boat sank. "The ship struck a sandbar and ran aground. The bow stuck fast and would not move, and the stern was broken to pieces by the pounding of the surf" (Acts 27:41).

The apostles tapped into a deeper—or more accurately, different—consciousness. They released an inner wisdom that came not merely from

human formulations but from a partnership between the human and the divine. This "wet-finger" partnership is what I am calling intuition—missional art #11 1/3.

> You don't need a weatherman
> to tell which way the wind blows.[4]
> —Bob Dylan

Common-Sense Gutenbergers, Intuitive Googlers

What "common sense" was to Enlightenment culture, intuition is to twenty-first-century culture. "Sharp intuition" was an oxymoron in the modern age. Enraptured by data, deadlines, and definitions, moderns understood intuition to be by its very nature something fuzzy and fairly off-kilter.

To emphasize intuition's inferior ranking, moderns assigned it to the "weaker sex." "Women's intuition" was something soft, emotional, unreliable, to be contrasted with the hard, quantifiable, dependable thinking that governed the thought processes of men. Intuition, like woman herself, was unpredictable and ultimately untrustworthy.

Despite the female stigma attached to the term "intuition," moderns could not totally reject intuitive processes. Intuitive insights and foresights lived on, socially sanctioned under male rubrics of "gut reactions" and "gut feelings."

"Trust your gut."

"Go with your gut."

"My gut says this just isn't right."

"Time for a gut check."

Thankfully, leadership requirements have moved intuition beyond the raging borders of the gender wars. Intuition is still spoken of in machismo terminology as an outgrowth of our most basic "primal instincts." There is an uncharted part of our being which, under the proper conditions, causes the hair on the back of our necks to "stand up," or our flesh to "crawl."

But we now recognize that intuition is not simply a physiological reaction but a mind-body-spirit response that relies less on numbers-driven processes than on intangibles and sensations. The "single intuitive glance," poet W. H. Auden believed, is what matters most when "completeness is impossible."[5] Scientists have now acknowledged "incompleteness" as at the heart of all knowledge. Advanced micro- and macro-physics now embrace uncertainty as part and parcel of the basic nature of the universe. A whole new profession called "medical intuitives" supplements traditional medical practice with gut-based diagnostics.[6]

Rare Necessities

The new scientific method has given up its love affair with linear consistency, rational prediction, and mathematical control. Soviet astrophysicist Andrei Linde goes so far as to admit that the universe may be even larger than we think it is already. He suggests the existence of many independent regions—"bubbles,"[7] he calls them—where the laws of physics would be very different than the ones we have so far uncovered.

Controversy still surrounds intuition. Some say it is universal (Carl Jung). Others say it is learned (Edward de Bono). Some call it "scientific intuition" (Hans Christian Oersted), a term that until recently sounded comically oxymoronic. Others say it is a form of "midwife thinking" (Gemma Corrado Fiumara), which helps others give birth to ideas.

Whatever it is, leaders can develop their intuitive capabilities. One book alone lists dozens of techniques.[8] The following are my favorite ten "rare necessities" for maximizing intuition in life:

1. Listen to music, especially unfamiliar pieces.
2. Get physical exercise, an essential part of the creative process.
3. Mix metaphors and match up opposites.
4. Use a variety of materials to build models and mock-ups.
5. Acquire dream skills and sleep learning.
6. Cultivate a "listening logic," a logic that hears both words and the feelings that lie behind the words.[9]

7. Develop "anticipatory consonance with nature."[10]

8. Read poetry aloud, and linger over every word until it sinks into the soul.

9. Practice extended seasons of prayer and fasting.

10. Stay away from people who are wave jammers.

Not only have scientists caught the slippery tail of intuitive thought processes, but philosophers have also found ways of making "seat-of-your-pants" decisions or moments of "inspired idiocy" sound downright reasonable. Why do our best-laid plans and choice arguments never seem to work out the way we planned? Debaters' intuitive senses are able to crunch together wildly variable data: the general state of public well-being or unease, the type of weather the day has to offer, the direction from which the wind is blowing, the shape of the room opponents are meeting in, the opponents' physical characteristics, educational disparities, and the fact that somebody is wearing a "lucky shirt." These unregistered perceptions "intuitively" provide debaters with insights that would not otherwise be part of the case.

Intuition is percussive enlightenment: rapping, tapping, and whacking uncharted depths where leaders can find passageways to wisdom's hidden insights and unrefined visions. In this sense, intuition may be less an accumulation of lifetime learning than a momentary openness to un-learning.

A Dance Aesthetic

Perhaps "intuition" is best paired with the word *aesthetics*. The intuitive sense is in fundamental ways an aesthetic sense. In street understandings of intuition there is too much passivity. Relying on one's intuition is not an excuse to sit back and wait for some bolt-of-lightning inspiration or some burst-across-your-brainstem revelation. Such intuitions can be ill-timed, ill-conceived, ill-willed—as every pioneer pushing against the long-established edges of a well-loved paradigm can attest.

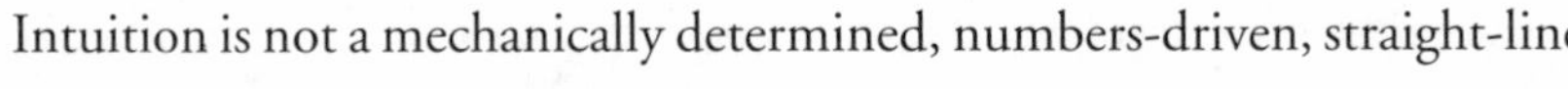
Intuition is not a mechanically determined, numbers-driven, straight-line

process. Intuition is an aesthetics of dance. There is no passivity in dancing, only creative motions coupled with stillness.

> Everything is copy.[11]
>
> —Mother of author Nora Ephron about her daughter's writing habits

The prime danger threatening every leader's intuitive dance is the natural tendency to copy. Mimicking observed behaviors is the best way children learn how to navigate their new world. But as every parent knows, children learn how to add their own unique spin to mimicked behavior. The greatest dancers of this past century have all happily admitted to imitating the styles and steps of the giants who preceded them. Baryshnikov borrowed from Kelly, who learned moves from Astaire, who found inspiration in Nureyev. Yet what made each one of these dancers great in their own right is that each imitated the masters while taking his own dance to new levels. Each flexed his own mind and muscle and melded individual imagination with intuition to create a style that precisely fit himself. As we watch them dance, it is their intuited uniqueness that skips our hearts and transposes our souls.

Imitate, Don't Impersonate

Emerging leaders hone their intuitive thrival skills to the unique needs of each church, each community, each situation. Unfortunately, leaders with the greatest ability to hear distant hoofbeats often find their heartbeat materializations to be more impersonation than innovation, more derivative than original. Without realizing it, leaders who turn up the volume of their context's uniqueness can find their mission marked more by sameness than difference.

Adding to the problem, Googlers are unconscious xerographiliacs. They love copying. They have a tremendous facility to impersonate. Xerographilia can substantially interfere with even the most attuned and attentive leader's

ability to distinguish his or her own intuitive heartbeat from that already being produced by others.

If you've seen one successful church, you not only haven't seen them all, you've not even seen two successful churches. When a church has been intuitively shaped and molded, it will necessarily take on its own individually created face. "Ministry by mimicry," George Barna writes, "almost invariably results in deterioration, rather than growth."[12]

I might quibble with Barna over definitions. When Barna talks about "imitation," he seems to be describing what I would define as "impersonation." Genuine "imitation" is adopting good ideas and then adapting them to one's own context. Impersonation is an attempt to cloak one's entire persona in another's identity, concealing oneself and trying to pass as someone or something else.

Every successful church is successful in its own way. However we may try to pass ministries off as our own "intuitive" insights, settling for mimicry and impersonation only offers up a recipe for extinction. How many Willow Creek clones—Garden Forks, I call them—have found themselves "up a creek without a Hybels."[13]

Ship-in-the-Bottle Mastery

The delicate feature of the missional art of intuition is that the very act of implementing intuition imperils it. Treating "intuition" like any other thrival skill is a little like staring at a beautiful swallowtail butterfly not darting about in the air, but poked on a pin, preserved and displayed in a specimen box. Marvel at its colors, shape, and elegance all we want, but we will never understand why this creature is called a "butterfly" unless we observe it flitting from flower to flower in the bright sunshine. Intuition cannot be boxed into a seminar study or specimen box. Intuitive leading is about going beyond the box, outside the boat, ignoring the boundaries, coloring outside the lines.

Ralph W. Neighbour Jr., the reigning expert on cell-group church, says that "I have asked every cell-group pastor I have met on my journeys, 'When you started, did you make a trip to see a model of what you have here? Did you attend someone's seminar before you started?' In each and every case, the answer has been, 'No, I went to my knees … I had no choice. [God] taught me as I went along.'"[14] The first intuitive step a missional leader must take is downward, onto the knees. From that kneeling position every perspective will necessarily be unique and unrepeatable.

> Get on your knees and fight like a man.
>
> —Petra

> Want to stay on your toes?
>
> Get on your knees.

What does prayer do? Some say prayer keeps us healthy and whole. Some say prayer heals us. The Scriptures teach us that prayer actually does both[15] by getting us on the right current. Mariners have learned that if they find the right current, they can send a signal that will travel all the way around the world. They learned this from whales, which are able to communicate with other whales on the other side of the planet. How? They find the right current and get connected.

Prayer is like jet streams of the sea and sky. Ride one, and all things are possible. Archbishop William Temple once said, "When I pray, miracles occur."

A friend traveling with him replied, "Perhaps what you call miracle is nothing more than mere coincidence."

The archbishop replied, "Yes, I suppose so, but I have noticed that when I do not pray, the coincidences do not occur."

All my ministry I have practiced various forms of "prayerwalking." I used to drive the streets of my parishes in Geneseo and Rochester, New York, praying for both parishioners and nonparishioners as I moved through various neighborhoods. Sometimes I would be "moved" to pull into a driveway and make a pastoral call. Other times I would pick up disturbances that I checked out later over the phone, at the store, during coffee hour, or on the racquetball court.

Nowadays I practice prayerwalking at churches, hotels, and in communities where I speak. Sometimes I invite other leaders to go on these prayerwalks with me. Prayerwalking the sidewalks and streets is a form of spiritual mapping that guides leaders in what to say and do. Prayerwalking paints a mural of the soul of a place, a spiritual diagnostic device that is tantamount to a CAT scan or MRI.

Although a rich prayer life threads all the missional arts together, a life of godliness that pivots on prayer makes "intuition" more than a message-in-a-bottle pitch into the unknown. In fact, a life of godliness transforms intuition into a ship-in-the-bottle virtuosity that boasts consummate skills of placement and strategy.

"Go Thou and Do … Otherwise"

Gerard Manley Hopkins wrote to Robert Bridges in 1888, "The effect of studying masterpieces is to make me admire and to do otherwise."[16] Leaders must not impersonate, but imitate and initiate what we can in our own way. This is a key component of leadership that was too often missing in a Gutenberg culture. If our model is Jesus, "Go Thou and Do … Likewise."

"Go Thou:" Sit at his feet, walk in his shoes, study his steps, and when you go home, "Do … Likewise."

But if our model is anyone else, "Go Thou and Do … Otherwise."

"Go Thou:" Sit at the feet of the best, study their strategies, but when you go home, "Do … Otherwise."

The greatest intuitive leader the world will ever know read his crowds perfectly. He knew when it was time for a story, when it was time to reach out and heal, when it was time to preach, and when it was time to eat, party, and relax. But Jesus knew his style was his own. He pointedly declared, "Who appointed me a judge or an arbiter between you?" (Luke 12:14). See to it yourself.

See to it yourself. Be yourself. Be your own person. Be your own church. Be the church God created you to be, not the church God created some other church to be.

> My Lord God I have no idea where I am going. I do not see the road ahead of me. I cannot know for certain where it will end. Nor do I really know myself, and the fact that I think I am following your will does not mean that I am actually doing so. But I believe that my desire to please you does in fact please you. And I hope that I have that desire in all that I am doing. I hope that I will never do anything apart from that desire. And I know that if I do this you will lead me by the right road though I may know nothing about it. Therefore will I trust you always though I may seem to be lost and in the shadow of death. I will not fear, for you are ever with me, and you will never leave me to face my perils alone.[17]
>
> —Prayer of Thomas Merton (1915–1968)

Beta & Biometrics

One way to help foster an intuition-friendly environment is to break out of old notions of what leadership structures look and act like. Perhaps the biggest shift is from an "alpha" approach to leadership to a "beta" approach. In alpha leadership structures the old pack mentality reigns. There is one alpha individual in charge—the big boss. Alpha leadership can work only when structures are uniformly hierarchical, relentlessly rational, and fixedly quantitative. New ideas or innovations are first eyed "critically," even suspiciously, and then are rigorously run through a wringer. No chart, no start: If the journey can't be mapped out, plotted, and predicted, it won't be launched.

Beta leadership finds its strength in flatness and diversity. Pulling ideas and inspirations from a variety of sources, beta leadership is synthesizing,

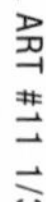

untaught, and indulging, encouraging the freest flow of energy and creativity. Sheer size is no longer an issue for beta leadership structures, for they recognize that, as Dwight D. Eisenhower is said to have observed from his experience in the Oval Office, "It is better to have one person working with you than three people working for you."[18]

Reading congregations, energy levels, or spirits takes a far lighter touch but heavier intuitive skills than learning to physically identify people and places. We are only now trying to find ways of positively identifying each other's bodies. It's called "biometrics," and there have been more than a hundred companies trying to create biometric identification systems that move beyond the traditional card key/PIN/password methods. Each one of these old methods eventually can be cobbled together by a crook.

Your body, however, has its own unique attributes, individualities, and idiosyncrasies that a computer can read, at least in theory. What are some of the characteristics computers are now busily trying to learn? Fingerprints, iris or retinal patterns, ear shapes, facial features, signatures, vocal waveforms, smell. PINs and passwords either are, or soon will be, history. If truth be told, human beings have always had available their own spiritual biometric PIN: It's called intuition. Intuitional skills help us identify ourselves to others as well as to ourselves. Spiritual biometrics help us access another's soul or reach across the data to find a new solution to a problem.

When's the last time you felt a "sense of rightness" about something? A beta leadership model's "all hands on deck" approach enables participants to intuitively feel it when what can only be called a "sense of rightness" begins to reign over congregational decisions and declarations. Honing intuitional radar helps leadership learn how to identify the shape and condition of each other's spirits.

Intuition's Etiquette and Ethics

Because intuition allows leaders to pick up vibrations and visions that others miss or miscarry, a certain etiquette is required of intuitional leaders. The ethical demands of this missional art extend beyond kindness and gentleness toward the people we serve.

Etiquette #1: Think it and sink it.

While some of the spiritual and emotional undercurrents you pick up may be pleasant and harmonic, some will be negative and discordant. A second level of the art of intuition is discerning when to act on an intuitive reading and when to let it pass. Sometimes you shouldn't do anything with the signals you pick up—other than pray. Pray for the person, pray for the situation, pray to be prepared for what you sense is coming.

But keep your mouth shut. How often do we forget that the commandment "Thou shalt not bear false witness" does not include "unless it is useful"? Pray your hunches, but don't say your hunches. In the words of a World War II refrain: "Loose lips sink ships."

Etiquette #2: Remember, this is **their** *story, this is* **their** *song.*

As any leader knows, every congregation, every team, every mission contains as many stories as it does individuals. If your intuition enables you to pick up and read one of these stories, don't be tempted to read between the lines as well. This is someone else's story, not your own. Respect their right to script and live their own story, to sing their own song.

Etiquette #3: Realize you could be wrong.

Finally, remember this: You and I boast no immaculate perceptions. Your intuition may be right. But you could be wrong.

Counterintuitive

Much of western culture initiates contact with another human being through a casual ritual and courteous gesture called "shaking hands." And yet, how many times has a simple handshake turned into a moment of confrontation and challenge? Grips squeeze, eyes lock, biceps flex—all in an attempt to send a subtle, nonverbal signal about who we are and what we are about. Every handshake may not be a contest, but every handshake is an inquest.

The dexterity of our fingers, the thousands of nerve endings at our fingertips, the sensitivity of our skin, make the human hand a tool virtually unsurpassed at bringing us information about the world and those we share it with. Does it seem like all your fingers have done lately is fly over a keyboard or click repeatedly on an electronic mouse? Do you wonder if the Internet and the anonymous intimacy of cyberspace will eventually reduce all human contact to electronic bleeps?[19]

Whole-hand interaction with cyberspace is called force feedback. Virtual technologist James Kramer, when asked whether the convergence of humans and machine through force feedback technology will precipitate the next evolutionary leap, responded: "On the contrary, people will de-evolve. We'll revert to the intuitive way of picking up an object we all learned as children—reach out and grab it with your hand. And your hand will open the door to whatever your imagination can hold."[20]

Forget the hand. One finger will do. As we have seen, the cache of unseen information gathered by a single digit is enough to determine the course of the ship.

Disciples of Jesus cruising the long, blue lanes of water will need to become highly skilled at using the natural powers of one finger to help them set course. But there is a difference between the nautical custom of the index finger pointed aloft by those who call themselves "Christian" and the same finger held up by others.

Christians poke into the air a wet finger. We are a baptized people—born of water and of Spirit. Nothing we do is without that water covering. The water is what enables the finger to distinguish between natural and supernatural breaths of wind, between the winds of time and the universal, culture-transcending winds of truth.

In many highly liturgical traditions, one wets one's fingers before walking into the sanctuary as a reminder of one's baptism. The wet finger the church lifts to the sky to seek which way the wind is blowing is washed with the waters of redemption. Just as you fight fire with fire, so we find our way in water with water. Aside from the North Star, the compass, and the anchor, there is no more trustworthy navigational aid than to take off your shoes and wet your fingers.

> But we have the mind of Christ.
>
> —1 Corinthians 2:16b

One of the greatest intuitive skills is in knowing when to be counterintuitive. The wetness of the finger ensures that the leader doesn't see things as the world sees things. The wetness of the finger enables leaders to give up their culture's fixed perspectives and finished answers and instead be open to God's new questions and approaches.

Of all the people who ever lived, the person most adept at counterintuitive knowledge and the counterintuitive use of power was Jesus of Nazareth. The cross is the ultimate counterintuitive move: to save the world by letting the world destroy you.

To the world, pointing a finger skyward is a way of determining which way the wind is blowing. The culture uses this information to put the wind to its back. Always taking the easiest route, culture changes its direction, morals, and values based on the momentary whims of the wind and trends of the times. The key for leaders is to distinguish the winds of time from the winds of eternity.

To the Christian who lifts a wet finger heavenward, the same information propels the church to tack into the winds. The winds of time are thus used as a power source, but the ship remains on its divinely appointed course. Cultural winds are thus used by the ship. But the winds of time do not blow the ship along ahead of them willy-nilly.

An angry *Christianity Today* subscriber from Palos Verdes, California, wrote to the editor and harrumphed, "No Christian should spend a moment of the time God has given him to listen to the 'Sex Pistols.'" When I discussed this mentality with my friend Landrum Leavell III of Phoenix,

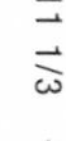

Arizona, he remarked, "Do you reckon this writer weeps over the people of Palos Verdes?"

Does our pagan culture offend us enough for us to pray over it and learn how to reach it? Did Paul refuse to listen to the first-century "Sex Pistols" the people were hearing and quoting? Didn't he learn to read and understand the culture of his day, and then tack into it?

The truly countercultural are not those who find which way the wind is blowing and then spit into the wind. The truly countercultural are those who use these winds as a power source to be more Spirit-driven, even to the point that the world deems our journey a "ship of fools."

To reach satisfaction in all
desire its possession in nothing.
To come to possess all
desire the possession of nothing.
To arrive at being all
desire to be nothing.
To come to the knowledge of all
desire the knowledge of nothing.
To come to the pleasure you have not
you must go by the way in which you enjoy not.
To come to the knowledge you have not
you must go by the way in which you know not.
To come to the possession you have not
you must go by the way in which you possess not.
To come to be what you are not
you must go by a way in which you are not.
When you turn toward something
you cease to cast yourself upon all.
For to go from all to the all
you must deny yourself of all in all.
And when you come to the possession of the all

you must possess it without wanting anything.
Because if you desire to have something in all
your treasure in God is not purely your all.[21]
—John of the Cross (1540–1591)

The Hum

There is an old nautical saying: "When the wind is not blowing, row." But that's not God's way. When the Winds of the Spirit are not blowing, don't move. "Stay in Jerusalem" is how the Scriptures put it.

A great organist was once playing a magnificent concert. The part of the program ended, and a stunned audience leapt to its feet in a booming chorus of bravos. Profoundly moved by the accolades, the organist made a brief speech in which he admitted, "Yes, that may have been one of my best performances ever."

As he spoke, the custodian who had been charged with making sure the air was blown into the pipes of the organ joined him on stage, bowed alongside him, and whispered, "I agree. That was one of our most magnificent performances."

When they walked off-stage, the stunned organist launched into a tirade. "What do you mean our performance? Did you attend music school? Did you practice every day? Did you reach deep into your soul to evoke that music?" At that, the embarrassed custodian disappeared into the darkness.

When the organist returned to play the second part of the program, he put his hands on the keys and his feet on the pedals. But nothing happened. No music came out. He tried again, and again nothing happened. Everyone began to realize what was going on: The custodian wasn't providing the air.

At that, the maestro stood up and thanked the custodian for his labor and his faithfulness through the years. Then he returned to the bench, put his hands on the keys and his feet on the pedals, and glorious music emerged.[22]

Spirit-driven leaders are utterly dependent on the unseen but unbridled Winds of the Spirit. When the Winds of the Spirit are not blowing, the best leaders can do is tack into the winds of the world. When the Winds of the Spirit are blowing, put them at your back and ride the waves. Let them take you into the future—even in directions "you do not wish to go" (John 21:18 NRSV).

> The wind is rising! …
> We must try to live.[23]
> —Paul Valéry

When a ship is maxed out in the wind, its sails unfurled and its lungs breathing in and out to their fullest capacity, the boat literally lifts out of the water and thrusts forward on a thin film of air. Sailors call this "planing." They know when a ship is "planing" because they hear what is called "The Hum."

Can you hear "The Hum" in your life? Can you hear "The Hum" in your church? The choice is yours: Leadership can either make the higher into the humdrum or into The Hum.

Which will it be?

Hoist the Sails.

Trust the Wind.

Come to the Water.

> What ship is this that will take us all home, Oh, glory hallelujah,
> And safely land us on Canaan's bright shore? Oh, glory hallelujah.
> Chorus: 'Tis the old ship of Zion, hallelujah. [repeated four times]
>
> The winds may blow and the billows
> may foam, Oh, glory hallelujah,
>
> But she is able to land us all home. Oh, glory hallelujah.
> Chorus: 'Tis the old ship of Zion, hallelujah. [repeated four times]

She landed all who have gone before, Oh, glory hallelujah,
And yet she is able to land still more, Oh, glory hallelujah.
Chorus: 'Tis the old ship of Zion, hallelujah. [repeated four times]

If I arrive there, then, before you do, Oh, glory hallelujah,
I'll tell them that you are coming up, too, Oh, glory hallelujah.
Chorus: 'Tis the old ship of Zion, hallelujah.
[repeated four times][24]
—"The Old Ship of Zion"

AQUACHURCH #11 1/3
THE OAKS FELLOWSHIP

Red Oak, Texas
www.oaksfellowship.org

Using intuition, The Oaks Fellowship shares the team leadership as a true AquaChurch. The staff consists of multiple senior and executive pastors. The Oaks Fellowship recognizes the importance of multiple voices at the helm and that sometimes it takes multiple wet fingers to feel the wind. The leaders at Oaks intuitively:

- Emphasize worship as a primary means to deepening the faith;
- Encourage the gifts of all in the community to minister and communicate God's love;
- Seek growth through relational evangelism;
- Speak the truth in love for the building of community;
- Strengthen faith through discipleship to Christ;
- Creatively use pop culture in the communication and propagation of the gospel.

CAPTAIN'S LOGBOOK

PERSONAL LOG

Use these ideas to stimulate your thinking about how the principles of this chapter could affect your ministry. Consider sharing these ideas with other church leaders.

1 After the New York Giants started the 2007 season with three losses, the much maligned New York quarterback Eli Manning, who had yet to live up to his first round draft status, said, "Time for a gut check." Consider:

- As you think about your readiness for the future, how does your "gut" feel?
- What quality results in more Olympic medals: guts, strength, speed, or skill? Think about the "why" behind your answer.

2 There are three "high-touch" components of leadership—intuition, inclusion, and authenticity. Think about how these components show themselves in your ministry.

- Which is the most difficult for you? the easiest? Why?
- Which is most needed in your congregation?
- How can you strengthen your leadership in the area you sense the most need?

3 Think about a time you made a decision based significantly on "intuition." Write down what happened: Make side-by-side lists of negative and positive results. Then compare the two, and decide if following your intuition was positive or negative. Then consider:

- How did that experience encourage or discourage your "gut-feeling" responses to leadership decisions?
- How might you want to change your use of intuition in the future?

4 Analyze the advantages and disadvantages of relying on "intuition" as a major piece of your decision-making process. Think about:

- How is the missional art of intuition "the culmination and completion of all the other missional arts" (p. 324)?

- When has someone you know prematurely utilized a "gut-feeling" and regretted it? Look over the previous eleven missional arts, and try to determine which ones may have been bypassed in that person's decision.

Develop a plan to grow in the missional arts you feel weakest in, to better prepare you to use intuition appropriately.

5 Not the easiest of Bible books, Hebrews offers an intriguing look at how the spiritually mature "have trained themselves to distinguish good from evil" (Heb. 5:14). Study Hebrews 5:13—6:1. Consider:

- How has your maturation process borne out the description in Hebrews 5:14?
- In what ways is intuition a learned behavior?
- What can you do to optimize your intuitive capabilities?

Look at the list of "rare necessities" on pages 327–28. Choose at least two, and make them a part of your regular study time.

6 Explore the distinction made between imitation and impersonation: "Genuine 'imitation' is adopting good ideas and then adapting them to one's own context. Impersonation is an attempt to cloak one's entire persona in another's identity, concealing oneself and trying to pass as someone or something else" (p. 330). Do you think the apostle Paul would agree with this definition? Check out what Paul says about "imitators" in 1 Corinthians 4:16; Ephesians 5:1; 1 Thessalonians 1:6; 2:14. How do your discoveries fit with what this chapter describes?

7 Os Guinness says, "The theme of tutoring and imitation, which goes far deeper than current notions of 'mentoring,' is conspicuous in the teaching of the early church. We grow through copying deeds, not just listening to words, through example as well as precept, through habit and not just insight and information."[25]

- How is Guinness's perspective similar to that of this chapter? How is it different?
- What kinds of things should you seek to "copy" from other churches?
- What kinds of things should you seek to adapt from other churches?

Ship's Log

Use these activities with your church leadership to help them understand and own the principles of this chapter and how they relate to your church's ministry.

1 Skitch Henderson, the musician, once quoted a saying among piano players: "If you can play 'Melancholy Baby,' you'll always get a job." Talk about the implications of that quote with your leaders:

- What place does pessimism have in our culture? in our church? In election races?
- Who gets the "gigs" within our church? Why?
- What types of messages get the most response within our culture? within our church?
- What effect do pessimistic messages and people have on our ministry?

2 Examine the depth and breadth of a coming plague of pessimism and acquiescence in apathy. Read the following three voices, the first predictable, the next two not:

a) Alexandr Solzhenitsyn lambasts popular culture and its imperialistic influence on the world in these words: "The iron curtain did an excellent job of defending our country against everything good in the West … But the curtain didn't quite go all the way down, and allowed the liquid dung of a debauched and decadent pop mass culture to ooze underneath, along with the most vulgar fashions and public displays."[26]

b) The second voice comes from one of the architects of the future, a cofounder of Apple Computer, founder of NeXT Software and 80 percent owner of Pixar Animation Studios, rescuer of Apple Computer, Steve Jobs. "The world's getting worse," he cries. "It has gotten worse for the last fifteen years or so. Definitely."[27]

c) The third voice comes from one of the greatest psychotherapists in the world, the former head of the Jung Institute. James Hillman complains, "The world is getting worse; ask the animals, ask the trees, ask the wind—but also ask the citizens declared mentally ill."[28]

Form groups of three, and assign each group one of the above quotes. Have groups discuss the questions below as they relate to the assigned quote:

- What is accurate about this view? What is inaccurate?
- How does the message of this book compare with this view?
- What should our view be as Christians?

Have groups report, and then ask: How will our view of the future affect the future ministry of this church?

3 I'm a natural, hard-nosed, unrepentant pessoptimist. I wait for the worst while I wish for the best. Discuss:

- How has the Christian tradition tied its future on psychological attitudes, intellectual aptitudes, or human emotions like "pessimism" or "optimism"?
- How do these attitudes, aptitudes, and emotions affect the ministry of the church at large?
- How fully do Christians look to the theological virtue of "hope" and hope's spiritual reading of history?
- What can we do to focus our attitudes more on the hope that we have through Jesus?

4 Ask your team to analyze the following: "The more technologically progressive, the more interconnected humans and machines, the more intuitively adept leaders must become" (p. 324). Ask:

- Why is this true?
- What makes intuition so important in leading the twenty-first-century church?
- How do technology and a faster pace of change actually make the art of intuition even more critical?
- How can we assist the church in recognizing the role of intuition for decision-making in the future?

5 Study together Acts 15, and evaluate what role the Holy Spirit played in the "intuitive" process of the historic meeting held in Jerusalem with Peter, Paul, James, and the other apostles. Then consider:

- How does the Holy Spirit work today?
- When have you seen the Holy Spirit function in such clarifying and unifying ways?
- How can the Holy Spirit enhance our team's intuition capabilities?

Now form groups of three or four. Have each group look back at Acts 15 and think about what might be the subject of this council if it were being held at your church this month. Have each group choose a subject and prepare arguments for both sides of the issue. Give groups at least ten minutes to prepare, and then have them present their arguments. After the presentations, discuss:

- How might the Holy Spirit help us deal with these issues in a unifying way?
- How can we as leaders be more in tune with the Holy Spirit in our intuition?

6 Have your leadership team respond to the observation that "in every place in the Scriptures where majority ruled, the result was a disaster" (p. 325). Discuss:

- When is majority rule used as a guiding principle for decision-making in our church?
- How could we make decisions based on "a partnership between the human and the divine" (p. 326)?
- What dangers are inherent in leading by intuition?
- What can we do to make sure that all of our decisions are based on God's desires for our church?

NOTES

Part One

1. Robert Ballard, "We're All Explorers," *Fast Company*, Sept. 1998, 162.
2. "Too Little, Too Late" in Robert Christiansen, *Tales of the New Babylon: Paris, 1869–1875* (London: Sinclair Stevenson, 1994), 142–62, esp. 143.
3. A.C. Grayling, ed., *Philosophy* (New York: Oxford University, 1995), v.
4. Salman Rushdie, "Outside the Whale," in *Imaginary Homelands* (London: Granta, 1991), 100.
5. The best presentation of "mind mapping" is Nancy Margulies and Nusa Maal, *Mapping Inner Space*, 2nd ed. (Tucson, AZ: Zephyr, 2002). See also Jamie Nast, *Idea Mapping* [electronic resource] (Hoboken, NJ: John Wiley & Sons, 2006). For an example of one of many mind-mapping software programs, see Open Mind2: Professional Mind Mapping Software by MatchWare: Software for Creative Minds.
6. Tony Buzan and Barry Buzan, *The Mind Map Book* (New York: Dutton, 1994, ©1993). For a verbal explanation, see also YouTube: Maximize the Power of Your Brain: Tony Buzan, Mind Mapping, www.youtube.com/watch?v=MlabrWv25qQ (accessed May 21, 2008).
7. Ernest Gellner, "What Do We Need Now?" *TLS: Times Literary Supplement,* July 16, 1993, 4. Gellner's realization that "we are facing a new situation in which the old polarities of thought no longer apply, or at the very least require scrutiny" is stronger than ever. "The concepts we use to describe the world," he contends, "urgently need to be reformulated" (3).
8. Philippa Berry and Andrew Wernick, ed., *Shadow of Spirit* (New York: Routledge, 1993), 11–108. See especially Mark C. Taylor, "Reframing Postmodernism," 11–29, and Mark Milbank, "Problematizing the Secular Post-Modern Agenda," 30–44.
9. As reported in Robert M. Knight, "Re-engineering: The Business Buzzword," *Sky*, Jan. 1995, 22.
10. Steffen Böhm, *Repositioning Organization Theory* (New York: Palgrave Macmillan, 2006).

11. Henry Miller, *Big Sur, and the Oranges of Hieronymus Bosch* (New York: New Directions, 1957), 25.
12. Mark S. Monmonier, *How to Lie with Maps* (Chicago: University of Chicago, 1991), 2.
13. Herman Melville, *Moby-Dick*, ed., John Bryant and Haskell Sringer (New York: Pearson, 2007), 67.
14. Raymond Lister, *Antique Maps and Their Cartographers* (Hamden, CT: Archon, 1970), 14.
15. Jorge Luis Borges, "On Exactitude in Science," in *Collected Fictions* (New York: Viking, 1998), 325.
16. François Aussemain's "Pensées" are the fabrication of Scottish writer Don Paterson and are used as epigraphs throughout his works. This one precedes his poem "Nil Nil," in his *Nil Nil* (Boston: Faber and Faber, 1993), 51.
17. Lewis Carroll, "Sylvie and Bruno Concluded" (1893), in *The Complete Sylvie and Bruno* (San Francisco: Mercury, 1991), 265.
18. This story was one of Gregory Bateson's favorites. See Gregory Bateson and Mary Catherine Bateson, *Angels Fear* (New York: Macmillan, 1987), 161.
19. Actually, it hinges on how you count bodies of water. With more precise computer measurements, the Census Bureau can now measure inland ponds and streams that once were considered land.
20. Quoted in Anna Muoio, "We're All Explorers," *Fast Company*, August 1998, www.fastcompany.com/magazine/17/ballard.html (accessed June 3, 2008)
21. As quoted in William R. Hutchison's review of *The Encyclopedia of the American Religious Experience, Religious Studies Review* 17 (April 1991): 115.
22. The actual date is 2019. See Ray Kurzweil, "The Paradigms and Paradoxes of Intelligence: Building a Brain," *Library Journal* 117 (Nov. 1992): 53–54. Available online at www.kurzweilai.net/meme/frame.html?main=/articles/art0253.html (accessed May 22, 2008).
23. Pauline Marie Rosenau, *Post-Modernism and the Social Sciences* (Princeton, NJ: Princeton University, 1992), 183.
24. This quote appeared in a newsletter called "Funny Business" at some point. Used by permission of the author in a telephone conversation on May 23, 2008.
25. Jeremy Black, *Maps and Politics* (Chicago: University of Chicago, 1997). See also his *Maps and History* (New Haven, CT: Yale University, 1997).
26. All of these maps can be found in Black, *Maps and Politics*.
27. The English translation of his paper appeared as *On Formally Undecidable*

Propositions of Principlia Mathematica and Related Systems, trans., B. Meltzer (New York: Basic, 1962).

28. Margaret Wheatley, *Leadership and the New Science* (San Francisco: Barrett-Koehler, 1992), xi.
29. Susan Resneck Pierce, "Can the Center Hold: The Challenge for the Liberal Arts," *Presidential Papers*, 10 (Sept. 1994): 5.
30. As quoted in John Noble Wilford, "Revolutions in Mapping," *National Geographic* 193 (Feb. 1998): 32.
31. George Santayana, *Winds of Doctrine* (New York: Charles Scribner's Sons, 1913), 1.
32. Frances Hesselbein, "'How to Be' Leader," in *The Leader of the Future*, ed., Frances Hesselbein, Marshall Goldsmith, and Richard Beckhard (San Francisco: Jossey-Bass, 1996), 122.

Part Two

1. Gary A. Phillips, "Drawing the Other: The Postmodern and Reading the Bible Imaginatively," in *Good Company: Essays in Honor of Robert Detweiler*, ed., David Jasper and Mark Ledbetter (Atlanta: Scholars, 1994), 409.
2. José Saramago calls this "Erratic Odyssey" a movement "From Novel to Poem." See his commentary, "Erratic Odyssey: The Novel's Return Toward the Condition of Poetry," *TLS: Times Literary Supplement*, 20 (Nov. 20, 1998): 14.
3. Gilles Deleuze, *Difference and Repetition*, trans., Paul Patton (New York: Columbia University, 1994), 23.
4. Quoted in Andrew Blauvelt, "In and Around Cultures of Design and the Design of Cultures," part 1, *Emigree*, 32 (1994): note 4, www.emigre.com/Editorial.php?sect=1&id=23 (accessed May 22, 2008).
5. George Cladis, *Leading the Team-Based Church* (San Francisco: Jossey-Bass, 1999), preface. See also John Milbank's contention that the "post-modern embracing of a radical linguisticality, far from being a 'problem' for traditional Christianity, has always been secretly promoted by it" in his *The Word Made Strange* (Cambridge, MA: Blackwell, 1997), 85.
6. Raphael Patai, *The Children of Noah* (Princeton, NJ: Princeton University, 1998), 108.
7. Clement of Alexander, *The Instructor* (3:11) in *The Ante-Nicene Fathers*, ed., Alexander Roberts and James Donaldson (New York: Charles Scribner's Sons, 1905), 2: 285–86.

8. As Romans 5:20–21 reminds us.
9. As quoted in John Barton, *People of the Book?* (Louisville, KY: Westminster/John Knox, 1988), 3. John Muddiman took this metaphor and made an entire book out of it. See his *The Bible: Fountain and Well of Truth* (Oxford: Basil Blackwell, 1983).
10. Lewis Carroll, *The Hunting of the Snark* (London: Macmillan, 1876), 15–16.
11. For more on the "Platinum Rule" that is now ruling the corporate world, see Tony Alessandra and Michael J. O'Connor, *The Platinum Rule* (New York: Warner, 1996).
12. The Titanium Rule in the business world is "Do unto others, keeping their preferences in mind." (Claire Raines, *Connecting Generations* [Menlo Park, CA: Crisp, 2003], 34.) For more on the Platinum Rule that is still operating in the corporate world, see for example, Anthony J. Alessandra, Ronald Finklestein, and Scott Zimmerman, *The Platinum Rule for Small Business Success* (New York: Morgan Jones, 2007).
13. As quoted in Elizabeth A. Johnson, *She Who Is* (New York: Crossroad, 1993), 128.
14. St. Gregory of Nyssa, *Commentary on the Song of Songs* (Brookline, MA: Hellenic College, 1987), 201. The paradox of the instability of motion and stability in motion was exemplified by the fountain as well for St. Gregory: "This is indeed paradoxical. All wells contain still water; only the bride has running water with both a well's depth and a continuous flow of water. Who can worthily comprehend the wonders applied to the bride? It seems that she has no further to reach once she has been compared to beauty's archetype. She closely imitates her bridegroom's fountain by one of her own; his life by hers, and his water by her water." (184)
15. For more of this, see David Martin, *Divinity in a Grain of Bread* (Cambridge: Lutterworth, 1989), 65.
16. Translation of Kyrie eleison from the fifteenth century Wanderings of Felix Fabri, as cited in John Davies, Pilgrimage Yesterday and Today (London: SCM, 1988), 54.

Missional Art #1

1. This is the inscription etched on the Maggi Hambling memorial to Oscar Wilde, on Adelaide Street, off Trafalgar Square, titled "A Conversation with Oscar Wilde."

2. Ghalib, "For the Raindrop" in Roger Housden, *Risking Everything* (New York: Harmony, 2003), 82.
3. See Jacques Ellul, *The Betrayal of the West*, trans., Matthew J. O'Connell (New York: Seabury, 1978), where he writes, "The West was the first civilization in history to focus attention on the individual and on freedom" (17).
4. Robertson Davies, *The Merry Heart: Reading and Writing* (New York: Penguin, 1998), 230.
5. The exact quote is: "He knew everybody and talked easily with the great but easiest with the humble, poor and lost. When he dropped a name it was always the name of Jesus." Unpublished "Address" by the Rev. Dan Beeby, February 8, 1998, Dulwich Grove United Reformed Church. With thanks to Donald Barber Jr. for showing me this material.
6. Gerhard E. Frost, "Nativity," in *Journey of the Heart* (Minneapolis: Augsburg, 1995), 35.
7. Peter Koenig, "To Be 'Values Driven' Means Escaping the Profitability Trap," *At Work,* July/Aug. 1997, 12–13.
8. James F. Keenan, S.J., "Proposing Cardinal Virtues," *Theological Studies,* 56 (1995): 723–28.
9. See Lawrence G. Brandon, *Let the Trumpet Resound* (Malvern, PA: CPCU-Harry J. Loman Foundation, 1996), 161.
10. Edward Hopper, "Jesus Savior Pilot Me," in James Gilchrist Lawson, *The Best Loved Religious Poems Gleaned From Many Sources* (New York: Fleming H. Revell, 1933), 101.
11. Teilhard de Chardin, *Meditations with Teilhard de Chardin* (Santa Fe, NM: Bear, 1988), 125.
12. Basil Hume, *To Be a Pilgrim* (Middlegreen, UK: St. Paul, 1984), 39–40.
13. George Sylvester Viereck, "What Life Means to Einstein, an Interview," *Saturday Evening Post,* Oct. 1929, 117.
14. Ella Wheeler Wilcox, "Faith," in Lawson, *The Best Loved Religious Poems*, 60.
15. John Wesley, "The General Spread of the Gospel" in *Sermons*, vol. 2, ed., Albert Outler; in *The Works of John Wesley*, ed., Frank Baker (Nashville: Abingdon, 1985), II: 495.
16. Nadya Aisenberg, "The Home Museum," in her *Before We Were Strangers: Poems* (Boston: Forest, 1989), 13.
17. Isaac Watts, "King Triumphant," in Lawson, *The Best Loved Religious Poems*, 73.
18. No one has stated this more forcefully than Bill Easum in *Sacred Cows Make Gourmet Burgers* (Nashville: Abingdon, 1995).

19. Quoted in Margaret Pawley, *Prayers for the Pilgrims* (London: Triangle/SPCK, 1991), 39.
20. Quoted in H. Grady Davis, *Design for Preaching* (Philadelphia: Fortress, 1958), 244.
21. D. H. Lawrence, *The Trespasser* (New York: Cambridge University, 1981), 130. I am grateful to Dolores La Chapelle for introducing me to the importance of the morning star in American Indian culture and D. H. Lawrence's writings. See her *Sacred Land, Sacred Sex: Rapture of the Deep: Concerning Deep Ecology and Celebrating Life* (Durango, CO: Kivakí, 1988), 223.
22. Quoted in *US Magazine* and referenced in Terry Beahm, "No Kidding! Quick News Items That You Need to Know," *Arizona Republic,* Jan. 3, 1999, E2.
23. Quoted in John Kaye, *Some Account of the Writings and Opinions of Clement of Alexandria* (London: J. G. & F. Rivington, 1835), 31.
24. All Web sites mentioned through this book were accessed in May 2008.
25. James D. Smith III, "Wordsmiths of Worship," in *Christian History* 12 (1993), 1: 30.
26. Melito of Sardis, *On Pascha and Fragments,* trans. and ed., Stuart George Hall (Oxford: Clarendon, 1979), 3, 5, 7.
27. See Henry Sloane Coffin's "Preaching in an Age of Disillusionment," the foreword to *Best Sermons* (1947-48), 4th ed., ed., G. Paul Butler (New York: Harper, 1947), xv.
28. Tom Robbins, *Jitterbug Perfume* (New York: Bantam, 1990), 85.
29. Michael Riddell, *Threshold of the Future* (London: SPCK, 1998), 123.

Missional Art #2

1. Samuel Taylor Coleridge, "The Rime of the Ancient Mariner," in *The Poetical Works of S. T. Coleridge* (New York: Thomas Y. Crowell, n.d.), 109.
2. P. T. Forsyth, *The Person and Place of Jesus Christ* (London: Hodder & Stoughton, 1909), 171. "If he died to make a church, that church should continue to be made by some permanent thing … by a book which should be the real successor of the apostles, with a real authority on the vital matters of truth and faith." Or, from P. T. Forsyth, *The Church and the Sacraments* (London: Independent, 1953), 64: "The real successor of the apostolate … was not the hierarchy but the canon of Scripture written to prolong their voice and compiled to replace the vanished witness."
3. The quote, attributed to several, including Howard Hendricks, Vance Havner

(1901–1986), as quoted in *Leadership* 17 (Spring 1996): 71; and Walter L. Stone and Charles G. Stone in *Recreation Leadership* (New York: William-Frederick, 1952), 19.

4. W. S, Merwin, "The Estuary," in *Selected Poems* (New York: Atheneum, 1988), 233.
5. Emmanuel Levinas, "The String and the Wood," in *Outside the Subject*, trans., Michael B. Smith (Stanford, CA: Stanford University, 1994), 129.
6. Eugene H. Peterson, *Eat This Book* (Grand Rapids, MI: Eerdmans, 2006), 20.
7. Northrop Frye, *The Great Code* (New York: Harcourt Brace Jovanovich, 1982), xviii–xix.
8. C. H. Spurgeon, "The Last Words of Christ on the Cross: Intended for Reading on Lord's Day, Oct. 15, 1899," in *The Metropolitan Tabernacle Pulpit,* rev. and published in 1899 (Pasadena, TX: Pilgrim, 1977), 45: 495.
9. See the character Calla in Joyce Carol Oates, *I Lock My Door Upon Myself* (New York: Ecco, 1992), 85.
10. The image is that of Donna Markova, *No Enemies Within* (Emeryville, CA: Publisher Group West, 1994), as quoted in Robert Hargrove, *Mastering the Art of Creative Collaboration* (New York: BusinessWeek, 1998), 65.
11. Sara Maitland, *A Big-Enough God* (New York: Henry Holt, 1995), 7.
12. Quoted in Paul Yanick, *Quantum Medicine* (North Bergen, NJ: Basic Health, 2003), 18.
13. Clark H. Pinnock, *Tracking the Maze* (New York: Harper & Row, 1984), 224.
14. R. D. Laing, *The Facts of Life* (New York: Pantheon, 1976), 16.
15. John Ruskin, "To Henry Acland, 24 May 1851," in *Letters of Ruskin, 1827–1869*, vol. 36 of *The Works of John Ruskin*, ed., E. T. Cook and Alexander Wedderburn (London: George Allen 1909), 115.
16. See Alan Levy, *The Wiesenthal File* (Grand Rapids, MI: Eerdmans, 1993), 29–30. The other three are "Technology, Crisis or War, and Minority as Victim."
17. Iain Crichton Smith, "The Village," in his *Collected Poems* (Manchester: Carcanet, 1995, ©1992), 289. Originally published in his *The Village and Other Poems* (Manchester: Carcanet, 1989).
18. Augustine's quote is "Love and do what you will," his most famous quote from his *Homilies, Augustine*, "Seventh Homily: 1 John 4:4–12," in his *Later Works*, ed., John Burnaby (Philadelphia: Westminster, 1955), 316.
19. For the latest developments in Global Navigation Satellite Systems (GNSS), see Paul D. Groves, *Principles of GNSS, Inertial and Multi-Sensor Integrated Navigation Systems* (Boston: Artech, 2008).

20. See Leonard Sweet, *The Gospel According to Starbucks* (Colorado Springs: WaterBrook, 2007).
21. A. E. Harvey, "The Evidence of Cave 7," *TLS: Times Literary Supplement*, March 22, 1996, 6.
22. Biblical scholar Thomas Boomershine asks pointedly: "Could a movement that was so radically literate and distinguished by documents have emerged out of someone who 'wrote nothing'?"
23. For a history of the newspaper, see most recently Joad Raymond, *The Invention of the Newspaper: English Newsbooks 1641–1649* (Oxford: Clarendon, 1996); see most comprehensively Joseph Frank, *The Beginnings of the English Newspaper 1620–1660* (Cambridge, MA: Harvard University, 1961).
24. David Paul Nord, "Religious Reading and Readers in Antebellum America," *Journal of the Early Republic* 15 (Summer 1995): 241–72, esp. 246.
25. Evangelicals understood, for example, that a traditional sermonic style would not work to get the new world's attention. The American Tract Society's *American Messenger* declared bluntly that "We would not be misunderstood. Our ideal of a religious paper would not be met by giving it the method and stateliness of a sermon. We would not repel the general reader by elaborate expositions, or abstract discussions, or incessant exhortations. No: the newspaper requires varied and lively talent in a style of its own." Quoted in Nord, "Religious Reading," 252.
26. "He rubbed his fist under my nose, and swore he would smash my face into jelly" is how one colporteur described a reaction of a person to an offer of Richard Baxter's *Call to the Unconverted.* Quoted in Nord, "Religious Reading," 267.
27. Quoted in M. T. Clanchy, "Parchment and Paper: Manuscript Culture 1100–1500," in *A Companion to the History of the Book*, ed., Simon Eliot and Jonathan Rose (Malden, MA: Blackwell, 2007), 195.
28. As referenced in "NB," *TLS: Times Literary Supplement,* Nov. 4, 1994, 16.
29. Alvin B. Kernan, *The Death of Literature*, new ed. (New Haven, CT: Yale University, 1992), 140.
30. John W. De Gruchy, *Faith for a Time Like This* (Cape Town, Rondebosch United Church, 1992), 8.
31. With thanks to Ted M. Stump in *Cell Church Magazine* 2 (1994), 4: 11, for first making this point.
32. With thanks to John Baker-Batsel of Boulder, Colorado, for this "Amandaism."
33. Bob Benson, "We Are Going to a Celebration," in *"See You at the House"* (Nashville:

Generoux/Nelson, 1989), as quoted in Harold Ivan Smith, *On Grieving the Death of a Father* (Minneapolis: Augsburg, 1994), 94.

34. New Zealand theologian Michael Riddell, *Threshold of the Future* (London: SPCK, 1998), 58.
35. Evan E. Schwartz, "Advertising Webonomics 101," *Wired*, Feb. 1996, 77.

Missional Art #3

1. Quoted in Richard Foster, "Going Deeper," *Perspective* 6 (Oct. 1996), 4: 5.
2. Nigel Barley, *Adventures in a Mud Hut* (New York: Vanguard, 1983), 190.
3. Pope John Paul II, letter to Agostino Cardinal Casaroli, secretary of state, May 20, 1982, as quoted in J. M. Waliggo, A. Roest Crollius, T. Nkéramihigo, and J. Mutiso-Mbinda, *Inculturation* (Kampala, Uganda: St. Paul, 1986), 7. Quoted from letter to Agostino Cardinal Casaroli on the occasion of the creation of the Pontifical Council for Culture, *Osservatore Romano* (English edition), June 28, 1982, 7.
4. From a 2003 radio interview of Jaroslav Pelikan by Krista Tippetts, "The Need for Creeds," on the program *Speaking of Faith.* The transcript of the March 20, 2008 rebroadcast is available online at http://speakingoffaith.publicradio.org/programs/pelikan/transcript.shtml (accessed May 26, 2008).
5. Faith Popcorn and Lys Marigold, *Clicking* (New York: HarperCollins, 1996), 13.
6. The slogan, dating back to Graham's days with Youth for Christ, is quoted in Harold Lawrence Myra and Marshall Shelley, *The Leadership Secrets of Billy Graham* (Grand Rapids, MI: Zondervan, 2005), 231–32, 306.
7. Thanks to New England pastor Randall P. Scheri for this illustration.
8. See James Alexander Thom, *The Children of First Man* (New York: Ballantine, 1994), 40–42.
9. For another look at this AncientFuture methodology, see Leonard Sweet, *Faithquakes* (Nashville: Abingdon, 1994). See especially page 19 where this theme for the entire book is introduced.
10. William Blake, "Proverbs of Hell," *The Marriage of Heaven and Hell in Full Color* (New York: Dover, 1994), 31.
11. For an alternative typology, see Donald G. Bloesch's extremely helpful typology of options relative to cultural interaction in *A Theology of Word and Spirit* (Downers Grove, IL: InterVarsity, 1992), 253–64. First, a theology of restoration that goes after modernity without seriously entering into conversation with it (B.

B. Warfield, Carl Henry, R. C. Sproul). Second, a theology of accommodation that unites the secular and sacred (Schleiermacher, David Tracy, John Hick). Third, a theology of correlation that synthesizes Christian religion with modern claims (Paul Tillich, Hans Küng, Wolfhart Pannenberg). Finally, a theology of confrontation that calls modern issues into question on the basis of Christian truth (John Calvin, Karl Barth, Abraham Kuyper).

12. Wade Clark Roof, *A Generation of Seekers* (San Francisco: HarperSanFrancisco, 1993), 34.
13. Stanley Hauerwas and William H. Willimon, *Where Resident Aliens Live* (Nashville: Abingdon, 1996), 39, 46.
14. Eddie Gibbs, *I Believe in Church Growth* (London: Hodder & Stoughton, 1981), 70–83.
15. Marcus J. Borg, *Conflict, Holiness & Politics in the Teachings of Jesus* (Lewiston, NY: Edwin Mellen, 1984), esp. 163–99.
16. Episcopalian/editor Douglas L. LeBlanc, "Two Cheers For TV," *Books & Culture,* July/Aug. 1998, 12. Also available online: www1.Christianity.net/bc/8B4/8B4010.html.
17. Lesslie Newbigin, "The Enduring Validity of Cross-Cultural Mission," *International Bulletin of Missionary Research* 12 (1988): 50.
18. One of Robertson Davies' novels has a marvelous section, "Of Water and the Holy Spirit," in which an eighteenth-century Wesleyan takes on a gang of hostile Welsh youths with storytelling and a cursing competition, and then preaches the gospel to them. That's Paul's inculturation model at work. See Davies, *Murther & Walking Spirits* (New York: Viking Penguin, 1991), 91–155.
19. Johann B. Metz, "The 'One World': A Challenge to Western Christianity," in *Christ and Context*, ed., Hilary D. Regan and Alan J. Torrance (Edinburgh: T&T Clark, 1993), 210–23, esp. 214.
20. Max L. Stackhouse, "Contextualization, Contextuality and Contextualism," in *One Faith, Many Cultures*, ed., Ruy O. Costa (Maryknoll, NY: Orbis, 1988), 6.
21. Michael Carrithers, *Why Humans Have Cultures* (New York: Oxford University, 1992).
22. See George G. Hunter III, *How to Reach Secular People* (Nashville: Abingdon, 1992). See also his "The End of the 'Home Field Advantage,'" *Epworth Review* 19 (May 1992): 69–76; and his "Can the West Be Won," *Christianity Today,* Dec. 16, 1991, 43–46.
23. Peter C. Phan, "Contemporary Theology and Inculturation in the United States"

in *The Multicultural Church*, ed., William Cenkner (New York: Paulist, 1996), 111. Phan's article is the best short introduction to the topic that I have found.

24. "The challenge of an in-but-not-of faith is knowing when to stand, timeless and transcendent as a rock, and when to surrender and let go, releasing oneself to be swept along by the relevant currents." See Leonard Sweet, *Quantum Spirituality* (Dayton, OH: Whaleprints, 1991), 2.
25. This is the argument of Jean Baudrillard. See especially his *America*, trans., Chris Turner (New York: Verso, 1988); and his *Selected Writings*, ed., Mark Poster (Stanford, CA: Stanford University, 1988).
26. Livia Kent, "Seek and Ye Shall Find," *Common Boundary*, Jan./Feb. 1999, 48.
27. Aylward Shorter, *Toward a Theology of Inculturation* (Maryknoll, NY: Orbis, 1988). The word *inculturation* implies a degree of desyncretization, which is a prime temptation in the twenty-first-century world.
28. William Reiser, "Inculturation and Doctrinal Development," *Heythrop Journal* 22 (1981): 135.
29. Ary Roest Crollius, "Inculturation: Newness and Ongoing Process," in Waligoo, et al., *Inculturation*, 43.
30. For an excellent alternative approach to how to contextualize theology, but one that is too close to Niebuhr's typologies for my tastes, see the five models presented by Stephen Bevans, *Models of Contextual Theology* (New York: Orbis, 1992). He calls these models Translation, Anthropological, Praxis, Synthetic, and Transcendental.
31. Recapitulation, a central theme for Irenaeus, is defined as a "'fresh start' … a taking up again and restitution of God's original plan for man by the reproduction in the incarnation of the features of the original creation, and the reversal of the features of the fall. The immediate effect of this 'fresh start' is to bring about, or rather, to restore a 'communion' between … the human race and God." See Joseph P. Smith's introduction to Irenaeus, *Proof of the Apostolic Preaching*, trans., Joseph P. Smith, Ancient Christian Writers, vol. 16 (Westminster, MD: Newman, 1952), 30.
32. David Tracy, *Plurality and Ambiguity* (San Francisco: Harper & Row, 1987), 77, 79. Elsewhere he says, "The best road to hermeneutical retrievals of tradition is through critique and suspicion." See his "God, Dialogue and Solidarity: A Theologian's Refrain," *Christian Century*, Oct. 10, 1990, 904.
33. Irenaeus wrote that Jesus came "for the recapitulation of all things." See Irenaeus, *Proof of Apostolic Preaching*, 51.
34. Larry L. Welborn calls this text "The Dangerous Double Affirmation: Character

and Truth in 2 Cor. 1, 17," *Zeitschrift für die neutestamentliche Wissenschaft* 86 (1995): 52; where he describes how Paul portrays beautifully both the gospel as God's "Yes" to the world as well as his own "gracelessness"—"as a man locked in combat with his own character, parrying doubts and suspicions, countering charges of vacillation and self-interestedness, stumbling over words as over cobblestones, colliding with his own promises, forced to repeat, to recite, to reiterate, to establish the truth of his every statement by employing what amounts to an oath."

35. Magen Broshi, "Evidence of Earliest Christian Pilgrimage to the Holy Land Comes to Light in Holy Sepulchre Church," *Biblical Archaeology Review*, Dec. 1977, 42–45. Thanks to Glenn Letham of Falls Church, Virginia, for pointing out this reference to me.
36. Jaroslav Pelikan, *Vindication of Tradition* (New Haven, CT: Yale University, 1984), 65.
37. John Wesley, *Letters 1740–1755*, ed., Frank Baker, The Works of John Wesley, vol. 26 (Oxford: Clarendon, 1982), 113–14.
38. Geoffrey Anketall Studdert-Kennedy, "Roses in December," *Best Loved Poems of the American People*, comp., Hazel Felleman (Garden City, NY: Doubleday, 1936), 363. Quoted in *Brewer's Famous Quotations* (London: Weidenfeld and Nicholson, 2006), 449.

Missional Art #4

1. Quoted in Gerald R. McDermott, *Seeing God* (Downers Grove, IL: InterVarsity, 1995), 221.
2. Michel de Montaigne, "Of Repentance," in *The Complete Essays of Montaigne*, trans., Donald M. Frame (Stanford, CA: Stanford University, 1965), 610.
3. Gary Hamel and C. K. Prahalad, *Competing for the Future* (Boston: Harvard Business School, 1994), 51–52.
4. This compares with nine in ten for the average American company. Thirty-three percent of Rubbermaid's sales each year come from products introduced in the past five years.
5. See Joshua Cooper Ramo and Debra Rosenberg, "The Puzzle of Genius," *Newsweek*, June 28, 1993 50.
6. Jorie Graham, *The Errancy by Jorie Graham* (Manchester: Carcanet, 1998), back cover.
7. Joyce Carol Oates, *The Faith of a Writer* (New York: HarperCollins, 2003), 53.

8. *The Wit and Wisdom of Oscar Wilde*, ed., Ralph Keyes (New York: HarperCollins, 1996), 121.
9. Nicolo Machiavelli, *The Prince*, trans., W. K. Marriot (Stilwell, KS: Digireads.com, 2005), 27.
10. For a sermon on this theme, see Leonard Sweet, "Risks Create Realities," *Homiletics,* Nov. 14, 1993.
11. In his last SCLC presidential address, Martin Luther King Jr. said, "We have a task and let us go out with a 'divine dissatisfaction.'" "Where Do We Go from Here," August 16, 1967, in *A Testament of Hope*, ed., James Melvin Washington (New York: Harper & Row, 1986), 151. Prior to this sentence, he talked about America and its "high blood pressure of creeds and an anemia of deeds." Probably true in the church too!
12. Beatrice Bruteau, "Freedom: 'If Anyone Is in Christ, That Person Is a New Creation,'" in *Who Do People Say I Am?* ed., Francis A. Eigo (Villanova, PA: Villanova University, 1980), 125.
13. Ibid., 126.
14. Bryan W. Mattimore, *99% Inspiration* (New York: American Management Association, 1994), 72–73.
15. John Naisbitt, "From Nation States to Networks," in *Rethinking the Future*, ed., Rowan Gibson (London: Nicholas Brealey, 1997), 214.
16. "Look at the biggest industry there is: tourism. It employs one out of nine people in the world. And it will get even bigger in the twenty-first century ... But apart from a few big players like the airlines, who provide the infrastructure, tourism is made up of millions and millions of entrepreneurs." Naisbitt, "From Nation States to Networks," 215.
17. Horace, "To Lollius Maximus," *The Epistles of Horace: Bilingual Edition*, trans., David Ferry (New York: Farrar Straus & Giroux, 2001), 15.
18. Note the argument of Michael Hammer, as referenced by Rowan Gibson, "Rethinking Business," in *Rethinking the Future*, ed., Gibson, 8.
19. Words from a *Sunday Telegraph* interview in October 1979; in May 1979 she became prime minister. Laura Ward, *Foolish Words* (London: PRC Publishing Ltd., 2003), 92.
20. For more on this, see Leonard Sweet, "Spiritual Leadership: What Potter A. Qoyawayma Taught Me About Spiritual Leadership," *Sweet's SoulCafe* 2:6–7 (Oct.–Nov. 1996).
21. James Martin, *Cybercorp* (New York: Amacom, 1996) ii, 7–15.
22. Thomas M. Finney, *The Life and Labors of Enoch Mather Marvin, Late Bishop*

of the Methodist Episcopal Church, South (St. Louis: James H. Chambers, 1880), 574.

23. Manfred Kets de Vries, *The Leadership Mystique* (New York: Prentice Hall, 2001), 55.
24. See Ilya Prigogine and Isabelle Stengers, *Order Out of Chaos* (New York: Bantam, 1984).
25. As cited in Hillel Schwartz, *Century's End* (New York: Doubleday, 1990), 245.
26. Robert Dale, *Seeds of the Future* (St. Louis: Old Hickory, 2005), 203.
27. Dan Benedict and Craig Kennet Miller, *Contemporary Worship for the 21st Century* (Nashville: Discipleship, 1994), viii.
28. Dava Sobel, *Longitude* (New York: Penguin, 1996), 138.
29. Thornton Wilder, *The Matchmaker* (New York: Samuel French, 1957), 113–14.
30. Coventry Patmore, "Fragments," in *The Poems of Coventry Patmore*, ed., Frederick Page (London: Oxford University, 1949), 479.
31. Quoted in Polly La Barre, "Ben Zander," *Fast Company,* Dec. 1998, 112–14.
32. D. J. Enright, *Interplay* (New York: Oxford University, 1995), 230.
33. Oscar Wilde, *The Picture of Dorian Gray* (New York: Three Sirens, 1931), 10.
34. Harry Emerson Fosdick, *The Meaning of Service* (New York: Abingdon, 1920), 67.
35. F. B. Meyer, *Life of Paul* (Lynnwood, WA: Emerald, 1995), 69.
36. Michael Riddell, *Threshold of the Future* (London: SPCK, 1998), 83.
37. John Sanders, *The God Who Risks* (Downers Grove, IL: InterVarsity, 1998).

Missional Art #5

1. "How Firm a Foundation," words by "K" in Rippon's *A Selection of Hymns, 1787, The United Methodist Hymnal: Book of United Methodist Worship* (Nashville: The United Methodist Publishing House, 1989), 529.
2. This account is based on Wesley's journal entries for this trip, October 21, 1735, to February 5, 1736, as found in John Wesley, *Journal and Diaries I (1735–1738),* ed., W. Reginald Ward and Richard P. Heitzenrater, The Works of John Wesley, vol. 18 (Nashville: Abingdon, 1988), 138–45.
3. Wesley had earlier compared the Moravians' hymns to his own Church of England's metrical psalm-singing and found the stilted English tunes both musically and spiritually lacking.
4. Quoted in Ivan Hewett, "A Wryer Humor, a Deeper Calm," *TLS: Times Literary Supplement,* July 31, 1998, 18.
5. Caroline Alexander, *The Endurance* (New York: Alfred A. Knopf, 1999), 94.

6. For more on Shackleton, see Leonard Sweet, *Summoned to Lead* (Grand Rapids, MI: Zondervan, 2004).
7. One of the surprise findings of the 1994 Louisville Institute Conference on "Baby Boomers and the Changing Shape of American Religion" was that the most effective way to attract boomers was "expressive music—music that touches the heart." Number 2? Preaching and the pastor. Number 3? "Experiential dimension" of worship. Almost nonexistent was denominational linkages. Bill Owens, *The Magnetic Music Ministry* (Nashville: Abingdon, 1996), 19–20.
8. Edward Foley, "Toward a Sound Theology," *Studia Liturgica*, 23 (1993), 2: 132. Another writer to understand this early on was British sociologist David Martin: "Thus music picks up signals of unfocused, inchoate, religious sensibility and the word is partially replaced by sound. The record begins to take over from the book, the concert audience—or the rock festival—replaces the congregation, and the quest for ecstasy displaces concern for dogmatic ascent." David Martin, *The Breaking of the Image* (New York: St. Martin's, 1979), 140.
9. Mendelssohn's actual quote is "Individual words ... seem to me so ambiguous, so vague, so easily misunderstood in comparison to genuine music, which fills the soul with a thousand things better than words. The thoughts that are expressed to me by music ... are not too indefinite to be put into words, but on the contrary, too definite." Felix Mendelssohn, "To Marc-André Souchay, Berlin, Oct. 15 1842," in *Letters*, ed., G. Selden-Goth (New York: Pantheon, 1945), 314.
10. Andrew Ford, *Composer to Composer* (London: Quartet, 1993), 155.
11. From Martin Luther's *Table Talk*. See Robin A. Leaver, *Luther's Liturgical Music* (Grand Rapids, MI: Eerdmans, 2007), 100; note 153 contains additional source information about this passage. See also a variation of the quote in Roland Bainton, *Here I Stand* (New York: Abingdon, 1950), 341.
12. John Calvin's preface to the Geneva Psalter (1543), as quoted by Susan McClary, "Same As It Ever Was," in *Microphone Fiends*, ed., Andrew Ross and Tricia Roise (New York: Routledge, 1994), 31, fn. 6.
13. Saint Augustine, *Confessions*, trans., R. S. Pine-Coffin (Baltimore: Penguin, 1961), 238. Thanks to Andrew Ross and Tricia Roise, editors of *Microphone Fiends*, who pointed me not only to Augustine but also to John of Salisbury.
14. Roger Cohen, "A Novelist at the Crossroads of Soviet Society," *New York Times*, Feb. 15, 1990, C21.
15. David W. Wolfe, *Tales from the Underground* (Cambridge, MA: Perseus, 2001), 116.

16. Henry Van Dyke, "Joyful, Joyful We Adore Thee," *The United Methodist Hymnal*, 89.
17. "Remote sensing" now includes altimeter readings from satellites, which can trace underwater topography.
18. The "Mark Twain" or two fathoms is the one made most famous by Samuel Clemens.
19. Adrian C. North, David J. Hargreaves, and Jennifer McKendrick, "Music and On-Hold Waiting Time," *British Journal of Psychology* 99 (1999): 161–64.
20. Music theorist Alfred Tomatis plays these in the background as he works, and he now requires only three to four hours of sleep a night. Tomatis is reviewed in Marilyn Ferguson, *Book of Pragmagic* (New York: Pocket, 1990), 168.
21. See Alfred Tomatis, *The Conscious Ear* (Barrytown, NY: Station Hill, 1991).
22. Physicist Henry Stapp, quoted in Kevin Sharpe and Jon Walgate, "Patterns of the Real: Quantum Nonlocality," *Science & Spirit* 10 (April/May 1999): 11.
23. For a fuller elaboration of this one point, see Leonard Sweet, "What Emanuel Levinas and Bill and Gloria Gaither Have Taught Me About Prayer," *Sweet's SoulCafe*, 3:7–9 (1998); "Creation: The Sound (Song) of God," in Sweet, *A Cup of Coffee at the SoulCafe* (Nashville: Broadman Holman, 1998), 58–71; and "The Music Gene," in Sweet, *Eleven Genetic Gateways to Spiritual Awakening* (Nashville: Abingdon, 1998), 154–69.
24. Quoted in Leslie Montgomery, *Redemptive Suffering* (Wheaton, IL: Crossway, 2006), 13.
25. Ted Gideonse and Marian Westley, "Music Is Good Medicine," *Newsweek*, Sept. 21, 1998, 103.
26. Cynthia Serjak makes the case for music as the model for global civilization in chapter 2 of her *Music and the Cosmic Dance* (Washington, D.C.: The Pastoral Press, 1987), 35; where she argues that "We are caught by rhythm, allured by melody, surrounded and expanded by harmony."
27. Foley, "Toward a Sound Theology," 127.
28. Carlos Castaneda, *The Teachings of Don Juan* (Berkeley, CA: University of California, 1998), 72.
29. Annie Dillard, *Pilgrim at Tinker Creek* (New York: Harper's Magazine, 1974), 34.
30. Tomatis, *Conscious Ear*, 47.
31. Ralph Waldo Emerson, "Self-Reliance," *Selected Essays* (Chicago: Peoples Book Club, 1949), 32.
32. Henry Mitchell, *Black Preaching* (San Francisco: Harper & Row, 1979), 163. See

also Evans E. Crawford with Thomas H. Troeger, *The Hum* (Nashville: Abingdon, 1995).

33. Foley, "Toward a Sound Theology," 134.
34. Quoted in Plato, *The Republic*, bk. 3, trans., C. D. C. Reeve (Indianapolis: Hackett, 2004), 84.
35. With thanks to Jeremy Fretts (jcfretts@iquest.net).
36. Thomas Torrance, "Einstein and God," *CTI Reflections* 1 (Spring 1998): 7.
37. John of Salisbury, *Policratus*, trans., William Dalglish, "The Origin of the Hocket," *Journal of the American Musicological Society* 13 (1978): 7.
38. To listen to Bernstein's explanation, go to "Leonard Bernstein and Glenn Gould Don't See Eye to Eye" in the CBC Archives, http://archives.cbc.ca/arts_entertainment/music/clips/4000/ (accessed May 28, 2008).
39. Quoted in Serjak, "Music and the Cosmic Dance," 35.
40. John C. Maxwell, *Developing the Leaders Around You* (Nashville: Thomas Nelson, 1993), 73.
41. With thanks to John Yarrington of Little Rock, Arkansas, for this poem.
42. Donald P. Hustad, *Jubilate! Church Music in the Evangelical Tradition* (Carol Stream, IL: Hope, 1981), 202.
43. See the SPPA estimates for 1997 in *Survey of Public Participation in the Arts, Summary Report*, 67, available online at www.nea.gov/research/Survey/Survey58-92.pdf (accessed May 28, 2008).

Missional Art #6

1. Quoted in Liam Hudson, "Captured Souls," *TLS: Times Literary Supplement,* Jan. 8, 1993, 15.
2. Pierre Babin and Mercedes Iannone, *The New Era in Religious Communication*, trans., David Smith (Minneapolis: Fortress, 1991), 7.
3. Oliver Sacks, "To See and Not See," *The New Yorker,* May 10, 1993, 59–73.
4. Ibid., 63, 65.
5. N. W. Clerk [pseud. C. S. Lewis], *A Grief Observed* (New York: Seabury, 1963, ©1961), 37.
6. Ralph Waldo Emerson, "The Rhodora," *Poems* (Boston: Houghton-Mifflin, 1904), 38.
7. Personal communication with author.
8. For more in-depth discussion of the dual requirements of complexity, see Mihaly

Csikszentmihalyi, *The Evolving Self* (New York: HarperCollins, 1993), esp. 156–62.

9. See Leonard Sweet, "Spiritual Leadership: What Potter A. Qoyawayma Taught Me About Spiritual Leadership," *Sweet's SoulCafe*, 2:6–7 (Oct.–Nov. 1996).
10. Robert Burns, "To a Mouse," *The Works of Robert Burns* (London: T. Tegg, 1840), 224.
11. For another way of approaching the double ring of vision, see Leonard Sweet, *SoulTsunami* (Grand Rapids, MI: Zondervan, 1999), 162.
12. T. S. Eliot, last line of "Little Gidding," from his *Four Quartets*, in *The Complete Poems and Plays 1909–1950* (New York: Harcourt Brace, 1971), 145.
13. Al Ries and Jack Trout, "Focused in a Fuzzy World," in *Rethinking the Future*, ed., Rowan Gibson (London: Nicholas Brealey, 1997), 188.
14. For postmodern writers trying to do this, see Gillian Rose, *Shadow of Spirit*, ed., Philippa Berry and Andrew Wernick (New York: Routledge, 1992), 49–54. See also Gillian Rose, *The Broken Middle* (Oxford: Blackwell, 1992).
15. L. C. Bezuidenhout, "Sing to Jahweh! … Cursed Be the Day on Which I Was Born: A Paradoxical Harmony in Jeremiah 20:7–18," *Hervormde Teologiese Studies* 46 (1990): 359–66.
16. Paul M. Kennedy's question in *Preparing for the Twenty-First Century* (New York: Random, 1993), 137.
17. W. N. Herbert, *Forked Tongue* (Newcastle Upon Tyne: Bloodaxe, 1994), 93.
18. For more on the and/also double ring, see Sweet, *SoulTsunami*, 167, 370–71.
19. The article began: "It's a paradox of global proportions … the closer that trade and technology bind nations together, the bolder the moves to break nations apart." Bob Davis, "Global Paradox; Growth of Trade Binds Nations, But It Also Can Spur Separatism; Dissident Groups Worry Less About the Economic Cost of Going Their Own Way; A World of 500 Countries," *The Wall Street Journal*, June 20, 1994, A1. Thanks to Jessica Lipnack and Jeffrey Stamps, *The Age of the Network* (Essex Junction, VT: OMNEO, 1994), 219.
20. "Christianity Showing No Visible Signs of a Nationwide Revival: Annual Survey by Barna Research Reveals Current Trends Regarding Spiritual Behavior," 1998, www.barna.org/ViewFrames.htm (accessed May 20, 2008).
21. Michel Foucault, *The Order of Things* (New York: Pantheon, 1971), 377.
22. This is the question of Jean Bethke Elshtain, *Democracy on Trial* (New York: Basic, 1995), 1.
23. For more on local-food options, see www.localharvest.org, or www.foodroutes.org.

24. F. Scott Fitzgerald, *The Crack-up*, (New York: New Directions, 1993), 69.
25. Blaise Pascal, *Pensées*, ed. and trans., Roger Ariew (Indianapolis: Hackett, 2005), 33.
26. So says Arie de Geus, *The Living Company* (Boston: Harvard Business School, 1997), 154.
27. Jon Berry, "We Want It All!" *American Demographics,* March 1999, 45–48.
28. Peter Elbow, *Embracing Contraries* (New York: Oxford University, 1986); Albert Rothenberg, *The Emerging Goddess* (Chicago: University of Chicago, 1979), 237–46; Richard Tanner Pascale, *Managing on the Edge* (New York: Simon & Schuster, 1990), esp. "Disturbing Equilibrium," 110–15.
29. Ogden Nash, *The Face is Familiar* (Garden City, NY: Garden City, 1941), 17.
30. More than 3.5 million households in the United States enjoy a net worth at or above $1 million—the greatest in history. Also for the first time in U.S. history, more millionaires are below age fifty than are above it. The faster we are gaining wealth, the more people are being diagnosed with depression.
31. The poem was composed in Czernowitz in late 1944, not long after the Russian army had liberated Celan from a forced labor camp in Romania. See Paul Celan, *Death Fugue*, in Paul Celan, *Poems: A Bilingual Edition*, trans., Michael Hamburger (Manchester: Carcanet, 1980), 51. For an example of its influence, see David Hartnett's *Black Milk* (New York: Random, 1995).
32. This will be the number one political issue of the future—the bottom 80 percent is getting worse, and the top 20 percent is getting dramatically richer. The inequality of wealth now stands at a 63-year high. The top 1 percent controls 42 percent of the nation's household assets and 50 percent of its financial assets, such as stocks and bonds. Ninety-eight percent of two decades of increases in household income have gone to the top one-fifth of earners. For the statistics on USAmerican poverty, see William O'Neill, "Poverty in the United States," in *Reading the Signs of the Times*, ed., T. Howland Sanks and John A. Coleman (New York: Paulist, 1993), 68–77.
33. In 1991, 85 percent of the world's population received only 15 percent of the global income, while in 1996 the total wealth of the world's top 358 billionaires equaled the combined incomes of the world's 2.3 billion poorest people, almost half of the world's population.
34. Robert Reich, *I'll Be Short* (Boston: Beacon, 2003), 7.
35. The number of African Americans who go to college has never been higher. At the same time, the number of black men in prison has never been higher, either. Wealth has exploded in USAmerica across all ethnic lines. Michael Jordan took in

$65 million in 1996. Oprah Winfrey earned $97 million in 1996. In the 1980s there was a 52 percent increase in black managers, professionals, technicians, and government officials. The percentage of black families earning more than $50,000 increased from 10 percent to 14 percent between 1970 and 1990. Simultaneously, the percentage of black families earning less than $10,000 increased from 21 percent to 26 percent.

36. Even among African Americans, one segment of the community is rising to the top in historic dimensions while another large segment is crashing to the bottom harder than ever before. In 1980, 13.8 percent of black households boasted incomes of $50,000 (in 1992 dollars). In 1992, that figure had risen to 16.1 percent.
37. Quoted in John Greenwald, "The New Service Class," *Time,* Nov. 14, 1994, 73.
38. For one example, see Kathryn Phillips, *Tracking the Vanishing Frogs* (New York: St. Martin's, 1994), where she argues that the very vulnerabilities of amphibians (such as permeable skin and land/water life cycles) make them good bio-indicators, whose health measures the health of an ecosystem. How's this for another "double ring": The more bird populations decline and species go extinct (in the past 2000 years, one-fifth of all bird species in the world have gone extinct, with 11 percent of the remaining 9,040 species currently threatened or endangered), the greater the numbers of people who enjoy watching and feeding birds (65 million in 1994) and the more money is spent on birdwatching ($5.2 billion was spent in 1994 by USAmericans to enjoy birds; that compares with $5.8 billion on movie tickets and $5.9 billion on sporting events like football and baseball). See "A Bird in the Bush Is Worth Big Bucks," *National Wildlife,* Dec. 1995/Jan. 1996, 8.
39. Discuss this quote from the British columnist and novelist Julie Burchill, perhaps the most famous journalist in the world today: "I want a quiet life, and a big noise career. I shall continue to wander through the global village like the global village idiot savant I am, keeping an eye peeled for the next thing to do for pleasure and profit … I now maintain that I have no ambition.… But then, the last person to say that was, I believe, Napoleon." (Julie Burchill, *Sex and Sensibility* [London: Grafton, 1992], 263.)
40. In 1970, there were ten churches in America that reported an attendance of two thousand. By 1990, there were three hundred plus churches, forty-three of which reported five thousand or more in attendance on a weekly basis. By 1997, another church went "mega" every three weeks.
41. Cynthia Crossen, *Tainted Truth* (New York: Simon & Schuster, 1994), 36.

42. Just like how some years ago words like *bad* began to be used to describe something that's good—when someone says, "He's a bad dude," they really mean he's good. Or, more recently, the word *sick* is now used to describe something that's good or cool.

43. The charismatic movement around the world has reached a plateau after a century of unprecedented growth, partly because almost every branch of Christianity that is growing is now charismatic in some fashion. Everybody now has their hands up—even the Baptists. See Laurence W. Wood, "Third Wave of the Spirit, Pentecostalization of American Christianity: A Wesleyan Critique," *Wesleyan Theological Journal* 31 (Spring 1996): 110–40.

44. Stephen M. Miller, "Charismatic Episcopalians: 100 Churches Have Joined New Denomination," *Christianity Today*, May 16, 1994, 51.

45. For two hundred years, the size of the average U.S. household has been shrinking: from 5.8 in 1790 to 2.6 in 1993 to a projected 2.4 in 2000, at which time the two-hundred-year trend should reverse slightly. (See the editorial by Brad Edmondson, "Do You Want to Be Alone?" *American Demographics* 16 [Oct. 1994]: 2.) Yet while household size is decreasing, the number of homes built with two or more bathrooms tripled from 1970 to 1992. New homes built in USAmerica have grown from an average 102 square meters in 1949 to over 187 today, with floor space per person more than doubling. (In one four year period—1988 to 1992—the typical house grew by one hundred square feet [6 percent] to about 1,900 square feet on average.) Move-up buyers, whose households are shrinking, are looking for larger homes. According to *American Demographics*, the more recent the dates the more severe the statistics: "The average new single-family home grew from 1,645 square feet in 1975 to 2,095 square feet in 1995. (See Marcia Mogelonsky, "Reconfiguring the American Dream (House)," *American Demographics* 19 [Jan. 1997]: 32; and Diane Crispell, "How Small a Household?" *American Demographics* 16 [Aug. 1994]: 59.) Gopal Ahluwalia, of the U.S. National Association of Homebuilders, says frustratingly, "Everybody wants a media room, a home office, an exercise room, three bathrooms, a family room, a living room, and a huge, beautiful, eat-in kitchen that nobody cooks in." Quoted in David Malin Roodman and Nicholas Lenssen, "Our Buildings, Ourselves," *World Watch* 7 (Nov./Dec. 1994), 22.

46. Karl Raymond Popper, *Conjectures and Refutations* (New York: Routledge, 2002), 38.

47. America is getting more spiritual at the same time fewer people are interested in organized religion. Ninety-eight percent of USAmericans profess to be "believers"

in God, but only 40 percent worship in church on an average Sunday. In other words, over half of USAmericans feel no need to worship with other believers the God in whom they believe. Fewer people in France believe in God, while more of the French believe in the Devil. (See the Le Monde newspaper poll, as reported in *National & International Religion Report* 8 [May 30, 1994]: 8.) As a historian of American religion and culture, I am privileged to live in one of the greatest spiritual awakenings in American history, a time some are calling America's "Fifth Great Awakening." As a bureaucrat in an old-line denomination, while in the midst of a spiritual heat wave in the wider culture, I find the church in a deep freeze, its paradigms frozen in the past.

48. What do you say of the *Money* magazine survey that showed USAmericans are becoming less honest? In 1987, 15 percent said they would not correct the waiter if undercharged. In 1994, 24 percent said they wouldn't. In 1984, 20 percent said they would keep the cash if they found a wallet containing $1,000. In 1994, 24 percent said they would keep it. Almost 25 percent said they would commit a crime if they would make $10 million and never get caught. One-third of us said we would cheat on taxes. Discuss the movie *Pulp Fiction* (1994). Here is a movie filled with violence that is gratuitous and savage. It is also packed with passionate moralizing. See Lance Morrow's "Yin and Yang, Sleaze and Moralizing," *Time*, Dec. 27, 1994–Jan. 2, 1995, 158.
49. In Holland, Multatuli's *Max Havelaar or the Coffee Auctions of the Dutch Trading Company* (London: Penguin, 1987) sells better in English than in the original Dutch (first published in 1860), according to Paul Kegan of Penguin Modern Classics. There are 360 megalanguages out there, and one world language.
50. *Boomer Report,* Oct./Nov. 1994, 8.
51. From "The Cloud Minders," *Star Trek*, episode 74, Feb. 28, 1969, quoted in David C. Korten, *When Corporations Rule the World* (San Francisco: Berrett-Kohler, 2001), 107.
52. "Where Boomers Shop," *Boomer Report,* Oct./Nov. 1994, 8.
53. Heraclitus, of Ephesus, *The Art and Thought of Heraclitus*, trans., Charles H. Kahn (New York: Cambridge University, 1999), esp. 200.
54. Heraclitus, of Ephesus, *Fragments*, trans., Brooks Haxton (New York: Penguin, 2003), 31.
55. James H. Snider, "Education Wars: The Battle Over Information-Age Technology," *The Futurist,* May–June 1996, 28.
56. Charles Handy, *The Age of Paradox* (Boston: Harvard Business School, 1994), 12–13.

57. All of these recommended books are available through books.google.com.
58. Quoted in John Heilemann, "It's the New Economy, Stupid," *Wired,* March 1996, 70.
59. David C. Korten, *When Corporations Rule the World* (San Francisco: Berrett-Koehler, 1995), 20.
60. Quoted in "Inequality: For Richer, for Poorer," *The Economist,* Nov. 5, 1994, 20.
61. Quoted in "Denominations Urged to Turn Focus 'Outward,'" *Christianity Today,* Oct. 3, 1994, 72, www.christianitytoday.com/ct/1994/october3/4tb72a.html (accessed May 28, 2008).

Missional Art #7

1. Thanks to classics professor Stephen Bertman in *Hyperculture* (Westport, CT: Praeger, 1998), 5–6, for this analogy.
2. Kathy Gallo, personnel director at Andersen Consulting, says that at least 30 percent of her audience at seminars check their voice and e-mail after ten o'clock each evening. See the report by Alison Maitland, "Slaves on Technology's Treadmill," *Financial Times,* Jan. 14, 1999, 10.
3. Quoted in Mardy Grothe, *Oxymoronica* (New York: HarperCollins, 2004), 159.
4. For a more complete discussion of these concepts, see Bernard F. Batto, "The Sleeping God: An Ancient Near Eastern Motif of Divine Sovereignty," *Biblica* 68 (1987): 153–77.
5. For more information, see Dennis C. Smolarski, *Liturgical Literacy* (New York: Paulist, 1990); J. G. Davies, ed., *A New Dictionary of Liturgy and Worship* (London: SCM, 1986); Gerhard Podhradsky, *New Dictionary of the Liturgy* (Staten Island, NY: Alba, 1966); William J. O'Shea, *The Worship of the Church* (Westminster, MD: Newman, 1957). Merrill Ware Carrington, whose work first alerted me to this lost tradition, is coming out with a book titled *Ensouling Our Embers.* Unfortunately, the "fire" imagery is alien to what the "embers" stood for in the Christian tradition.
6. Quoted in Jurriaan Kamp, *Because People Matter* (New York: Paraview, 2003), 92.
7. The full story is told in Raphael Patai, *The Children of Noah* (Princeton, NJ: Princeton University, 1998), 60–61.
8. Mrs. Charles E. Cowman, *Streams in the Desert* (Grand Rapids, MI: Zondervan, 1997), 372.

9. Stephen Strauss, *The Sizesaurus* (New York: Kodansha International, 1995), 150.
10. Barbara Moses, *Career Intelligence* (San Francisco: Berrett-Koehler, 1998), 240-241.
11. Quoted in Emmanuel Levinas, "Jean Wahl: Neither Having Nor Being," in *Outside the Subject*, trans., Michael B. Smith (Stanford, CA: Stanford University, 1994), 77.
12. David Sutton, *Absences and Celebrations* (London: Chatto and Windus: Hogarth, 1982), 47.
13. Nancy S. Hill, *Actual Factuals* (Wheaton, IL: Tyndale, 1997), 53–54. With thanks to Judge Jesse B. Caldwell III of Gastonia, North Carolina, for pointing me to this story.
14. Mitch Albom, *Tuesdays with Morrie* (New York: Doubleday, 1997), 103–8. Available through books.google.com.
15. See also Wayne Muller's *Sabbath* (New York: Bantam, 2000). Available through books.google.com.
16. Marva J. Dawn, *Keeping the Sabbath Wholly* (Grand Rapids, MI: Eerdmans, 1989).
17. Eugene H. Peterson, *Working the Angles* (Grand Rapids, MI: Eerdmans, 1987), 72–73.

Missional Art #8

1. Alexandr Solzhenitsyn, "A World Split Apart," in *Finding God at Harvard*, ed., Kelly Monroe (Grand Rapids, MI: Zondervan, 1996), 101.
2. Hank Hanegraaff argues that the eye, the egg, and the earth are three other examples of organized complexity that can only be explained by "in the beginning God created the heavens and the earth." See his "Fat Chance: The Failure of Evolution to Account for the Miracle of Life," *Christian Research Journal* 21 (July–Sept. 1998): 10–15. Complexity theologian Catherine Keller's *The Face of the Deep* elaborates a constructive theology based not on creatio ex nihilo but creatio ex profundis.
3. One version of the Lloyd list is found in John Horgan's *The End of Science* (New York: Broadway, 1997), 303, note 11.
4. David M. Kennedy, *Over Here* (New York: Oxford University, 1980), 17, 87.
5. Bill Gates, with Nathan Myhrvold and Peter Rinearson, *The Road Ahead*, 2nd ed. (New York Penguin, 1996) 299.

6. Howard Rheingold, *The Virtual Community* (Reading, MA: Addison-Wesley, 1994), 7–8.
7. Learning, growing, and diversity are the "three essential complexities for a model of changing culture or life." See Kevin Kelly, *Out of Control* (Reading, MA: Addison-Wesley, 1994), 448. See also his "The Nine Laws of God," 468–72.
8. F. Barbara Orlans, Tom L. Beauchamp, Rebecca Dresser, David B. Morton, and John P. Gluck, *The Human Use of Animals* (New York: Oxford University, 1998), 89.
9. Ninety percent of the 2.7 million jobs produced by the U.S. economy in 1994 were due to service firms, as reported in John Greenwald's "The New Service Class," *Time,* Nov. 14, 1994, 72. The "gods/clods" language was introduced by Jack London to distinguish the "school of God" from the "school of clod," as he called these different styles of short-story writing. See James I. McClintock, *Jack London's Strong Truths* (East Lansing, MI: Michigan State University, 1997), 41–44, 53.
10. For a sampling of digitalization programs, see "Collaborative Digitalization Programs in the United States," www.mtsu.edu/~kmiddlet/stateportals.html; and "BCR's Collaborative Digitalization Programs," www.bcr.org/cdp/ (accessed May 29, 2008).
11. Granted, it is necessary to procure the printed or digitized book in order to read it in its entirety (books.google.com suggests online sites where you may purchase the book, and directs you to the nearest library where you may borrow the book), and there are copyright issues still to be settled, but my research assistant tells me that she now needs to visit libraries (to view hard copy materials) for only a small percentage of the items she researches. The rest of the time she works at home with her laptop.
12. Leonard Sweet, ed., *Communication and Change in American Religious History* (Grand Rapids, MI: Eerdmans, 1993).
13. Gerald M. Levin, "The World on a String: Media Responsibility in a Wired Universe," *Vital Speeches of the Day* 64 (Sept. 1, 1998): 689.
14. See Dick Lilly, "Videoconference Wedding Lets Guests Attend with No Travel," *Seattle Times,* July 26, 1998, B1, B8.
15. My gratitude goes to Tex Sample, author of *The Spectacle of Worship in a Wired World* (Nashville: Abingdon, 1998), for helping me name and define this concept.
16. Quoted in Ron Zemke, "Wake Up! And Reclaim Instructional Design," (Interview with M. David Merrill), *Training,* June 1998, 337–39.

17. Quoted in Douglas S. Robertson, *The New Renaissance* (New York: Oxford University, 1998), 112.
18. Films and sports are two of the most prominent shared cultural reference points. Leaders ignore both at their peril.
19. John Ortberg, "Let There Be Wit & Wisdom, Weekly …" *Leadership* 14 (Summer 1993): 38.
20. Quoted in David A. Aaker and Erich Joachimsthaler, *Brand Leadership* (New York: Free, 2000), 77.
21. Howard Gardner, *Leading Minds* (New York: Basic, 1995), esp. "The Leader's Stories," 41–65.
22. Quoted in "Job Titles of the Future," *Fast Company,* Sept. 1998, 64.
23. See, for example, Alycia Perry and David Wisnom, *Before the Brand* (New York: McGraw Hill, 2003).
24. *John Naisbitt's Trend Letter,* March 30, 1995, 4–5.
25. I am indebted to Laurie Coots, chief marketing officer for TBWA Chiat/Day in Los Angeles, for this insight. See "Fast Pack 1999," *Fast Company*, Feb./Mar. 1999, 138.
26. With gratitude for and acknowledgment of Patricia Nakache's "Secrets of the New Brand Builders," *Fortune*, June 22, 1998, 168, 170.
27. I am an Amazon.com franchisee through leonardsweet.com.
28. Robert Ballard, "We're All Explorers," *Fast Company,* Sept. 1998, 166.
29. Curtis Sittenfeld, "Minister of Comedy," *Fast Company,* Sept. 1998, www.fastcompany.com/magazine/18/jtfdlevin.html (accessed May 30, 2008).
30. This is the position of many writers like Georges Bernanos and Marcel Proust. See, for example, Proust's *The Captive* (Vintage, 1970).
31. Oswald Chambers, *The Psychology of Redemption* (London: S. Marshall, 1930), 136.
32. Mark Allan Powell, "Rocking the Church," *Christianity Today,* March 1, 1999, 66.
33. P. J. Huffstutter, "God Is Everywhere on the Net," *Los Angeles Times*, Dec. 14, 1998, A1, A18.
34. This is from *Home Evangelization* (New York: American Tract Society, 1850), 139–40.

Missional Art #9

1. With thanks to Warren Bennis, as cited in Anna Muoio, "Boss Management," Fast Company, April 1999, 92 (www.fastcompany.com/online/23/one.html).
2. Caroline Alexander, *The Endurance* (New York: Alfred A. Knopf, 1999), 4, 13, 153.
3. Ibid., 193.
4. Ibid., 194.
5. Ibid., 56.
6. Ibid., 93.
7. E-mail correspondence.
8. Pauline Maier, *American Scripture* (New York: Alfred A. Knopf, 1997), 100, 104–7, 114–16, 124–39. Robert Hargrove first pointed this out to me in his *Mastering the Art of Creative Collaboration* (New York: BusinessWeek, 1998), 10.
9. See Richard C. Lewontin, "Genes, Environment, and Organisms," in Lewontin and Richard Levins, *Biology Under the Influence* (New York: Monthly Review, 2007), 221–34.
10. Harvard Law School Professor Martha Minow elaborates on this concept in her book *Between Vengeance and Forgiveness* (Boston: Beacon, 1998), 52.
11. Cited in Raphael Patai, *The Children of Noah* (Princeton, NJ: Princeton University, 1998), 105.
12. First line of Charles Albert Tindley's hymn, "Stand By Me," as printed in Ralph H. Jones, *Charles Albert Tindley* (Nashville: Abingdon, 1982), 175.
13. Allen Hammond, *Which World? Scenarios for the 21st Century* (Washington, D.C.: Island, 1998), 45.
14. Stephen Crane, "The Open Boat" (1897), *The Open Boat and Other Stories* (New York: Dover, 1993), 58.
15. George Cladis, *Leading the Team-Based Church* (San Francisco: Jossey-Bass, 1999). See also Shirley Guthrie, *Christian Doctrine*, rev. ed. (Louisville, KY: Westminster/John Knox, 1994), 91–92.
16. For more on Jesus' team ministry, see Leonard Sweet, *Eleven Genetic Gateways to Spiritual Awakening* (Nashville: Abingdon, 1998), esp. "The Team Gene," 69–99.
17. Quoted in Olivier Clément, *Taizé* (Chicago: GIA, 1997), 31.
18. With gratitude to Catherine Keller's "The Subject of Complexity: Autonomy and Autopoiesis," in *Die autonoma Person,* ed., Klaus-Peter Köpping, Michael Welker, and Reiner Wiehl (München: Wilhelm Fink, 2002).

19. Stuart Kauffman, *At Home in the Universe* (New York: Oxford University, 1995), 274. Kauffman, who credits Kant for this concept, is more than a key name in the sciences of complexity. His earlier book, *The Origins of Order* (1993), has been called "perhaps the most significant work ever written" in terms of the exploration of the emergence and origin of life.
20. John Briggs and F. David Peat, *Turbulent Mirror* (New York: Harper & Row, 1989), 154.
21. For more on this, see Hargrove, *Mastering the Art of Creative Collaboration*; and Sarah and Paul Edwards, *Teaming Up* (New York: Tarcher/Putnam, 1998).
22. Emily Dickinson, "Wild Nights!" *The Complete Poems*, ed., Thomas H. Johnson (Boston: Little, Brown, 1960), 114.
23. Charles Arn, "A Closer Look at Church Dropouts," vol. 45, *The Growth Report* as reprinted in *Ministry Advantage* 5 (May/June 1994): 5–7.
24. Warren Bennis and Patricia Ward Biederman, *Organizing Genius* (Reading, MA: Addison-Wesley, 1997), 27.
25. Ibid., esp. 15, 94–95.
26. Michael Abrashoff, *It's Your Ship* (New York: Warner, 2002), 13.
27. Reggie McNeal, *Revolution in Leadership* (Nashville: Abingdon, 1998), 45.
28. The Pew Research Center for People and the Press, *Deconstructing Distrust*, March 10, 1998, www.people-press.org/trustrpt.htm (accessed May 20, 2008). The report says, "The national mood and trust are both up from the mid-1990s, but still just 20 percent of Americans are highly satisfied with the state of the nation and only 34 percent basically trust the government."
29. Robert E. Quinn, *Deep Change* (San Francisco: Jossey-Bass, 1996), 83.
30. Ralph Ellison, "The Charlie Christian Story," in *Shadow and Act* (New York: Random, 1964), 234.
31. Hargrove, *Mastering the Art of Creative Collaboration*, 62.
32. Quoted in Arthur Block, *Murphy's Law* (New York: Parigee, 2003), 138.
33. Quoted in Peter Hay, *Canned Laughter* (New York: Oxford University, 1992).
34. Thomas Wright, *The New Testament and the People of God* (Minneapolis: Fortress, 1992), 45.
35. George Cladis, *Leading the Team-Based Church* (San Francisco: Jossey-Bass, 1999), 2. See also Kevin Freiberg and Jackie Freiberg, *Nuts!* (Austin, TX, Bard, 1996), 316.
36. Ibid., 316.
37. Patricia McLagan and Christo Nel, *The Age of Participation* (San Francisco: Berrett-Koehler, 1995), 247.
38. Os Guinness, *The Call* (Nashville: W. Publishing Group, 2003), 49.

Missional Art #10

1. Quoted in Walter Isaacson, *Einstein* (New York: Simon & Schuster, 2007), 287.
2. David Buttrick, "God Is Coming," *Pulpit Resource* (Logos Productions), Nov. 27, 1994.
3. I am dependent here on the insight of researchers at the Institute of HeartMath in Boulder Creek, California, and their book *The HeartMath Solution* (San Francisco: HarperSanFrancisco, 1999), which argues that the heart boasts its own parallel brain and nervous system.
4. *The Works of Francis Bacon*, ed., James Spedding, Robert Leslie Ellis, and Douglas Denon Heath (New York: Hurd & Houghton, 1864), 8: 68.
5. Julia Cameron and Mark Bryan, *The Artist's Way* (New York: G.P. Putnam's Sons, 1992), 119.
6. For more on the "chaordic," see Leonard Sweet, *SoulTsunami* (Grand Rapids, MI: Zondervan, 1999), esp. "'Chaordic' Churches & 'Chaordic' Leaders," 72–83.
7. Lawrence Miller, *Barbarians to Bureaucrats* (New York: Fawcett Columbine, 1989), 181.
8. Carola Giedion-Welcker, *Constantin Brancusi* (New York: Graziller, 1959), 220.
9. Quoted in Sandra Silberstein, *War of Words* (New York: Routledge, 2004), 29.
10. Elizabeth Barnes, *The Story of Discipleship* (Nashville: Abingdon, 1995), 50, 67–68.
11. Ibid., 49.
12. Richard Dawkins and Steven Pinker, "Is Science Killing the Soul," *Edge* 53 (April 8, 1999), www.edge.org/documents/archive/edge53.html (accessed June 1, 2008).
13. Pierre Babin and Mercedes Iannone, *The New Era in Religious Communication* (Minneapolis: Fortress, 1991), 13.
14. Nancy Gibbs, "Angels Among Us," *Time,* Dec. 27, 1993, 56.
15. David Bosch, *Transforming Mission* (Maryknoll, NY: Orbis, 1991) 352–53.
16. David Lindley, *The End of Physics* (New York: Basic, 1993), 255.
17. Andrew Harvey and Mark Matousek, *Dialogues with a Modern Mystic* (Wheaton, IL: Quest, 1994), esp. "The Concentration Camp of Reason," 27–41.
18. Donald H. Juel, "The Baptism of Jesus (Mark 1:9–11)," in *All Things New*, ed., Arland J. Hultgren, Donald H. Juel, and Jack D. Kingbury (St. Paul, MN: Luther Northwestern Theological Seminary, 1992), 126.
19. The report is chronicled in Richard Tanner Pascale, *Managing on the Edge* (New York: Simon & Schuster, 1990), 110. The original study, conducted by Albert

Rothenberg, is the basis for his *The Emerging Goddess* (Chicago: University of Chicago, 1979).

20. The story is told by Bryan W. Mattimore, *99% Inspiration* (New York: American Management Association, 1994), 66.
21. "Paradox has to be accepted, coped with, and made sense of, in life, in work, in the community, and among nations." Charles Handy, *The Age of Paradox* (Boston: Harvard Business School, 1994), 13.
22. See Elizabeth Smart, *On the Side of the Angels*, ed., Alice Van Wart (London: Harper Collins, 1994).
23. David Weeks and Jamie James, *Eccentrics* (New York: Villard, 1995), 64–65.
24. Ibid., 16, 27–28.
25. Gary Hamel, "Reinventing the Basis for Competition" in *Rethinking the Future*, ed., Rowan Gibson (London: Nicholas Brealey, 1997), 91.
26. Saul Bellow, "Facts that Put Fancy to Flight," in *It All Adds Up* (New York: Viking, 1994), 66.
27. Quoted in Stephen E. Ozment, *When Father Ruled* (Cambridge, MA: Harvard University, 1983), 224, note 32.
28. Ginghamsburg Church (United Methodist) is located in Tipp City, Ohio (www.ginghamsburg.org). See also Michael Slaughter, *Out on the Edge* (Nashville: Abingdon, 1998).
29. Mary Warnock, *Imagination* (Berkeley, CA: University of California, 1976), 33. She concludes, "There is a power in the human mind which is at work in our everyday perception of the world, and is also at work in our thoughts about what is absent; which enables us to see the world, whether present or absent as significant, and also to present this vision to others, for them to share or reject" (196).
30. I borrow this concept from George Lakoff and Mark Johnson, *Metaphors We Live By* (Chicago: University of Chicago, 1980), 235–36.
31. Quoted in Jeffrey Goldsmith, "The Geometric Dreams of Benoit Mandelbrot," *Wired*, August 1994, 93.
32. Cameron M. Ford and Dennis A. Gioia, ed., *Creative Action in Organizations* (London: Sage, 1995). *Leadership* magazine published an entire issue on the theme of creativity in the summer of 1993.
33. Gary A. Phillips, "Drawing the Other: The Postmodern and Reading the Bible Imaginatively," in *In Good Company*, ed., David Jasper and Mark Ledbetter (Atlanta: Scholars, 1994), 408–9.
34. Raymond Williams, *Keywords* (Oxford: Oxford University, 1976), 72.

35. Thom and Joani Schultz, *The Dirt on Learning* (Loveland, CO: Group, 1999), 31.
36. For a fuller elaboration of this theme, see chapter 3 in Leonard Sweet, *Strong in the Broken Places* (Akron, OH: The University of Akron, 1995), 105–28.
37. Benjamin Franklin's notes listing questions to be asked includes this one that defines, in good Enlightenment fashion, wisdom as the self's knowledge of itself:

    Q. What is Wisdom?

    A. The knowledge of what will be best for us on all Occasions and the best Ways of attaining it.

    See Leonard W. Larabee, ed., *The Papers of Benjamin Franklin* (New Haven, CT: Yale University, 1959), 1: 262.
38. J. G. Ballard, *The Atrocity Exhibition* (London: Triad/Panther, 1979), 11.
39. Steven Levy, *Insanely Great* (New York: Viking, 1994), 165.
40. Mihaly Csikszentmihalyi, *Creativity* (New York: Harper Collins, 1996), 347–52, 357, 364–69.
41. "The Grand Inquisitor" episode is in book 5, chapter 5. One of many editions is Fyodor Dostoevski, *The Brothers Karamazov*, trans., Constance Garnell (New York: Modern Library, n.d.), 255–74.
42. Robert J. Sternberg and Todd I. Lubart, "Ten Tips Toward Creativity in the Workplace," in *Creative Action in Organizations*, ed., Ford and Gioia, 173–80. Quote is from Table 23.1, "Ten Tips for Fostering Creativity," 180.
43. Quoted in James Goldsmith, "Superstate of Europe," *Resurgence* 159 (July/Aug. 1993): 12.

Missional Art #11

1. John Locke, *An Essay Concerning Human Understanding* (Yorkshire: Scholar, 1970 reprint), 3.
2. As told in Morris A. Graham and Melvin J. LeBaron, *The Horizontal Revolution* (San Francisco: Jossey-Bass, 1994), 79.
3. Harlan Cleveland makes these distinctions in *The Knowledge Executive* (New York: E. P. Dutton, 1985), 22–23; as referenced in Walter Truett Anderson, *Evolution Isn't What It Used To Be* (New York: W. H. Freeman and Company, 1996), 59. One of the best statements of "The Case for the Learning Community" is the

chapter by that title in Reggie McNeal, *Revolution in Leadership* (Nashville: Abingdon, 1998), 43–51.

4. Rudyard Kipling, "The Elephant's Child," in *Just So Stories for Little Children* (New York: Charles Scribner's Sons, 1903), 87.
5. Quoted in Paul McClure, *New Entrepreneur's Guidebook* (Menlo Park, CA: Crisp, 1998), 81.
6. It is not only social and political but also ecclesiastical and theological exchanges that are often reduced solely to power.
7. Rosabeth Moss Kanter, *Rosabeth Moss Kanter on the Frontiers of Management* (Cambridge, MA: Harvard University, 1997), 135–36.
8. Clive Ponting, *Progress and Barbarism* (London: Chatto and Windus, 1998). This quotation from the book is cited from Sunil Khilnami's review, "Counting Their Dead," *TLS: Times Literary Supplement*, Oct. 23, 1998, 11.
9. For example, overreactions range from deifying technology to dethroning technology.
10. I learned this metaphor from Sandra Postel, "Carrying Capacity: Earth's Bottom Line," in *State of the World: 1994* (New York: W. W. Norton, 1994), 19.
11. This is now being explored by scientists at Okanagan Biotechnology, Inc., in British Columbia, and Ag-West Biotech, Inc., in Saskatchewan.
12. This has already been done by researchers in China, where "super beets" can survive at minus 6.5 degrees Celsius. For more about this and the genetic engineering exhibition at the Science Museum in London, see the Web site www.maff.gov.uk/maffhome.htm.
13. Directly tapping into the brain seems to me a violation of God's design, with perhaps one exception: bringing light impulses to the visual cortex of a blind person. See also Michael L. Dertouzos, *What Will Be* (San Francisco: HarperEdge, 1996) 77–80.
14. For more, see artificial-intelligence expert Raymond Kurzweil, *The Age of Spiritual Machines* (New York: Viking, 1999).
15. For other examples along these lines, see Sweet, *SoulTsunami* (Grand Rapids, MI: Zondervan, 1999), esp. "Get Bionomic: The Loss of Genetic Innocence," 241–81.
16. Quoted in *Executive Speechwriter Newsletter* 8 (1993): 6.
17. Quoted in David Marcum, Steve Smith, and Mahan Khalsa, *BusinessThink* (New York: Wiley and Sons, 2002), 68.
18. David Kolb, *Experiential Learning* (Englewood Cliffs, NJ: Prentice-Hall, 1983), esp. 68–69, 77–78.
19. Daniel Safer, Julia M. Zito, and Eric M. Fine, "Increased Methylphenidate Usage for Attention Deficit Disorder in the 1990s," *Pediatrics* 98 (Dec. 1996): 1084.

Lawrence H. Diller, MD, in his book *Running on Ritalin* (New York: Bantam, 1998), mentions a Tennessee and Indiana experiment in which classroom size reduction to fifteen children dramatically reduced the number of referrals for behavior problems in general. ADD is a nonspecific cover for a host of acting-out "behavior problems" in children.

20. Quoted in Barbara Kantrowitz and Pat Wingert, "Learning at Home: Does It Pass the Text," *Newsweek,* Oct. 5, 1998, 65ff.
21. Gordon Dryden and Jeannette Vos, *The Learning Revolution* (Rolling Hills Estates, CA: Jalmar, 1994), 77.
22. Quoted in Arthur C. Clarke, "Technology and Humanity—The Shape of What's to Come," in Anne Leer, *Masters of the Wired World* (London: Financial Times/Pitman, 1999), 35.
23. Quoted in Paul Levinson, "Sacred Genes," *Wired,* Dec. 1995, 140.
24. See Ralph D. Stacey, *Complexity and Creativity in Organizations* (San Francisco: Berrett-Koehler, 1997), esp. 286–87; where Stacey explains, "Double-loop learning occurs when a system adapts its behavior to the stimuli presented to it in a beneficial way as a result of changing its schema … Double-loop learning results in innovation and creativity."
25. According to the laws of chaos, systems are not uniform in their disbursements of unpredictability. "You can't predict far," chaos physicists like to say, but "you can predict short." In other words, there are "pockets of predictability" or "local predictability" that organisms exhibit and can be exploited.
26. Lewis Carroll is credited with the first use of the word *galumphing* in *Through the Looking Glass* (1872). Karl Weick, *Making Sense of Organization* (Reading, MA: Addison-Wesley, 2001), 417. Much of the recent studies of galumphing are based on Stephen Miller, "Ends, Means, and Galumphing: Some Leitmotifs of Play," *American Anthropologist* 75 (1973): 87–98.
27. Peter F. Drucker, *Managing for Results* (Woburn, MA: Butterworth-Heinemann, 1999), 162.
28. Nicholas of Cusa, quoted in Jasper Hopkins, *On Learned Ignorance* (Minneapolis: A. J. Benning, 1981); Charles F. Kettering, "'Research' is a High-hat Word," in *Prophet of Progress* (New York: E. P. Dutton, 1961), 96: "To be a good research worker, one should have a certain amount of intelligent ignorance, for if he knows too much he won't try anything."
29. Quoted in John Geirland, "Complicate Yourself," *Wired,* April 1996, 137.
30. Donella H. Meadows, "State of the Village Report," updated in 2005, www.odt.org/popvillage.htm (accessed June 2, 2008).

31. Emily Dickinson, "There is no Frigate like a Book," *The Complete Poems of Emily Dickinson*, ed., Thomas H. Johnson (Boston: Little, Brown, 1960), 553.
32. Quoted in Peter Goodman, "Inside the Archives of the Inquisition: How Abelard, Machiavelli, and Darwin Were Placed on the Index," *TLS: Times Literary Supplement,* Jan. 16, 1998, 15.
33. Nadya Aisenberg, "At Akumal," in *Before We Were Strangers* (Boston: Forest, 1989), 75.
34. James Hornell, "The Role of Birds in Early Navigation," *Antiquity* 20 (Sept. 1946): 142–49.
35. In June 1991, the National Institutes of Health (NIH) filed for a patent on several hundred strands of complementary DNA (cDNA), which were discovered in human brain cells by then-NIH researcher Dr. Craig Venter. A storm has been raging in the scientific community ever since. Dr. Venter left NIH for his own nonprofit cDNA-identification organization, The Institute for Genomic Research, which has licensed patent rights to Human Genome Sciences, a Gaithersburg, Maryland–based biotechnology company.
36. Philip Leder and Patricia Thomas, "Making Drugs from DNA," *Harvard Health Letter*, July 1994, 9–12.
37. Stan Davis and Bill Davidson, *2020 Vision* (New York: Simon & Schuster, 1991), 184.
38. This explains why neurocomputing is already being utilized by financial services industries (machine vision, speech processing, and general-purpose robots).
39. Seth Lloyd, quoted in Charles Platt, "A Million MhzCPU?" *Wired*, March 1995, 127. Also on www.wired.com/wired/archive/3.03/limits.html.
40. "In 1988, ... scientists at the University of California, Berkeley, built a working 100-micron motor (two hair-widths) that rotated five hundred times a minute [and was] powered by static electricity, not by magnetic attraction like a conventional electric motor." For more, see Davis and Davidson, *2020 Vision*, 191–92.
41. Davis and Davidson, *2020 Vision*, 194.
42. Ibid., 192.

Missional Art #11 1/3

1. Leland Gregory, *Hey Idiot* (New York: Andres McMeel, 2003), 107.
2. One of the few resources that acknowledges the increasing importance of this missional art is Reggie McNeal, *Revolution in Leadership* (Nashville: Abingdon, 1998). Here is his definition of intuition: "The ability of the leader to engage information at a level

that is fundamentally different from logical cognition, to gather decision-making data from hunches and feelings that extend beyond surface analysis" (44).

3. See Bryan Garner, *A Dictionary of Modern American Usage* (New York: Oxford University, 1998), 39–40, 519, 616–17.
4. Quoted in Anthony Scaduto, *Bob Dylan* (New York: Grosset & Dunlap, 1971), 241.
5. W. H. Auden, *The Dyer's Hand and Other Essays* (New York: Random, 1962), 313.
6. Mona Lisa Schulz is a neuropsychiatrist with a traditional medical practice who runs a parallel "medical intuitive" practice on the side. See her *Awakening Intuition* (New York: Harmony, 1998), 10.
7. "Instead of one single big bang producing a single-bubble universe, we are speaking now about inflationary bubbles producing new bubbles, producing new bubbles, *ad infinitum*." Quoted in Rem Edwards, *What Caused the Big Bang* (New York: Rodopi, 2001), 126.
8. Sandra Weintraub, *The Hidden Intelligence* (Butterworth-Heinemann, 1998), 35–87.
9. Gemma Corrado Fiumara, *The Other Side of Language*, trans., Charles Lambert (New York: Routledge, 1990).
10. Quoted in Gerald Holton, "On Doing One's Damnedest: The Evolution of Trust in Scientific Findings," in *The Fragile Contract*, ed., David H. Guston and Kenneth Keniston (Cambridge, MA: MIT, 1994), 63.
11. Quoted in Barbara Ellen Levy, *Ladies Laughing* (Amsterdam: Gordon & Breach, 1997), 42.
12. George Barna, *User Friendly Churches* (Ventura, CA: Regal, 1991), 16.
13. I have adopted this phrase from Allan Dunbar, former pastor of Bow Valley Christian Church and host of the television program *To You With Love, in Calgary, Alberta*. He is currently president of Puget Sound Christian College in Edmonds, Washington.
14. Ralph W. Neighbour Jr. and Lorna Jenkins, *Where Do We Go From Here? A Guidebook for the Cell Group Churches* (Houston, TX: Touch, 1990), 8.
15. In this I agree with Larry Dossey, *Healing Words* (San Francisco: HarperSanFrancisco, 1994).
16. *Letters of Gerard Manley Hopkins to Robert Bridges* (New York: Oxford University, 1955), 291.
17. Thomas Merton, *Thoughts in Solitude* (New York: Farrar, Straus & Giroux, 1958), 79.
18. Often attributed to Eisenhower, the author of this quote is unknown, according to

George R. Goethals, Georgia Sorensen, and James Macgregor Burns, *Encyclopedia of Leadership* (Thousand Oaks, CA: Sage, 2004), 220.

19. After I wrote this, I discovered David Owen's description of online communication as "intimate anonymity." See his "Ripoff!" *The New Yorker,* Feb. 22/Mar. 1, 1999, 76.
20. Quoted in Jordan S. Gruber, "Gropethinks: James Kramer Wants to Get in Touch With Your Feelings," *Wired,* Oct. 1998, 169.
21. John of the Cross, "The Ascent of Mount Carmel," in *John of the Cross: Selected Writings*, ed., Kiernan Kavanaugh (New York: Paulist, 1987), 78–79.
22. I got this story from the Rev. Samuel T. Lloyd III, "Making the Shift to Sanity," *Trinity Church, Boston*, Oct. 18, 1998.
23. Paul Valéry, "Graveyard by the Sea," in *Selected Writings of Paul Valéry* (New York: Penguin, 1964), 49.
24. "The Old Ship of Zion," author unknown, in *Original Sacred Harp: Denson Revision* (Cullman, AL: Sacred Harp, 1971), 79. Later edition available online at http://fasola.org/indexes/1991/?p=79 (accessed June 3, 2008).
25. Os Guinness, *The Call* (Nashville: Thomas Nelson, 2003) 81.
26. Quoted in Michael Scammeli, "A Great Man Eclipsed," *TLS: Times Literary Supplement,* Nov. 16–22, 1990, 1234.
27. Steve Jobs continues, "For two reasons. On a global scale, the population is increasing dramatically and all our structures, from ecological to economic to political, just cannot deal with it. And in this country, we seem to have fewer smart people in government, and people don't seem to be paying as much attention to the important decisions we have to make." Quoted in Gary Wolf, "Steve Jobs: The Next Insanely Great Thing," *Wired,* Feb. 1996, 158, www.wired.com/wired/archive/4.02/jobs_pr.html (accessed June 3, 2008).
28. James Hillman quotes a 1989 report of the Public Citizen Health Research Group: "Not since the 1820s have so many mentally ill individuals lived untreated in public shelters, on the streets, and in jails." See James Hillman and Michael Ventura, *We've Had a Hundred Years of Psychotherapy—And the World's Getting Worse* (San Francisco: HarperSanFrancisco, 1992), 137.